The
Airbus
A380

A History

The
Airbus
A380

A History

Graham M Simons

Pen & Sword
AVIATION

First Published in Great Britain in 2014 by
Pen & Sword Aviation
an imprint of
Pen & Sword Books Ltd
47 Church Street, Barnsley, South Yorkshire S70 2AS

Copyright © Graham M Simons
ISBN .9781783030415

A CIP catalogue record for this book is
available from the British Library.

Typeset in 10/11 Times
by GMS Enterprises

Printed and bound in India by Replika Press Pvt Ltd.

Pen & Sword Books Ltd incorporates the Imprints of Pen & Sword
Aviation, Pen & Sword Family History, Pen & Sword Maritime, Pen & Sword
Military, Pen & Sword Discovery, Wharncliffe Local History, Wharncliffe
True Crime, Wharncliffe Transport, Pen & Sword Select, Pen & Sword
Military Classics, Leo Cooper, The Praetorian Press, Remember When,
Seaforth Publishing and Frontline Publishing.

For a complete list of Pen & Sword titles please contact
PEN & SWORD BOOKS LIMITED

47 Church Street, Barnsley, South Yorkshire, S70 2AS, England
E-mail: enquiries@pen-and-sword.co.uk
Website: www.pen-and-sword.co.uk

Contents

Acknowledgements

A book of this nature would not have been possible without the help of many people and organisations.

Thanks are offered to all at Airbus SAS at all their facilities around Europe including Stefan Schaffrath, Vice President Media Relations; Jacques Rocca, Deputy Head of Media Relations; Justin Dubon, Head of Global News; Marie Caujolle, Eduardo Galicia-Roquero, Alizée Genilloud, Heidi Carpenter, Agnès Carmes, Marcella Muratore, Martin Fendt, Anne Galabert, Aude Lebas, Marion Brochart; Chloé Hetelle and Christelle Cossiaux. To Bill McPherson, Manager Emirates Airport Services and Lisa Poole, Senior Administration Assistant, Emirates Airport Services, London Heathrow; to Julia Gillam, Head of PR, Heathrow Airport Ltd. To George Banks, Catering Manager Concept development at Emirates; to Gudrun Gorner, Corporate Communications Executive UK & Ireland Lufthansa German Airlines and to to Kerstin Roßkopp, Deutsche Lufthansa AG; to Zoë Hatton PR Manager UK & Ireland, Singapore Airlines; the personnel of a number of airlines including Air Austral, Air France, Asiana Airlines, British Airways, China Southern Airlines Korean Air, Malaysia Airlines, QANTAS, Qatar Airways and Thai Airways.

Thanks are also offered to Captain Roger Cooper, John Stride, David Lee, John Hamlin, Brian Cocks, Martin Bowman, Mick Oakey and Ian Frimston. Finally, thanks also go to Laura Hirst, Jon Wilkinson and Charles Hewitt of Pen & Sword!

I am indebted to many people and organisations for providing photographs for this story, but in some cases it has not been possible to identify the original photographer and so credits are given in the appropriate places to the immediate supplier. If any of the pictures have not been correctly credited, please accept my apologies.

Introduction

'The Boeing 747 was the flagship of the twentieth century; the A380 is the flagship of the twenty-first century'. So said John Leahy, Chief Operating Officer - Customers and Chief Commercial Officer of Airbus before the assembled media at New York's John F Kennedy Airport. The occasion was the arrival of the first Airbus A380 to touch down on American soil when MSN007 arrived on 19 March 2007.

That day not one but two A380s touched down on either side of the continent within minutes of each other and in many ways was the cumulation of years of hard work, commercial fear and political infighting.

The hard work was that it was the result of years of incredible effort put in by thousands of Airbus employees and their suppliers. The commercial fear was the amazing gamble taken by Airbus and it's parent EADS in building such an aircraft and the political infighting involved not only Airbus' great rivals the Boeing Aircraft Corporation, but also the American political establishment and rabid jingoistic flag-waving from the American media.

The Airbus A380 may not be the prettiest of airliners - beauty is definately in the eye of the beholder, and it must be admitted that that title probably goes to either Concorde, Comet or the Lockheed Constellation, but it is certainly the most technologically advanced.

Airbus began as as a *Groupement d'Interet Économique* - Economic Interest Group or GIE - organisation on 18 December 1970. It was formed by a government initiative between France, Germany and the UK that originated in 1967 and was intended to be a consortium of European aviation firms to compete with American companies such as Boeing, McDonnell Douglas, and Lockheed.

The Americans - and in particular Boeing - could and would not believe that the Europeans dared to challenge their dominance. They just did not take the fledgling Airbus seriously. But then in April 1978 Airbus received an order for twenty-three wide-bodied A300s from Eastern Airlines. This gave much needed credibility.

With the launch of the narrow-bodied A320 in the early 1980s Airbus was really going head-to-head with the Boeing 727 and 737 and with McDonald Douglas and their DC-9 derivations. But it was more than that, for the new Airbus A320 was equipped with a fly-by-wire flight control system that was generationally streets ahead of anything the Americans were using on their airliners.

It was not long before Airbus were making huge inroads into the market - McDonald Douglas started to struggle, and Boeing started to scream 'foul' over what they saw as illegal government subsidies and loans to the Europeans, convieniently forgetting that they had received Federal and State tax breaks and benificial military cross funding and research on their civil projects that went back as far as the early 1950s with the Boeing 367-80, that was the two-generation precursor to the 707, 720, 727 and 737.

On 30 September 1968, the first of their 747 'jumbo-jets' was rolled out of the Everett assembly building before the world's press and representatives of the 26 airlines that had ordered the airliner, which had came out of a losing entrant in the contest for the USAF's 'Cargo Experimental Heavy Logistics System' aircraft. Since that moment Boeing had enjoyed a monopoly in the large, wide-bodied airliner market.

The emergence of a whole raft of ultra large airiliner studies in the late 1980s and early 1990s saw a plethora of acronyms: UHCAs, VLCTs, NLAs.... and that's not counting the 7X7s and A3XXs!

Airbus came out with their own designs, Boeing proposed a number of their own completely new designs along with new versions of their 747. The two companies were working alone, then together, then on their own again.

The whines from Seattle and Chicago about subsidies kept surfacing only to appear to be apparently settled, only to flare up again.

Eventually, Boeing pulled out of any co-operation and Airbus went on alone.

The design work was incredible, the cost phenomenal, the logistics a planning nightmare - but eventually all was overcome and the design took to the skies.

Just as with Concorde before it, it was not long before the doom-mongering environmental campaigners came out of the woodwork, as demonstrated by this piece from 2006: *'Over 90% of residents will be disturbed by noise from the new A380 Super Jumbo, according to a survey by a London council. The news came as the world's largest commercial airliner flew into Britain for the first time, visiting Heathrow for airport compatibility tests.*

The Airbus A380 is being promoted by its manufacturers as an 'environmentally friendly' aircraft, claiming that it will be 'a 'good neighbour' at even the most noise-sensitive airports around the world.'

But aviation campaigners have warned that the A380 will be 'one of the noisiest beasts in the sky'.

Media reports have also highlighted potential problems with 'wake vortices' from the giant aircraft sucking roof tiles off houses, throwing other aircraft off course and causing delays to planes waiting to take off.

Local residents in Hounslow are now voicing concerns that the Super Jumbo will have a significant impact on the levels of noise pollution in the London Borough of Hounslow.

According to a Hounslow Council survey conducted in the run up to Noise Action Week (May 22 to 26), 92% of people living in the borough think residents will be disturbed, bothered or annoyed by noise from the new aircraft.

Responding to the news, Hounslow's Head of Environmental Strategy, Rob Gibson, said: 'It is clear from our survey that the vast majority of residents are concerned that the A380 will have a negative impact on the environment.

'Any testing done today will do nothing to allay those fears, as well as being meaningless because the aircraft will not be carrying passengers. Airbus should come clean and publish proper test results showing the noise impact and vortex effects of a fully laden A380.'

One has to wonder where people like this got their information from, for it has been proven that the A380 is the quietest airliner around by a large margin.

Then there was the strange matter of how the media reported some of the problems Airbus had with the A380. The world's press was flooded with wall-to-wall reports on the early wiring problem, the weight issues, the QANTAS engine failure and a defect, located in the wings, relating to brackets that attached the wing ribs to the wing's metal skin. The press seemed to take great delight in splashing every problem to the public's attention.

Strange though that the early problems with battery fires on the Boeing 787 Dreamliner received little to no press attention until one spectacularly caught fire at London Heathrow.

Strange also that the mainstream media failed almost to a man to report that cracks had been discovered in over forty ship-sets of wings for the 787 Dreamliner under construction by Mitsubishi Heavy Industries.

Those in the industry know that both designs have no more or no less teething problems than previous new aircraft models being introduced and many claim that it is the omnipresence of social media information in today's age simply makes the information available on a global basis while in times past only aviation personnel and specialized media got hold of such details, and then by and large kept it to themselves to avoid alarming the general public. But the question remains, why one scattered across the press and not the other?

Before anyone complains that none of the dimensions mentioned in this book are in metric, this goes back to aeronautical engineer Roger Béteille, one of the key players in the formation of the Airbus consortium. It was he who decided that English should be the working language of Airbus and that measurements should not be metric because of the simple reason that most airlines already had American built aircraft.

The A380 has gone from strenth to strength, in terms of sales, performance, quietness and passenger appeal - this is the story so far!

Graham M Simons
Peterborough
June 2014.

Chapter One

Genesis of a Giant

During the summer of 1988, a group of Airbus engineers led by Jean Roeder started work on the secret development of an ultra-high-capacity airliner, termed, not unsurprisingly, the Ultra High Capacty Aircraft - the UHCA - to both complete its own range of products and in an attempt to break the dominance that the Boeing Company of the USA had enjoyed in this particular market segment since the early 1970s with its model 747.

Roeder had been given approval for further evaluations of the UHCA after a formal presentation to the President and CEO Jean Pierson of Airbus in June 1990. The megaproject was announced at the 1990 Farnborough Air Show in the UK, with the goal stated as being 15% lower operating costs than the 747-400 - the design used as the benchmark. Airbus organised four teams of designers, one from each of its partners - Aérospatiale, Deutsche Aerospace AG, British Aerospace and Construcciones Aeronáuticas Sociedad Anónima (CASA) - to propose new technologies for its future aircraft designs. The designs would be presented in 1992 and the most competitive designs would be used.

In January 1993, The Boeing Company and a number of companies in the Airbus consortium started a joint feasibility study of an aircraft known as the Very Large Commercial Transport (VLCT), with a supposed intention of forming a partnership to share the limited market. This was abandoned two years later, Boeing's interest having declined because their analysts thought that such a product was unlikely to cover the projected $15 billion development cost. It seems that Boeing – having seen in principal what 'the opposition' was thinking, decided to pursue stretching its own 747 design, at the same time pushing the suggestion that air travel was already moving away from the hub and spoke system that consolidated traffic into large aircraft - a concept that Boeing themselves had promulgated for many years - was now towards more non-stop routes that could be served by smaller machines.

Eighteen months later - in June 1994 - Airbus announced its plan to develop a very large airliner, designated the A3XX. Their designers had considered several designs, including a blended side-by-side combination of two fuselages from the A340, which was Airbus's largest jet at the time. From 1997 to 2000, as the East Asian financial crisis darkened the market outlook, Airbus refined its design, targeting a 15–20% reduction in operating costs over the existing Boeing 747-400 benchmark. After extensive market analysis the A3XX design converged into a double-deck layout that provided more passenger volume than a traditional single-deck design, to be operated in line with traditional hub-and-spoke theory as opposed to the point-to-point theory of the Boeing 777 at the time Boeing's latest product.

Going back in time...

However, the 1990s were by no means the start of the story. Double-deck aircraft - or very large commerical aircraft - have been around since the 1920s, initially often taking the form of flying boats. One of the earliest was the German Dornier company, itself a very early forerunner to the European Aeronautic Defence and Space Company N.V. (EADS) with their Do.X. At the time this huge flying boat was the largest, heaviest, and most powerful aircraft in the world. First conceived by Dr. Claudius Dornier in 1924, planning started in late 1925 and after over 240,000 work hours it was completed in June 1929. Only the Soviet Tupolev ANT-20 *'Maxim Gorki'* land-plane of a few years later was physically larger between the two world wars, but was not as heavy as the Do.X, at 53 metric tons maximum takeoff weight versus the Do.X's 56 tonnes.

The Do.X was a semi-cantilever monoplane and had an all-duralumin hull, with wings composed of a steel-reinforced duralumin framework covered in doped linen fabric. It was financed by the German Transport Ministry and built in a specially designed plant at Altenrhein, on the Swiss portion of Lake Constance, in order to circumvent the Treaty of Versailles which forbade any aircraft exceeding set speed and range limits to be built in Germany after World War One.

The aircraft was initially powered by twelve 524 hp Siemens-built Bristol Jupiter radial engines (six tractor propellers and six pushers), mounted in six tower nacelles on the wing. The nacelles were joined by an auxiliary wing whose main purpose was to stabilize the mountings. The air-cooled Jupiter engines were prone to overheating and proved to only be able to lift the Do.X to an altitude of 425 metres. The engines were supervised by an engineer, so the pilot would ask the engineer to adjust the power, in a manner similar to that used on maritime vessels. After completing 103 flights in 1930, the Do.X was refitted with 610 hp Curtiss Conqueror water-cooled 12-cylinder inline engines. Only then was it able to reach the altitude of 500 metres necessary to cross the Atlantic. Dr. Dornier designed the flying boat to carry 66 passengers long distance or 100 on shorter flights.

The luxurious passenger accommodation approached the standards of transatlantic liners. Although often referred to as a 'double deck aircraft', in fact the Do.X had three decks. On the main deck was a smoking room with its own bar, a dining salon, and seating for the passengers which could also be converted to sleeping berths for night flights. Aft of the passenger spaces was an all-electric galley,

lavatories, and cargo hold. The cockpit, navigational office, engine control and radio rooms were on the upper deck. The lower deck held fuel tanks and nine watertight compartments, only seven of which were needed to provide full flotation.

The Flugschiff, or 'flying ship' as it was called, was launched for its first test flight on 12 July 1929, with a crew of fourteen. From this point on, there are some doubts as to exactly what happened when – some sources say that in order to satisfy sceptics, on its 70th test flight on 21 October there were 169 souls on board; 150 passengers - mostly production workers and their families, a few journalists, ten aircrew and nine 'stowaways', who did not hold tickets. The flight set a new world record for the number of persons carried on a single flight, a record that was not broken for the next 20 years. After a takeoff run of 50 seconds the Do.X slowly climbed to an altitude of only 200 metres. Allegedly, as a result of the ship's size, passengers were asked to crowd together on one side or the other to help make turns. It flew for 40 minutes. Other sources – such as *Flug Revue* - claimed that it was the 42nd flight and lasted 53 minutes. A suriving historical film shows '*...fliegt mit 170 personen*' at a maximum speed of 170 km per hour before finally alighting back on Lake Constance.

To introduce the airliner to the potential United States of America market, the Do.X took off from Friedrichshafen in Germany on 3 November 1930, under the command of Friedrich Christiansen, for a transatlantic test flight to New York. The somewhat convoluted route took the Do.X to

Above: The Dornier Do.X under tow, but with at least four of the twelve Curtiss Conqueror engines turning.

Right: the engineers station inside the fuselage of the Dornier Do.X. As can be seen, the engine gauges and throttles were grouped in pairs, with which the engineer responded to instructions from the pilots.

the Netherlands, England, France, Spain, and Portugal. The journey was interrupted at Lisbon on 29 November, when a tarpaulin made contact with a hot exhaust pipe and started a fire that consumed most of the port wing. After sitting in Lisbon harbour for six weeks while new parts were made and the damage repaired, the flying boat continued - with several further mishaps and delays- along the Western coast of Africa so that by 5 June 1931 it had reached the Cape Verde Islands, from which it crossed the Atlantic to Natal in Brazil, where the crew were greeted as heroes by the local German émigré communities.

The flight continued north to the United States, finally reaching New York on 27 August 1931, almost nine months after departing Friedrichshafen – probably the longest time ever between departure and arrival for an Altantic crossing! The Do.X and crew spent the next nine months there as its engines were overhauled, and thousands of sightseers made the trip to Glenn Curtiss Airport - now LaGuardia Airport - to tour the leviathan of the air. The economic effects of the Great Depression dashed Dornier's marketing plans for the Do.X, however, and it departed from New York on 21 May 1932 via Newfoundland and the Azores to Müggelsee, Berlin where it arrived three days later and was met by a cheering crowd of 200,000 people.

Germany's original Do.X was turned over to Deutsche Luft Hansa, the national airline at that time, after the financially strapped Dornier Company could no longer operate it. After a successful 1932 tour of German coastal cities, Luft Hansa planned a Do.X flight to Vienna, Budapest, and Istanbul for 1933. The voyage ended after nine days when the flying boat's tail section tore off during a botched, over-steep landing on a reservoir lake near the city of Passau.

Above: The Dornier Do.X is seen low in formation with two other flying boats - thought to have been taken during the 1932 tour of German coastal cities.

Left: The interior of the Do.X, showing the internal structural bracing and the four-abreast seating!

While never a commercial success, the Dornier Do.X was the largest heavier-than-air aircraft of its time, a pioneer in demonstrating the potential of an international passenger air service. A successor, the Do-XX, was envisioned by Dornier, but never advanced beyond the design study stage.

Three Do.Xs were constructed in total: the original operated by Dornier, and two other machines based on orders from Italy - both Italian boats were based at the seaplane station at La Spezia, on the Ligurian Sea. Both orders originated with SANA, then the Italian state airline, but were requisitioned and used by the Italian Air Force primarily for prestige flights and public spectacles.

The British Contribution.

In the immediate pre-war years there were a number of other notable double-deck aircraft such as the Shorts 'C' Class flying boats of Great Britain's Imperial Airways and the Boeing 314 Clippers.

The Short 'C' Class – also known as the 'Empire flying boat' was a family of medium range four engined monoplane passenger and mail carrying flying boats, of the 1930s and 1940s, that linked together the outposts of the empire between Britain and the British colonies in Africa, Asia and Australia as well as providing service between Bermuda and New York City.

The origins of the Empire boats lay in an Air Ministry requirement for passenger and mail carriers that could provide air mail service to the colonies in Africa and Australia.

The Empire flying boat was officially known as the C-class by Imperial Airways and each aircraft operated by them was given a name beginning with C. The first aircraft, G-ADHL *Canopus*, was completed in June 1936 and launched on 3 July. A total of 42 Empires boats

Right: Cockpit of the S.23. Left of the control wheel there is an altimeter with an airspeed indicator below. The readout of the directional gyro is visible immediately above with a turn indicator beneath with a clock, variometer and gyro compass. Co-pilot has four oil pressure gauges at the top of his panel with vertical column-reading engine speed indicators mounted in pairs. Basic flight instruments were duplicated. Central at the very bottom of the picture are the airscrew pitch levers.

Below: The second of the S.23 Empire Flying Boats to be built, G-ADHM, beached next to RAF Short Singapore Mk.III, K6918. To facilitate beaching, the S.23 had special undercarriage legs that could be floated into position and attached while the boat was still in the water. A beaching trolley was then attached to the aft step and the vessel drawn ashore backwards.

21 July 1939 and Golden Hind is being readied for its first flight at Rochester. The S.26 flying-boats were fitted with De Havilland three-bladed constant-speed metal airscrews in place of the controllable-pitch two-position propellers of the smaller S.23.

Right: The forward passenger lounge of the prototype, S.23 G-ADHL Canopus. This offered rather spartan but nevertheless comfortable accommodation.

were built, all at Short's Rochester factory.

The first series of the Short Empires, the S.23, could carry 5 crew, 17 passengers, and 4,480 lb of cargo at a maximum speed of 174 knots and were powered by four 920 hp Bristol Pegasus radials.

The Short Empire was designed to operate along the Imperial Airways routes to South Africa and Australia, where no leg was much over 500 miles. After the design was finalized and production was started it was realised that it would be desirable to offer a similar service across the Atlantic. The range of the S.23 was such that they could not provide a true trans-Atlantic service, so two boats - *Caledonia* and *Cambria* - were lightened, given long range fuel tanks and experimented with in-flight refuelling so they could make the trip but that meant they could carry fewer passengers and cargo.

The S.30 series were fitted with the more efficient, but lower power 890 horsepower Bristol Perseus sleeve valve engines and had a strengthened airframe allowing the take off weight to be increased to 46,000 pounds, giving a range of 1,500 miles. *Cabot, Caribou, Clyde* and *Connemara* were fitted with in-flight refuelling equipment and extra fuel tanks so they could be used for a regular trans-atlantic airmail service.

Initially, they were designed for a 40,500 lb gross weight but by 1939 aircraft were strengthened for 53,000 lb. Wartime experience in operating at overload resulted in the realisation that the Empires could take off at considerably higher weights than the conservative maxima provided by Shorts and, although the last Empire crossings to America were made in 1940 (by *Clare* and *Clyde*), many more flights were made on the long, demanding and vital over-water Lisbon-Bathurst flights.

A completely new flying boat, designed as an enlarged Short C-Class Empire flying boat, also incorporating features from the Short Sunderland, the S.26 G class was produced for year-round use on the North Atlantic route (although it was used instead between the UK and West Africa). Of similar appearance to the C-class boats but about 15% larger in all dimensions with the more powerful Hercules engines and an improved hull design, they had a wing span of 134 feet and a length of 101 feet. Three aircraft were built for Imperial Airways, subsidised by the Air Ministry in anticipation of military use.

Greater use of extrusions in the structure, rather than bent sheet sections, compared to the C-Class aircraft, helped to keep the weight down. It was powered by four 1,400 hp Bristol Hercules sleeve valve radial engines, and it was designed with the capability of crossing the Atlantic without refuelling, and was intended to form the backbone of Imperial Airways' Empire services. The plan was for the first aircraft to make long range runs, the second would operate medium length (2,000 miles) flights with a dozen passengers, and the third would make short range (1,000 miles) trips with 24 passengers. It could fly 6,000 miles unburdened, or 150 passengers for a 'short hop'.

On 21 July 1939, the first aircraft, (G-AFCI *Golden Hind*), was first flown at Rochester by Shorts' chief test pilot, John Lankester Parker. On 24 February 1940, the second (G-AFCJ *Golden Fleece*) flew, and the third (G-AFCK *Golden Horn*) flew on 8 July 1940.

French efforts
Over in France - and based on the same specifications as the Potez-CAMS 161 for a large trans-ocean flying boat for Air France, the Loiré et Olivier works started in 1936 with the design of a similar six-engine large flying boat

under the designation H-49 with the name *Amphitrite*. After nationalisation of LeO as SNCASE (Société Nationale de Constructions Aéronautiques du Sud-Est), the H-49 was re-designated as the SE-200. Just like the Potez-CAMS 161 it was a modern all-metal flying boat fitted with six of the most powerful engines available. The SE-200 had a twin vertical tail layout and two fixed wingfloats with a double deck inside the hull for accommodation of up to 40 passengers and a crew of 8. The French government ordered in 1938 four SE-200s for the Air France transatlantic route, but when the war broke out none of these were completed at the Marignanne works near Marseille. After the armistice, construction on all the machines continued. The SE-200.01 made its first flight on 11 December 1942 from Lake Berre with the civil registration F-BAHE. It was named *Rochambeau*, although it is not certain this name was ever carried on the fuselage nose. The SE-200.01 was confiscated by the Germans and later ferried to Friedrichshafen carrying German Luftwaffe markings 2D:UT. On 17 January 1944 it was destroyed during an allied air raid. when moored on Lake Constance together with the Potez-CAMS 161 and the Laté 631.01.

American Clippers
The Boeing 314 Clipper came slightly later than the 'C' Class – This was a long-range flying boat produced by the Boeing Airplane Company between 1938 and 1941 and was comparable to the

Above: the Potez-CAMS 161 on its beaching trolley.

Left: the Société Nationale de Constructions Aéronautiques du Sud-Est SE-200.03 F-BAIY seen in flight It made its first flight on 2 April 1946 and was tested for the French navy until it made a bad landing on 18 October 1949 and scrapped.

British Short S.26. Twelve Clippers were built for Pan American Airways, three of which were sold to BOAC in 1941 before delivery.

The 314 was a response to PAA's request for a flying boat with unprecedented range capability that could augment the airline's trans-Pacific Martin M-130. Boeing's bid was successful and on July 21 1936, Pan American signed a contract for six. Boeing engineers adapted the cancelled XB-15 bomber's 149 feet wing, and replaced the original 850 horsepower Pratt & Whitney Twin Wasp radial engines with the more powerful 1,600 horsepower Wright Twin Cyclone. Pan Am ordered an additional six aircraft with increased engine power and a larger carrying capacity of 77 daytime passengers as the Boeing 314A.

The huge flying boat was assembled at Boeing's Plant 1 on the Duwamish River and then towed to Elliott Bay for taxi and flight tests. The first flight was on 7 June 1938, piloted by Edmund T. 'Eddie' Allen. Originally built with a single vertical tail, Allen found that he was unable to keep the aircraft flying straight, due to inadequate directional control. The aircraft was returned to the factory and fitted with the endplates on the ends of the horizontal tail in place of the single vertical fin. This too was found to be lacking and finally the centreline vertical fin was restored.

Internally, the 314 used a series of heavy ribs and spars to create a robust fuselage and cantilevered wing. This sturdy structure obviated the need for external drag-inducing struts to brace the wings. Boeing also incorporated Dornier-style sponsons into the hull structure. The sponsons, which were broad lateral extensions placed at the water line, on both the port and starboard sides of the hull, served several purposes: they provided a wide platform to stabilize the craft while floating on water, they acted as an entryway for passengers boarding the flying boat and they were shaped to contribute additional lift in flight. With weight an extremely sensitive concern, passengers and their baggage were weighed, with each passenger allowed up to 77 pounds free baggage allowance (in the later 314 series) but then charged $3.25 per lb for exceeding the limit. To fly the long ranges needed for trans-Pacific service, the 314 carried 4,246 US gallons of fuel. The later 314A model carried a further 1,200 US gallons. To quench the radial engines' thirst for oil, a capacity of 300 US gallons was required.

Pan Am's Clippers were built for one-class luxury air travel, a necessity given the long duration of transoceanic flights. The seats could be converted into bunks for overnight accommodation; with a cruise speed of only 188 miles per hour, many flights lasted over twelve hours. The 314s had a lounge and dining area, and the galleys were crewed by chefs from four-star hotels. Passengers were provided with separate male and female dressing rooms, and white-coated stewards served five and six-course meals with a silver service. Although the transatlantic flights were only operated for three months in 1939, their standard of luxury has been rarely matched by heavier-than-air transport; they were a form of travel for the super-rich, at $675 return from New York to Southampton, comparable to a round trip aboard Concorde. Most of the flights were transpacific with a one-way ticket from San Francisco to Hong Kong, via the 'stepping-stone' islands posted at $760 (or $1,368 round-trip).

The first 314, *Honolulu Clipper,* entered regular service on the San Francisco-Hong Kong route in January 1939. A one-way trip on this route took over six days to complete. Commercial passenger service lasted less than three years, ending when the United States entered World War Two in December 1941.

At the outbreak of the war in the Pacific, the *Pacific Clipper* was en-route to New Zealand. Rather than risk flying back to Honolulu and being shot down by Japanese fighters, it was decided to fly west to New York. Starting on 8 December 1941 at Auckland, New Zealand, the *Pacific Clipper* covered over 8,500 miles via such exotic locales as Surabaya, Karachi, Bahrain, Khartoum and Leopoldville. The *Pacific Clipper* landed at Pan American's LaGuardia Field seaplane base at 7:12 on the morning of 6 January 1942.

The *Yankee Clipper* flew across the Atlantic on a route from Southampton to Port Washington, New York with intermediate stops at Foynes in Ireland, Botwood in Newfoundland, and Shediac in New Brunswick. The inaugural trip occurred on 24 June 1939.

The Clipper fleet was pressed into military service, the flying boats being used for ferrying personnel and equipment to the European and Pacific fronts. American military cargo was carried via Natal, Brazil to Liberia, to supply the British forces at Cairo and even the Russians, via Teheran. Since the Pan Am pilots and crews had extensive expertise in using flying boats for extreme long-distance, over-water flights, the company's pilots and navigators continued to serve as flight crew. In 1943, President Franklin D. Roosevelt traveled to the Casablanca Conference in a Pan-Am crewed Boeing 314. Winston Churchill also flew on them several times adding to the Clippers' fame during the war.

NC18603 - Boeing 314 Yankee Clipper *of Pan American Airways System at its moorings in 1939.*
(Photo: Authors collection)

American War Efforts

Also in the USA, in 1942, the US War Department was faced with the need to transport war materiel and personnel to Britain. Allied shipping in the Atlantic Ocean was suffering heavy losses to German U-boats, so a requirement was issued for an aircraft that could cross the Atlantic with a large payload. Due to wartime priorities, the design was further constrained in that the aircraft could not be made of metal.

The aircraft was the brainchild of Henry J Kaiser, a leading Liberty ship builder. He teamed up with aircraft designer Howard Hughes to create what would become the largest aircraft built at that time. It was designed to be capable of carrying 750 fully equipped troops or one M4 Sherman tank. The original designation 'HK-1' reflected the Hughes and Kaiser collaboration.

The HK-1 contract was issued in 1942 as a development contract and called for three aircraft to be constructed under a two-year deadline in order to be available for the war effort. Seven configurations were considered including twin-hull and single-hull designs with combinations of four, six, and eight wing-mounted engines. The

final design eclipsed any large transport then built. To conserve metal, it would be built mostly of wood; hence, the 'Spruce Goose' epithet tagged on the aircraft by the media, a nickname that Howard Hughes detested. It was also referred to as the Flying Lumberyard by some critics.

While Kaiser had originated the 'flying cargo ship' concept, he did not have an aeronautical background and deferred to Hughes and his designer, Glenn Odekirk. Development dragged on, which frustrated Kaiser, who blamed delays partly on restrictions placed for the acquisition of strategic materials such as aluminum, but also placed part of the blame on Hughes' well-known insistence on perfection. Although construction of the first HK-1 took place 16 months after the receipt of the development contract, Kaiser withdrew from the project.

Hughes continued the programme on his own under the designation 'H-4 Hercules', signing a new government contract that now limited production to one example. Work proceeded slowly, with the result that the H-4 was not completed until well after the war was over. It was built by the Hughes Aircraft Company at Hughes

The Hughes H-4 Hercules lies in Long Beach harbour undergoing last minute preparations before taxi trials. The size of the aircraft is not really noticable in this picture. (Photo: Authors collection)

Moving the pieces of Howard Hughes' huge flying boat brought its own problems - here wing sections were trucked from the Hughes Aircraft Company plant in Culver City along a Redondo Beach highway en route to the graving dock on Terminal Island Long Beach for assembly.

*The hull recieved a police escort and power cables had to be moved as it progressed along the Roosevelt Highway in San Pedro.
(Photos: Authors collection)*

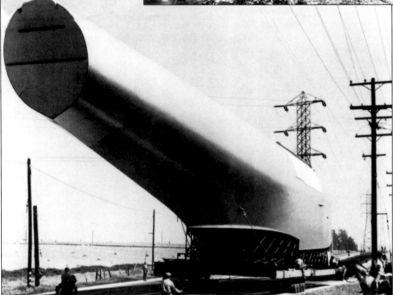

usage of government funds for the aircraft. During a Senate hearing on August 6, 1947 Hughes said:*'The Hercules was a monumental undertaking. It is the largest aircraft ever built. It is over five stories tall with a wingspan longer than a football field. That's more than a city block. Now, I put the sweat of my life into this thing. I have my reputation all rolled up in it and I have stated several times that if it's a failure I'll probably leave this country and never come back. And I mean it'.*

Airport, location of present day Playa del Rey, Los Angeles, California, employing the plywood-and-resin 'Duramold' process – a form of composite technology – for the laminated wood construction, which was considered a technological tour de force. It was shipped on streets to Pier E in Long Beach, California by a company specialising in house moving. The Spruce Goose was moved in three large sections consisting of the fuselage and each wing, and a fourth smaller shipment containing the tail assembly parts and other smaller assemblies. After final assembly a hangar was erected around the flying boat with a ramp to launch the H-4 into the harbor.

In 1947, Howard Hughes testifed before the Senate War Investigating Committee over the

On November 2, 1947, following a break in the Senate Hearings during which Hughes returned to California he began taxi tests on the H-4. His crew included Dave Grant as co-pilot, two flight engineers, Don Smith and Joe Petrali, 16 mechanics, and two other flight crew. In addition, the H-4 carried a number of invited guests from the press corps and additional industry representatives.

After the first two taxi runs, four reporters left to file stories, but the remaining press stayed for the final test run of the day. After picking up speed on the channel facing Cabrillo Beach, the Hercules lifted off, remaining airborne at 70 feet off the water and a speed of 135 miles per hour for around a mile. At this altitude and with the aircraft still in

Two views of the interior of the Hughes H-4 Hercules

Left: Looking towards the rear of the H-4 on the day before it flew.

Below: Howard Hughes watches Shell Bowen at work on the radio panel. He flew a lot with Hughes, but was not on board during the one and only flight of the H-4. (Photos: Authors collection)

ground effect Hughes proved to his detractors his masterpiece was flight-worthy, thus vindicating the use of government funds. Nevertheless, the H-4 never flew again. Its lifting capacity and ceiling were never tested.

It was during the senate hearings that Howard Hughes revealed some of the mathematical facts behind building very large aircraft in a simple, clearly understood way – facts and calculations that would have an impact in the future. '*We have discovered a great, great deal about the design and building of big airplanes*' he said. '*For example, it has long been considered that the bigger the airplane is, the more efficient it is. We have discovered, and I believe it to be quite important as a discovery - we have discovered that is not the fact.*

'*If I may be technical for just a minute. The body of the airplane becomes more efficient as it is larger. Now the reason for that is obvious. The skin area, which determines the drag, goes up as the square of the size; whereas the volume, which determines the cargo or passengers it can carry, the volume goes up as the cube.*

'*You can see that the cube will exceed the square, and therefore the carrying capacity will be greater in relation to drag as size goes up. But on the other hand, we have discovered that wing design is quite different, and that as the wing becomes larger, it weighs more per square foot than a smaller wing. In other words, a wing of 320-foot span, built according to the same design criteria, will weigh more in relation to its size than a smaller wing.*

'*Now, a point is reached, apparently, where the loss in wing efficiency, that is, in relation to its weight, exceeds the gain in body efficiency, and where those two lines cross, apparently, it is not desirable to build a bigger ship.*

'*Now, this one may have actually exceeded that point, but at least we will find out. And we have already found out a good deal in that direction. Now that, of course, is of some value. I think it is of considerable value in the design of further planes*'.

Immediately after the successful flight of the

flying boat everyone understood *Time* magazine's terse headline: 'It Flies!' The November hearing was an anticlimax. Senator Brewster had gone gunning for big game-Hughes and the connection with President Roosevelt. The committee instead bagged Brig. Gen. Bennett Meyers, whose financial misdeeds were uncovered during the Hughes investigation.

Partisan dissension delayed release of the Senate committee report of the Hughes investigation until April 1948, and even then it was fully approved by only the Republican members of the committee. The main conclusions of the report regarding the HK-1 flying boat were that the project, '...*which produced no planes during the war, was an unwise and unjustifiable expense as a wartime project. The manpower, facilities, and public funds devoted to it during the war were wasted at a time when military planes were urgently needed .... The conclusion is inescapable that the decision of the War Production Board was influenced because of the wide and favorable public acceptance of the proposal of Henry I. Kaiser for the mass production of huge cargo planes which Kaiser claimed would overcome the existing submarine menace to ocean transportation.*'

The aircraft never flew again. Some have suggested that Hughes was afraid of it – while others closely connected with it suggest that there was nothing wrong at all.

Evidently, however, the flying boat did have its weaknesses. According to one of Hughes's mechanics, '*Maybe one of the reasons why they didn't fly it again was there was a little fluctuation in the tail, and maybe it wasn't beefed up enough to suit him.*' Another mechanic said, '*There was a lot of little damage. I don't know whether I should say it or not, but there was. That's when they went out into the wing and put little metal stiffeners in there to hold the glue joints together. A lot of angles snapped loose. I guess the whipping of the wing is what did most of that.*'

The H-4 Hercules may have been the largest flying boat ever built, but it certainly was not the largest ever concieved. This may well have been the Saunders-Roe P192 - a giant of an aircraft that had been proposed following a scheme by a consultant for the P&O Shipping Company what wanted an enormous 1,000 seat airliner with accommodation similar to a luxury liner.

It was easily the largest aircraft ever seriously designed in Britain, the P192 'Queen' was enormous in every way; it was twice as long as a Boeing 757: 318 feet, and had a wing span - 313 feet - nearly half that again of a Boeing 747. The fuselage was of constant diameter, being 33 feet across, and the design also featured two large 'v' tails that stretched 88 feet high above the keel. Power was to be provided by twenty-four Rolls-Royce Conway jet engines of 18,500lb thrust, which were positioned within huge delta wings mounted above the fuselage.The engine bays were to be titanium, and big enough so as to be able to work on the engines in flight. Not that this would be needed; cruise power of 86% RPM could have been maintained with up to six engines shut down at once. Thus any engine changes could wait till the craft returned to its base at the end of the week. There were to have been split flaps below the engine exhausts. The engines themselves were to be mounted well outboard, clear of hull spray, and breathing through extra intakes on top of the wing when the machine was on the water. The main intakes were opened only in flight. There were 'hydroflaps' in the rear fuselage for good water

The Saunders Roe P192, supposedly named 'Queen' - it allegedly had five decks, 40 stewards and 53 toilets!

maneuverability; and interconnected spoilers and ailerons for roll control, as on the Boeing 707. All controls were fully powered.

There was to be a flight crew of seven, plus service staff including forty cabin stewards. The flight deck, or control deck, was of immense proportions, more akin to the bridge of a luxury liner.

The accommodation was laid out over five decks to enable passengers to eat and sleep on board, with lounges and bars. It included some fifty-three toilets and a purser's office. Seating was to have been divided into six-passenger compartments, as in old-fashioned sleeper trains, with the seats converting into sleeping berths at night. First-class passengers even had separate bars and dining rooms, lounges and dressing rooms. There was an elaborate galley from whence food was to be conveyed to the upper-decks by elevator. The crew had sleeping accommodation in the lowest deck inside the keel.

Designed for what was then the all-important Australian route, it was envisaged that, like the great liners, passengers would take-off from Southampton Water and then stop in Fanara in Egypt, Karachi, Calcutta (for a halfway stop), Singapore, and Darwin, before arriving in Sydney forty-eight hours later. The legs between Karachi and Calcutta, and Singapore and Darwin, were designed for sleep periods, while at the other stops, refuelling would have taken place while meals were served. The all-up weight of this massive design was 1,500,000lb

Double Deck land machines - Boeing

It is hard to decide which was the first land aircraft with double-deck features, but an early example was the Boeing 377, also called the Stratocruiser, a large

The flight deck of the Boeing 377 was roomy - someone once said it was like flying the bay window of your house!

Pan American World Airways' N1041V Clipper Yankee *rests between flights at Dusseldorf, Germany. (Photo: Authors collection)*

The main cabin (left) and lower lounge area of the Stratocruiser. (Photos: Authors collection)

long-range airliner built after World War Two. As was usual with many of the Boeing designs, the company used military projects and contracts to provide development of comparative civil designs - the 377 was developed from the C-97 Stratofreighter, itself a military derivative of the B-29 Superfortress used for troop transport. The Stratocruiser's first flight was on 8 July 1947.

Released in the late 1940s, the aircraft was powered by four piston engines, driving tractor propellers. It had a pressurized cabin, which was a relatively new feature to transport aircraft at the time, and two decks. Airlines were able to make transoceanic flights easier and faster with the new aircraft, which enabled easier international travel to places such as Hawaii.

The Stratocruisers did not have great reliability, mainly due to chronic problems with the four 28-cylinder Pratt & Whitney Wasp Major radial engines and their associated four-blade propellers.

Like the C-97, the 377 was developed towards the end of World War Two by adapting an enlarged upper fuselage onto the lower fuselage and wings, which were essentially the same as those of the B-50 Superfortress, itself the high-performance evolution of the B-29 Superfortress bomber. The 377 was larger and longer-ranged than the Lockheed Constellation and Douglas DC-6, with nonstop transatlantic range eastbound. Production ended in 1950.

The 'inverted-figure-8' double-deck fuselage design provided 6,600 cubic feet of interior space where the lower deck had a smaller diameter than the upper deck. It offered seating for over 100 passengers, or sleeping berths for up to 28

berthed and five seated passengers. It first flew on 8 July 1947. It had the speed and range to span ocean routes, enabling flying from New York to Hawaii in less than 24 hours. Pressurisation (previously introduced on the Boeing Stratoliner and also designed into the B-29) allowed sea-level cabin pressure at 15,500 foot altitude. At 25,000 feet passengers enjoyed a 'cabin altitude' of only 5,500 feet.

Despite a service record remembered for a number of disasters arising from propeller blade failures, the Stratocruiser was one of the capable post-war propeller-driven transports, and certainly among the most luxurious. Only 55 were built as airliners, joined eventually by the reconditioned prototype. Another 60 of this general design, with significant engineering differences, were built as C-97 military transports, but most were built as KC-97 tankers.

The Stratocruiser flew premier services to Hawaii, across both the Pacific and Atlantic Oceans, and elsewhere in the world. It was one of the few airliners with a double-decker seating arrangement (another was the French Breguet Deux-Ponts) until the arrival of the 747, though some airlines did have lower-level lounges on their L-1011 TriStar aircraft. The upper deck of the Stratocruiser was for 55–100 passenger seats or 28 sleeper berths, while the lower deck had a lounge and bar. Passengers could walk down and get a drink on the long flights, once the aircraft levelled off at cruising altitude.

In the late 1950s these aircraft were starting to become superseded by jets such as the De Havilland Comet, Boeing 707 and Douglas DC-8. A few survived to be sold to smaller airlines, used

The Air France's 'Deux Ponts' F-BASO seen between flights.

as freighters or converted into a specialised freighter called a Guppy.

French double-deckers

Breguet of France began design work on their Model 761 two-deck airliner in 1944. It was decided that a medium range airliner with seating for over 100 passengers would be built. The design envisaged using readily available engines with the aim of ease of manufacture and an early first-flight date. The design was known as Project 76-1.

The 761 featured a cantilever wing set at mid-height on the bulky fuselage. The retractable tricycle landing gear featured dual-wheel main units. The empennage, high on the rear fuselage had twin fins and rudders. The prototype was powered by four 1,580 hp SNECMA built Gnome-Rhône 14R radial engines.

The prototype was followed by three Br.761S pre-production aircraft powered by 2,020 hp Pratt & Whitney R-2800-B31 radial engines. These were fitted with 12 feet 1½in diameter Hamilton Standard propellors. The aircraft successfully completed their trials incident-free. Their first

flights were in 1951 or 1952. They also included a vestigial central fin. The French Government ordered 12 production aircraft, the Breguet 76-3 which were later redesignated Br.763. Six aircraft were to be operated by Air France and the other six by the Ministry of Transport. The 763 had more powerful engines, an 1.20 metres larger wingspan, strengthened wings and three-crew flight deck (earlier aircraft had four crew). The 763 first flew on 20 July 1951 and entered service with Air France during autumn 1952.

Air France aircraft had accommodation for 59 passengers on the top deck, and 48 on the lower deck, although the aircraft was capable of carrying 135 passengers in a high-density layout.

Projects to build versions powered with British engines (for possible United Kingdom buyers) did not come to fruition. These projects would have been the 766 (with the Bristol Hercules radial engine), and the 767 with British turboprop engines.

The first Br.761 entered service with Air Algérie in 1952 as a cargo aircraft, only to be withdrawn early the next year. The Breguet Br.763 Provence entered service with Air France on 10 March 1953. The

24

One of the two Lockheed R6V Constitutions seen in flight low over the California coastline.

Both machines were retired from the US Navy in 1953, The first was stored at Litchfield Park, Arizona. It was purchased and flown to Las Vegas, but was never put into civilian service, being used as a billboard to advertise Alamo Gasoline and eventually scrapped.

inaugural route was Lyon - Algiers. It was used on European routes from Paris, mainly to the Mediterranean, but occasionally to London. Domestic routes included Paris to Lyon, Marseille and Nice.

The US Military also came up with a number of designs - Lockheed Aircraft designed the R6V Constitution as a large, propeller-driven, double-decker transport aircraft developed from 1942 onwards by Lockheed as a long-range, high capacity transport and airliner for the US Navy and Pan American Airways. Initially designated the Lockheed Model 89, the Constitutions were identified as R6O until 1950.

Pan Am was involved in the study because such an aircraft had potential use as a commercial airliner. This transport would carry 17,500 pounds of cargo 5,000 miles at a cruising altitude of 25,000 feet and a speed greater than 250 mph. The aircraft would be fully pressurized and large enough so that most major components could be accessed and possibly repaired in flight. For instance, tunnels led through the thick wings to all four engines.

The aircraft was designed by a team of engineers led by Willis Hawkins and W A Pulver of Lockheed and Commander E. L. Simpson, Jr. of the Navy. The name Constitution was given to the project by Lockheed president Robert E Gross. The Constitution design had a 'double bubble' fuselage, the cross section of which was a 'figure eight'. This unorthodox design, originally created in 1937 by Curtiss-Wright's chief aircraft designer George A Page Jr and first introduced with the Curtiss C-46 Commando, utilized the structural advantages of a cylinder for cabin pressurisation, without the wasted space that would result from a single large cylinder of the same volume.

The original contract from the Bureau of Aeronautics called for 50 Constitutions for a total price tag of $111,250,000. On VJ Day, however, the contract was scaled back to $27,000,000 for only two aircraft. Only two of the aircraft were ever built, both prototypes.

The Constitution had operational difficulties which prevented it from meeting its original design objectives. The large airframe needed more power than the four Pratt & Whitney R-4360s could deliver. The engines also had cooling problems. While this could be compensated for by flying with engine cooling gills partially open, it increased drag and therefore decreased the overall range.

The Navy operated the two Constitutions through the end of the 1940s and into the 1950s. By 1949, however, the Navy announced that it could no longer afford to operate them, and offered them to airlines on a five-year lease. There was no interest from airlines in using the Constitutions

(the airline version was named the Model 189), so the Navy retired both aircraft in 1953. They went into storage at Litchfield Park, Arizona in 1955. Both aircraft and 13 spare engines were sold for $97,785. Lockheed proposed the Model 389 and Model 489 airliners based on the Constitution, which would have accommodated up to 169 passengers. Neither of these 'paper' projects received much interest from civil operators.

The Convair XC-99, 43-52436, was a prototype heavy cargo aircraft built by Convair for the United States Air Force. It was the largest piston-engined land-based transport aircraft ever built, and was developed from the B-36 bomber, sharing the wings and some other structures with it. The first flight was on 23 November 1947 in San Diego, California, and after testing it was delivered to the Air Force on 23 November 1949.

Design capacity of the XC-99 was 100,000 lb of cargo or 400 fully equipped troops on its double cargo decks. A cargo lift was installed for easier loading. The engines face rearward in a pusher configuration.

In July 1950 the XC-99 flew its first cargo mission, designated 'Operation Elephant'. It transported 101,266 pounds of cargo, including engines and propellers for the B-36, from San Diego to Kelly Air Force Base in San Antonio, Texas, a record it would later break when it lifted 104,000 lb from an airfield at 5,000 feet elevation. In August 1953, the XC-99 would make its longest flight, 12,000 miles, to Rhein-Main Air Base, Germany, by way of Bermuda and the Azores. It carried more than 60,000 lb each way. It attracted much attention everywhere it flew.

The US Air Force determined that it had no need for such a large, long-range transport at that time, and no more were ordered. The sole XC-99 served until 1957, including much use during the Korean War. It made twice weekly trips from Kelly

The Convair XC-99 - a civilian version - the Model 37 - was offered, but never built. It is seen here in the early colour scheme, without the nose-radar fitted and huge single wheel landing gear.

Above: the lower deck, looking towards the tail with opening lower fuselage doors.

Right: the upper deck, again looking towards the tail.

Below: the XC-99 at Kelly AFB, Texas while attached to the Military Air Transport Service 1700th Air Transport Group in 1954. By this time it had been fitted with the 'pinoccio' radome and 'bogie' landing gear.

Bottom: from a contemporary brochure for Pan American: 'A double-deck interior will embrace two-passenger staterooms, oversize berths, two lounges, and a number of rest rooms, with Henry Dreyfuss interiors assuring color and comfort for passengers on the long over-water routes'.
(Photos: Authors collection)

AFB to the aircraft depot at McClellan AFB, California, transporting supplies and parts for the B-36 bomber while returning by way of other bases or depots making pick-ups and deliveries along the way. During its operational life the XC-99 logged over 7,400 hours total time, and transported more than 60,000,000 lbs of cargo. The aircraft made its last flight on 19 March 1957, landing at Kelly Air Force Base, where it would remain for the next 47 years.

The Convair Model 37 was a large civil passenger design derived from the XC-99 but was never built. It was to be of similar proportions to the XC-99; 182 feet 6 inches length, 230 feet wingspan, and a high-capacity, double-deck fuselage. The projected passenger load was to be 204, and the effective range 4,200 miles.

Fifteen aircraft were ordered by Pan American for transatlantic service and supposedly given the name 'Pegasus'. However, the fuel and oil consumption of the six 3,500 hp Wasp Major radials powering the XC-99 and B-36 meant that the design was not economically viable, and the hoped-for 5000 hp turboprop powerplants did not materialize fast enough. The low number of orders were not sufficient to initiate production, and the project was abandoned.

MODEL 37—Consolidated Vultee's giant 204-passenger transport will make New York to London trip in 9 hours. It has two decks with luxurious accommodations for passengers, crew. Facilities will include rest rooms (above) and lounges (below). Fifteen are on order for PAA.

Chapter Two

Origins of the Wide-Body

The communists were on the move in South-east Asia and so in March 1961, President Kennedy authorized increasing aid to Laos, where rebel forces were attempting to overthrow the government. In neighboring Vietnam, the Viet Cong were killing more South Vietnamese every day in their drive to reunify their divided country as a Communist nation. The area was no longer a geographical nonentity as uneasy details splashed over the front pages of American newspapers. The domino theory became the prevalent wisdom as it was predicted that one by one, all of the countries of Southeast Asia would fall to the Communists.

As a result, the US Department of Defense began planning ways to move large numbers of troops and equipment rapidly to forward areas. The idea of a super-size logistics transport began to gain strength.

In 1961, several aircraft companies began studying heavy jet transport designs that would replace the Douglas C-133 Cargomaster and complement the Lockheed C-141 Starlifters. In addition to higher overall performance, the United States Army wanted a transport aircraft with a larger cargo bay than the C-141, whose interior was too small to carry a variety of their larger equipment. These studies led to the 'CX-4' design concept, but in 1962 the proposed six-engine design was rejected, because it was not viewed as a significant advance over the C-141. In 1963, the USAF began a series of study projects on a very large strategic transport aircraft. By late 1963, the next conceptual design was named CX-X. It was equipped with four engines, instead of six engines in the earlier CX-4 concept. The CX-X had a gross weight of 550,000 pounds, a maximum payload of 180,000 lb and a speed of Mach 0.75 (500 mph). The cargo compartment was 17.2 feet wide by 13.5 feet high and 100 feet long with front and rear access doors. To provide required power and range with only four engines required a new engine with dramatically improved fuel efficiency.

Meanwhile, over at Boeing, director of engineering for the Airplane Division, Maynard Pennell assigned William L. Hamilton, a young engineer and operations analyst, to study the factors involved in the movement of an entire army division by air. Pennell instructed Hamilton to analyse US Armed Forces airlift requirements for the next two decades. Hamilton gathered a team of engineers and set about building scale models of Army vehicles to load onto the floor plan of an advanced heavy aircraft layout. The central consideration became the maximising of the floor area.

Specific concepts were studied by Kenneth F. Holtby and his product development staff. Working with Hamilton's group they moved the cockpit up and over the body. The resulting configuration maximized the floor area on the main deck and allowed the entire nose of the aircraft to be hinged. The nature of operations studied - fast loading and unloading at unimproved runways in forward areas by an unarmed aircraft - further dictated design parameters. Boeing invested in excess of $10 million in the project and the final 4,272-page proposal submitted took the form of an aircraft that weighed over a half million pounds.

The criteria were finalized by the Department of Defense and an official request for proposal was issued in April 1964 for the 'Cargo Experimental Heavy Logistics System' (CX-HLS), previously the CX-X. Proposals were received from Boeing, Douglas, General Dynamics, Lockheed, and Martin Marietta. General Electric, Curtiss-Wright, and Pratt & Whitney submitted proposals for the engines. After a selection process, Boeing, Douglas and Lockheed were given one-year study contracts for the airframe, along with General Electric and Pratt & Whitney for the engines. All three of the designs shared a number of features; all three placed the cockpit well above the cargo area to allow for cargo loading through a nose door. The Boeing and Douglas designs used a pod on the top of the fuselage containing the cockpit, while the Lockheed design extended the cockpit profile down the length of the fuselage, giving it an egg-shaped cross section. All of the designs had swept wings, as well as front and rear cargo doors allowing simultaneous loading and unloading. Lockheed's design featured

The first Lockheed C-5A Galaxy (66-8303) was rolled out on 2 March 1968 and prepared for initial flight trials at Lockheed's Marietta plant, located adjacent to Dobbins AFB in Georgia. Hundreds of workers and invited guests gathered to witness the monumental occasion. (Photos: Authors collection)

With the name 'Galaxy' proudly in the forward fuselage and a huge nose probe fitted for test flying, the maiden flight took place on 30 June 1968 and lasted 94 minutes; Lockheed pilots Leo J. Sullivan and Walter E. Hensleigh were at the controls. (Photo: Authors collection)

a T-tail, while the designs by Boeing and Douglas had conventional tails.

The Air Force may have considered Boeing's design better than that of Lockheed, although Lockheed's proposal was the lowest total cost bid. and so the Lockheed design was selected the winner in September 1965, then awarded a contract in December. General Electric's TF-39 engine was selected in August 1965 to power the new transport aircraft. At the time GE's engine concept was revolutionary, as all engines beforehand had a bypass ratio of less than two-to-one, while the TF-39 promised and would achieve a ratio of eight-to-one, which had the benefits of increased engine thrust and lower fuel consumption.

The political saga of the C-5 is worthy of a book in its own right and is far too complex for here. It is sufficient to say that in the early sixties, with the 'military-industrial complex' under attack, President Kennedy had ordered Secretary of Defense Robert McNamara to do something about the poor image of the Defense Department for military procurement. McNamara responded by changing the rules.

Termed'Total Package Procurement', the major innovation of the new philosophy was the requirement for each manufacturer to present a single bid. The bid must not only include research and development, but the production phase as well—in short, a total price for the finished hardware. The C-5 was to be the first aircraft to come under the new rules.

The bid for 115 aircraft submitted by Boeing was $2.3 billion. Douglas asked $2 billion, and Lockheed, feeling that renegotiation would be a certain option at a later date, simply presented a bid low enough to be assured of winning. Their bid was $1.9 billion, $400 million less than Boeing, and even $300 million less than the Pentagon's own estimate.

When the Department of Defense announced the results of the competition for the C-5A. Thornton 'T' Arnold Wilson, Boeing's President, gave an emotional message over the public address system: *'I regret to report that Boeing has lost the C-5A competition. The award was made to Lockheed. It is an understatement to say we are disappointed; however, we are not disappointed in our people. What we learned will be applied to our other business efforts.'*

The C-5 is a large high-wing cargo aircraft. It has a distinctive high T-tail, 25 degree wing sweep, and four TF39 turbofan engines mounted on pylons beneath the wings. The C-5 has 12 internal wing tanks and is equipped for aerial refueling. It has both nose and aft doors for 'drive-through' loading and unloading of cargo. The C-5 is also known as FRED (Fantastic - often said as something much more rude - Ridiculous, Economic Disaster) by its crews due to its maintenance and reliability issues along with a large consumption of fuel.

It has an upper deck seating area for 73 passengers and two loadmasters. Passengers face the rear of the aircraft, rather than forward. Its takeoff and landing distances, at maximum gross weight, are 8,300 feet and 4,900 feet respectively. Its high flotation main landing gear has 28 wheels to share the weight. The rear main landing gear is steerable for a smaller turning radius and it rotates 90 degrees horizontally before it is retracted after takeoff. The 'kneeling' landing gear system permits lowering of the parked aircraft so the cargo floor is at truck-bed height to facilitate vehicle loading and unloading.

The C-5 features a cargo compartment 121 feet long, 13.5 feet high, and 19 feet wide, or just over 31,000 cu ft. The compartment can accommodate up to 36 master pallets or a mix of palletised cargo and vehicles. Nose and aft doors open the full width and height of the cargo compartment to permit faster and easier loading. Ramps are full width at each end for loading double rows of vehicles. The Galaxy is capable of carrying nearly every type of the Army's combat equipment, including bulky items such as the 74 short tons armoured vehicle launched bridge (AVLB), from the USA to any location on the globe. A C-5 is capable of transporting up to six Boeing AH-64 Apaches or five Bradley Fighting Vehicles.

As with many other aircraft, the C-5 soon became involved in politics that involved hidden cost-overruns and the doctoring of documents.

Advent of the Boeing 747

At Boeing the booming space and missile business of the sixties was being augmented by accelerating sales of the 707 and the 727. Nevertheless, the C-5 contract loss created a giant spike of anxiety.

As airline traffic continued a steep rise around the world, Europeans began talking about an airbus, and Boeing began looking into plans to stretch the 707. However, with Douglas already in the market with a stretched DC-8, the idea for a higher capacity 707 was abandoned.

Even before it lost the CX-HLS contract, Boeing was being pressured by Juan Trippe, president of Pan American World Airways, to build a passenger aircraft more than twice the size of the 707. Trippe thought that airport congestion, worsened by increasing numbers of passengers carried on relatively small aircraft could be addressed by a large new machine.

In 1965, Joe Sutter was transferred from Boeing's 737 development team to manage the design studies for a new airliner, already assigned the model number 747. Sutter initiated a design study with Pan Am and other airlines, in order to better understand their requirements. At the time, it was widely thought that the 747 would eventually be superseded by supersonic transport aircraft.

Boeing responded by designing the 747 so that it could be adapted easily to carry freight and remain in production even if sales of the passenger version declined. In the freighter role, the clear need was to support the containerized shipping methodologies that were being widely introduced at about the same time. Standard containers are 8 feet square at the front (slightly higher due to attachment points) and available in 20 and 40 feet lengths. This meant that it would be possible to support a 2-wide 2-high stack of containers two or three ranks deep with a fuselage size similar to the earlier CX-HLS project.

Ultimately, the high-winged CX-HLS Boeing design was not used for the 747, although technologies developed for their bid had an influence. The original design included a full-length double-deck fuselage with rows of eight-across seating and two aisles on the lower deck and seven-across seating and two aisles on the upper deck. However, concern over evacuation routes and limited cargo-carrying capability caused this idea to be scrapped in early 1966 in favour of a wider single deck design. The cockpit was, therefore, placed on a shortened upper deck so that a freight-loading door could be included in the nose cone; this design feature produced the 747's distinctive 'bulge'. In early models it was not clear what to do with the small space in the pod behind the cockpit, and this was initially specified as a 'lounge' area with no permanent seating.

One of the principal technologies that enabled an aircraft as large as the 747 to be conceived was the high-bypass turbofan engine. The engine technology was thought to be capable of delivering double the power of the earlier turbojets while consuming a third less fuel. General Electric had pioneered the concept but was committed to developing the engine for the C-5 Galaxy and did not enter the commercial market until later. Pratt & Whitney was also working on the same principle and, by late 1966, Boeing, Pan Am and Pratt & Whitney agreed to develop a new engine designated the JT9D to power the 747.

The project was designed with a new methodology called fault tree analysis, which allowed the effects of a failure of a single part to be studied to determine its impact on other systems. To address concerns about safety and flyability, the 747's design included structural redundancy, redundant hydraulic systems, quadruple main landing gear and dual control surfaces. Additionally, some of the most advanced high-lift devices used in the industry were included in the new design, in order to allow it to operate from existing airports. These included leading edge flaps running almost the entire length of the wing, as well as complex three-part slotted flaps along the rear. The wing's complex three-part flaps increase wing area by 21%and lift by 90%when fully deployed compared to their non-deployed configuration.

Extrapolation of historical passenger traffic growth to 1970 set the probable required seating capacity at about 375, and the 747 was born.

To John Yeasring, vice president of the Commercial Airplane Division, the project was a frightening one. It would take an investment of more than $500 million, dwarfing the investments on the 707, 727, and 737 combined. Sutter maintained his confident air. *'The 747 or something like it has to happen.'*

In April 1966, Pan Am ordered 25 747-100 aircraft for US$525 million. During the ceremonial 747 contract-signing banquet in Seattle on Boeing's 50th Anniversary, Juan Trippe predicted that the 747 would be *'... a great weapon for peace, competing with intercontinental missiles for mankind's destiny'.*

Boeing agreed to deliver the first 747 to Pan Am by the end of 1969. The delivery date left 28 months to design the aircraft, which was two-thirds of the normal time. The schedule was so fast paced that the people who worked on it were given the nickname 'The Incredibles'. Developing the aircraft was such a technical and financial challenge that management was said to have 'bet the company' when it started the project.

In spite of its cost of $22 million per copy, more than four times that of a 707-320, the world's airlines rushed to gain delivery positions. Including the Pan Am order, sales to fifteen airlines reached ninety-three within five months after the decision to go ahead was announced, and Boeing had a $1.8 billion commitment to produce. Both Boeing and Pan American had put their corporate existence on the line.

Problems abounded. The maximum empty weight of the airframe, which had been pegged at 274,094 pounds in the Pan Am contract, was

An early version of the 747 project was for a double-decker fuselage with six-abreast seating. Another model revealed three engines instead of four, mounted in the empennage topped by a high T-tail while yet another had the flight deck situated under the passenger cabin. Joe Sutter, Boeing's chief engineer, completely disregarded the 'turkeys' as he called them. Little did he realise that what he called a 'turkey' was really the Airbus A380 and the 'Beluga' heavy cargo lifter. (Photos: via Martin Bowman)

climbing alarmingly, and after the first year of engineering gestation, then stood at 308,924 pounds, threatening a payload reduction of more than 10%. The only remedy was to increase the gross takeoff weight, which was raised from 550,000 to 710,000 pounds.

Engine power then came into focus. A still more powerful engine would be needed, requiring larger nacelles and, in turn, major modifications to the wing design.

To produce such an aircraft in the quantities contemplated - seven machines a month at peak production - an assembly building, encompassing 160 million cubic feet would be required, larger in volume than any existing building in the world.

How this came into being is one of the legends of aviation. In January 1966 Bill Allen is supposed to have asked Mal Stamper, the former Vice President of the Boeing Turbine Division *'How would you like to build the worlds largest airplane?'*

Stamper's reply was *'...The only airplane I ever built had rubber bands on it.'*

Allen sat back in his chair. *'Do you want to build it or don't you?'* he demanded.

Allen pointed to an aerial photograph of Paine Field, near Everett, Washington, which had nothing much to offer except a 9,000-foot, little-used runway.

'We'll need an entirely new plant adjacent to the field, to build the 747. I want you to take responsibility for directing the program from start-up to fleet deliveries. The first airplane has been committed to Pan Am in September 1969.'

Beginning with 780 undulating acres of undeveloped and heavily forested land in the early summer of 1966, contractors cleared and leveled 250 acres and laid a two-mile-long railroad spur with a 5.6%gradient to serve the factory site.

The first locomotive, pulling outsized rail cars, was moving over the new spur by November. Working around the clock, contractors completed the first stage of construction by January 1967 - a low bay manufacturing and mockup building - allowing initial occupancy by Boeing workers. The huge mockup, completed at Plant II, at Boeing Field, Seattle, was immediately moved into place.

Only four months later, in May 1967, work was started on the first 747 in the main assembly building - still under construction - and by year end, with the building nearly complete, 5,000 employees were on the job.

The work force, eventually growing to 20,000, became Mal's Incredibles. *'I remember escorting workers to their cars, telling them to go home, that they'd put in enough hours, but they'd be back in the plant before I was.'*

The Everett 747 facility was essentially an assembly plant, with more than 65% of the aircraft subcontracted. Only the wing and the thirty-three-foot-long forward body section, enclosing the flight deck, were manufactured in Boeing plants. This commitment to spread the work throughout the United States was maximized on the 747, a continuing Boeing tradition, beginning early in the Company's history.

At the time, $2.1 billion in subcontracts were in effect, shared by approximately 20,000 companies residing in all fifty American States and several foreign countries.

In spite of major problems on every hand, production moved apace, and the first 747 rolled out of the Everett factory in September 1968, and flew on February 9, 1969.

Bill Allen masked his anxiety in a hearty handshake with test pilot Jack Waddell on that gray day at Paine Field, but his stark words left nothing unsaid: *'Jack, I hope you know the Boeing Company flies with you today.'*

Astonishing onlookers by its quietness, aircraft used only half of the runway for takeoff. At first flight, 196 machines had been sold to thirty-one airlines, and Boeing had committed to increase the production rate from seven to eight and one-half aircraft a month.

747 certification

Flying the first four aircraft off the line in an integrated plan, Boeing had compressed the certification programme into just ten months - by far the most ambitious in aviation history - and the 747 went into service for Pan Am on January 22, 1970.

However, the new Pratt and Witney JT9D series high bypass engines, the designated powerplant for the 747s, had ran into serious delays in development.

The engines suffered from distortion, the high pressure turbine blades and seals rubbing at the sides, and the high pressure compressor blades rubbing at the bottom of their casings. This phenomenon was not fully understood at the time, and took a considerable amount of time to fix.

Early in 1969, twenty-six completed 747s, representing almost the net worth of the Company, most of them without engines, were parked on the flight line at Everett, Washington, waiting to be delivered.

Similar problems occurred just over forty years later in 2013 that caused a grounding of the Boeing 787 Dreamliner following a series of incidents, mostly concerning fires with the lithium-ion batteries fitted to the aircraft. Boeing Chairman, President and CEO Jim McNerney was forced to issue a statement after the US Federal Aviation Administration issued an emergency airworthiness directive that required US 787 operators to temporarily cease operations and recommends other regulatory agencies to follow suit: *'The safety of passengers and crew members who fly aboard Boeing airplanes is our highest priority.*

'Boeing is committed to supporting the FAA and finding answers as quickly as possible. The company is working around the clock with its customers and the various regulatory and investigative authorities. We will make available the entire resources of The Boeing Company to assist.

'We are confident the 787 is safe and we stand behind its overall integrity. We will be taking every necessary step in the coming days to assure our customers and the traveling public of the 787's safety and to return the airplanes to service.

'Boeing deeply regrets the impact that recent events have had on the operating schedules of our customers and the inconvenience to them and their passengers.'

Nevertheless, back in 1969 confidence prevailed in the 747 because of the integrity of the airframe, which had sustained a wing loading of 116% of its ultimate design load during its structural test to failure. Those results guaranteed a significant improvement in airline performance, translating to either more fuel for extended range, or an increased passenger load.

The arrival of modified engines in sufficient quantities in late 1969 led to the 'year of the 747' in 1970. When the first twelve months of service were completed in January 1971, the operational statistics numbed the mind. Ninety-eight 747s, flying the colours of eighteen airlines, carried

The first Boeing 747 is rolled out from the Everett plant on 30 September 1968.
(Photo: Authors collection)

The plant at Everett, along with the 747 evolved into a huge facility, along with paint and testing facilities. It will always be associated with 'Mal's Incredibles'. The picture was taken at the height of the engine problems with 25 747s grounded - almost all without engines fitted. Present are aircraft for Pan Am, TWA, BOAC, Japan Airlines, Northwest, Air France and Lufthansa.(author's collection via David Lee)

seven million passengers a distance of more than 71 million miles. The 30,000 revenue flights represented 15.5 billion passenger-miles, five times that logged by the 707 at an equal point in service.

Wide-body trijets from Douglas and Lockheed
Douglas - who had also participated in the C-5 competition also attempted to salvage something

By 1966, the situation for Douglas was crucial as they attempted to configure the correct aircraft to challenge the 747. With sales of over $1 billion, the company reported a loss in excess of $27 million. On the verge of a financial crisis, they began exploring the possibility of a merger.

North American and General Dynamics were involved in early discussions, but the McDonnell Aircraft Company quickly moved to the fore as the most likely candidate. McDonnell, a strongly based manufacturer of military airplanes, had never built a commercial aircraft. The merger of the two capabilities seemed ideal.

Talks led to terms, and on a cold, rainy morning in April 1967, the stockholders gathered

at Beverly Hills to vote the Douglas Aircraft Company out of existence. Donald Douglas, Sr., then seventy-five years old, moved to semi-retirement, stepping down from chairman, and becoming a board member of the new company, the McDonnell Douglas Corporation.

The headquarters of the newly merged company was established in St. Louis, with James S McDonnell Jr, 'Mr Mac' as its chairman.

A relative newcomer to the community of aviation pioneers who started their own companies, Mr. Mac had become one of its giants.

At the time of the merger, McDonnell had completed a very successful year, showing a $43 million profit on sales of just over $1 billion.

McDonnell Douglas concentrated on an aircraft with three engines, somewhat smaller than the 747, believing that US airports would never be ready for the 'jumbo' that Boeing had announced. The capacity would be in the 250-to 300-passenger range.

Lockheed, after dropping out of commercial competition when the ill-fated Electra ended production - and with the C-5A safely in their

Lockheed's built TriStars for many airlines, but none so colourful than the two for UK holiday airline Court Line.

On the left and seen during assembly at Palmdale is the yellow, orange and red G-BAAA Halcyon Days, while below is the pink G-BAAB Halcyon Breeze basks in the California sunshine during flight testing. (Photo: Ed Posey/author's collection)

pocket - was thought to have an advantage in entering the wide-bodied competition. Dan Haughton, the eternal optimist, saw what appeared to be a new opportunity, and in the autumn of 1967, publicly announced that Lockheed was prepared to take orders for the L-1011, also a 250- to 300-passenger capacity trijet, to be known as the TriStar. Termed as the L-1011-385-1 by the FAA, (later called the TriStar L-1011-1) it had a 20/80% mixed-class configuration for 52 first class passengers seated six-abreast and 204 coach class passengers seated eight abreast. Alternative arrangements were for a maximum of 345 all-

economy passengers by the removal of interior bulkheads and the changing of seats. Two months later, McDonnell Douglas followed, taking orders for their DC-10.

Daniel 'Dan' Jeremiah Haughton was a shrewd man with numbers, and had majored in accounting and business administration at the University of Alabama. Starting as a systems analyst at Lockheed's Burbank headquarters in 1933, he rose rapidly through the company. In 1961, he was named president of Lockheed, and in 1967, became chairman.

With Boeing targeting for the global market

N10DC - the prototype McDonnell Douglas DC-10 first flew on 29 July 1970. (Photo: Authors collection)

and the longer routes, the early cut-throat competition was between McDonnell Douglas and Lockheed. For the trijets, the sale of each aircraft for one meant minus one to its competitor.

American Airlines was first to announce. The decision had been agonisingly close. There was hardly a day when there was not either a Lockheed or a McDonnell Douglas man in the head office. At the end of the evaluation, an American Airlines official called Dan Haughton in to inform him that Lockheed had lost the order.

The American Airlines order, made public on 16 February 1968, was for twenty-five aircraft, amounting to a contract price of $382 million, or about $15.3 million per machine. American also took options on twenty-five more, raising the potential of the order to over $800 million.

With his two-month sales lead having evaporated, Haughton decided to mortgage Lockheed's future a little deeper, slashing the price of each Tristar by $1 million.

By the end of March, Lockheed had orders for 118 Tristars from Eastern, Delta, and TWA. A fourth order for fifty machines by Air Holdings Ltd., a hastily conceived consortium launched by Lockheed itself, with Rolls Royce of England as a partner, was achieved. Thus, Haughton had tightened the loyalty of Rolls, the engine manufacturer. They were in the venture together - win or lose.

The score was suddenly 168 to 25, and McDonnell Douglas paused to consider. David Lewis, new president of the Douglas operations, convinced Mr. Mac they had to stay in the race. To show their determination, they chopped one-half million dollars from the price of each DC-10.

On April 25, 1968, United Airlines, the largest United States customer, and last to decide, ordered sixty DC-10s.

Meanwhile, over in Europe there were stirrings of creation of an alternative to American domination.

Chapter Three

Airbus

Airbus Industrie began as a consortium of European aviation firms to compete with American companies such as Boeing, McDonnell Douglas, and Lockheed.

While many European aircraft were innovative, even the most successful had small production runs. In 1991, Jean Pierson, then CEO and Managing Director of Airbus Industrie, described a number of factors which explained the dominant position of American aircraft manufacturers: the land mass of the United States made air transport the favoured mode of travel; an alleged 1942 Anglo-American agreement that entrusted transport aircraft production to the US; and World War Two had left America with '…a profitable, vigorous, powerful and structured aeronautical industry.'

Airbus published the following as it's *raison d'être '…for the purpose of strengthening European co-operation in the field of aviation technology and thereby promoting economic and technological progress in Europe, to take appropriate measures for the joint development and production of an airbus.'*

Formation of Airbus Industrie

It was in 1965 that member companies of the European aircraft industry, along with representatives of the British and French governments began to examine the likely requirements for a medium range, high capacity commerical passenger aircraft.

Tentative negotiations commenced regarding a

French aeronautical engineer Roger Béteille, one of the key players in the formation of the European Airbus consortium. It was he who decided that English should be the working language and that measurements should not be metric because most airlines already had American built aircraft. Béteille retired in March 1984.

European collaborative approach. Individual aircraft companies had already envisaged such a requirement; in 1959 Hawker Siddeley had advertised an 'Airbus' version of the Armstrong Whitworth AW.660 Argosy, which would '… *be able to lift as many as 126 passengers on ultra short routes at a direct operating cost of 2d. per seat mile.'* Numerous other designs were studied, including a whole tranche of designs under the Handley Page 126 designation that were, in effect, all-wing airliners. Other schemes suggested a 'double-bubble' Hawker Siddeley Trident which saw the airliner's original upper fuselege lobe combine with a new lower fuselage. The upper deck provided six-abreast seating while the lower deck provided five-abreast - up to 200 passengers were scheduled to be carried. The lower passenger deck would have been foward of the wing only, the rear portion being for freight.

European aircraft manufacturers were becoming aware of the risks of such any new development and began to accept, along with their governments, that collaboration was required to develop such an aircraft and to compete with the more powerful US manufacturers.

At the 1965 Paris Air Show major European airlines informally discussed their requirements for a new 'airbus' capable of transporting 100 or more passengers over short to medium distances at a low cost. The same year Hawker Siddeley (at the urging of the UK government) teamed with Breguet and Nord to study airbus designs. The Hawker Siddeley - Breguet - Nord group put forward five proposals, the main one being the HBN100 which became the basis for the continuation of the project. This was a nine-abreast, 261-seat widebody design with a low-mounted wing of 30-degree sweepback fitted with leading and trailing edge lift devices. Propulsion would come from either a pair of Pratt & Witney JT9D-1s or Rolls Royce RB-198 engines mounted in underwing pods. With development, a 300 seater was expected to be available by 1975.

The other main project against the HBN100 was the HBN101, a twin-engined, bulbous-looking horizontal double-bubble aircraft with a high wing.

By 1966 the partners were Sud Aviation, later Aérospatiale (France), Arbeitsgemeinschaft Airbus, later Deutsche Airbus (Germany) and Hawker Siddeley (UK). A request for funding was made to the three governments in October 1966.

Germany was soon brought into the picture and on 26 September 1967 the three governments signed a Memorandum of Understanding (MoU) in London for what was now being referred to as the Airbus A300 - a 300 seat twin-jet wide-bodied airliner. Under the terms of the agreement France and the UK would each contribute 37.5% while Germany would contribute 25%. It was also agreed that Rolls-Royce would manufacture the engines.

Following the agreement, Roger Béteille was appointed technical director of the A300 development project. In 1952, he joined Sud-Aviation in Toulouse and held senior posts; Head of Flight Testing, Head of Rockets and Satellites division and the deputy technical director. He was to become A300 programme manager.

Béteille developed a division of labour which would be the basis of Airbus' production for years to come: France would manufacture the cockpit, flight control and the lower centre section of the fuselage; Hawker Siddeley, whose Trident technology had impressed him, was to manufacture the wings; Germany should make the forward and rear fuselage sections, as well as the upper centre section; the Dutch would make the flaps and spoilers; finally Spain would make the horizontal tailplane.

In the two years following this agreement, both the British and French governments expressed doubts about the project. The MoU had stated that 75 orders must be achieved by 31 July 1968. The French government threatened to withdraw from the project due to the concern over funding development of the Airbus A300, Concorde and the Dassault Mercure concurrently, but was persuaded otherwise. Having announced its concern at the A300B proposal in December 1968, and fearing it would not recoup its investment due to lack of sales, the British government announced

F-OCAZ, the first A300 takes to the skies on a test flight. (Photo: Airbus SAS)

its withdrawal on 10 April 1969. Germany took this opportunity to increase its share of the project to 50%. Given the participation by Hawker Siddeley up to that point, France and Germany were reluctant to take over its wing design. Thus the British company was allowed to continue as a privileged subcontractor. Hawker Siddeley invested £35 million in tooling and, requiring more capital, received a £35 million loan from the German government.

On 18 December 1970 Airbus Industrie was formally set up as a Groupement d'Intérêts Economique (GIE) to manage the development, manufacture and marketing of the A300B. The name 'Airbus' was taken from a non-proprietary term used by the airline industry in the 1960s to refer to a commercial aircraft of a certain size and range, for this term was acceptable to the French linguistically. Aérospatiale and Deutsche Airbus each took a 36.5% share of production work, Hawker Siddeley 20% and Fokker-VFW 7%. Each company would deliver its sections as fully equipped, ready-to-fly items. In addition to the original partners, Construcciones Aeronáuticas SA (CASA) of Spain joined the programme having acquired a 4.2% share of Airbus Industrie, with Aérospatiale and Deutsche Airbus reducing their stakes to 47.9%. In January 1979 British Aerospace, which had absorbed Hawker Siddeley in 1977, acquired a 20% share of Airbus Industrie. The majority shareholders reduced their shares to 37.9%, while CASA retained its original stake and was given responsibility for manufacturing the tailplane, forward fuselage passenger doors and all undercarriage doors. Of the three major partners, Aérospatiale was to manufacture the entire nose section including the flight deck, lower centre-section fuselage, four inboard spoilers, wing/body fairings and engine pylons, while also undertaking final assembly at Toulouse. Deutsche Airbus manufactured the forward fuselage between the flight deck and the wing box, the upper centre fuselage, rear fuselage including the tailcone, the fin, ten outboard spoilers and some cabin doors as well as equipping the wing and installing interiors and seats. Hawker Siddeley (later British Aerospace) had design authority for the wings, building the fixed wing structures while also working in collaboration with Fokker-VFW in the Netherlands, which produced the wingtips, moving wing surfaces and main undercarriage fairings.

Retention of production and engineering assets by the partner companies in effect made Airbus Industrie a sales and marketing company. This arrangement led to inefficiencies due to the inherent conflicts of interest that the four partner companies faced; they were both GIE shareholders of, and subcontractors to, the consortium. The companies collaborated on development of the Airbus range, but guarded the financial details of their own production activities and sought to maximise the transfer prices of their sub-assemblies. It was becoming clear that Airbus was no longer a temporary collaboration to produce a single aircraft design as per its original mission statement, it had become a long term brand for the development of further aircraft.

The original 300 seat airliner design matured into a smaller 250 seater, the A300 designation gaining a `B' suffix to denote the change. Two prototype A300B1s were built, the first of these flying from Toulouse, France on 28 October 1972, the second on 5 February the next year. The General Electric CF6 was the powerplant choice for initial A300s. Following the prototype A300B1s was the 2.65m longer A300B2, the first production version which first flew in April 1974. The B2 entered service with Air France on 23 May 1974.

Subsequent versions included the B2-200 with Krueger leading edge flaps and different wheels and brakes; the B2-300 with increased weights for

Eastern Airlines A300B4-203 N234EA in service. It was this order that gave Airbus a foothold in the USA. (Photo: Airbus SAS)

Dan Air's A300B4-103 G-BMNC seen outside the company's new engineering hangar at Gatwick in 1990.
(Photo: Authors collection)

greater payload and multi stop capability; the B4-100 a longer range version of the B2 with Krueger flaps; and the increased max takeoff weight B4-200 which featured reinforced wings and fuselage, improved landing gear and optional rear cargo bay fuel tank. A small number of A300C convertibles were also built, these featured a main deck freight door behind the wing on the left hand side. Late in the A300B4's production life an optional two crew flightdeck was offered as the A300-200FF (customers were Garuda, Tunis Air and VASP).

Although a notable engineering achievement, the A300 failed to impress many of the world's airlines. With slow sales, the big twin limped almost unnoticed through the early 1970s. The giant US aircraft manufacturers scoffed at it, and the global recession that the oil crisis in the Middle East sparked severely hampered it. These were vulnerable years for Airbus, which held onto life by a thread, selling only a single aircraft in 1976 and producing only one aircraft per month.

In 1977, the A300B4 became the first 'ETOPS compliant' aircraft – its high performance and safety standards qualified it for Extended Twin Engine Operations over water, providing operators with more versatility in routing.

As the airlines that were forced to adjust to higher fuel prices in the late 1970s they gradually recognized the economic appeal of a wide-body twin. The basic concept of a large twin, ironically, had come from an early American Airlines specification, but it was another US-based carrier, Eastern Airlines, that provided the sales breakthrough. The April 1978 order for 23 A300B4s by Eastern, the first North American customer for Airbus, instantly gave the fledgling manufacturer a new measure of credibility that it has kept to this day.

Production of the A300B4 ceased in May 1984, with manufacture switching to the improved A300-600. Eventually, in 1987, American Airlines did order a fleet of A300-600Rs, which served it well into the twenty-first century.

By the late 1980s work had begun on a pair of new medium-sized aircraft, the biggest to be

Jean Pierson served as Airbus' chief executive officer from 1985 to 1998. Pierson dropped his trousers to seal a key US order in 1997 and the resulting order helped Airbus take on Boeing in its own backyard, setting up the biggest rivalry in global business. He was at US Airways' headquarters for what he thought would be a short meeting to tie up an aircraft deal - at the last minute, US Airways' then-chairman Stephen Wolf started arguing for a 5% discount on the selling price. Pierson began slowly lowering his trousers and saying 'I have nothing more to give.' He then allowed the trousers to fall around his ankles. Wolf is supposed to have replied: 'Pull up your pants. I don't need any more money,' and the deal was signed. Shortly afterward, US Airways announced the purchase of 124 single-aisle Airbus A320 family jets with options for 276 more, a stab into the heart of Boeing's competing 737 programme. It put the European company on track to overtake Boeing in global orders only two years later. (Photo: Airbus SAS)

The Airbus 'family' just before the turn of the millenium. From top to bottom: A319, A320, A321, A310-300, A300-600, A330-200, A340-300 and the Super Transporter, later named 'Beluga' (Photo: Airbus SAS)

produced at this point under the Airbus name, the Airbus A330 and the Airbus A340. In the early 1990s the then Airbus CEO Jean Pierson argued that the GIE should be abandoned and Airbus established as a conventional company. However, the difficulties of integrating and valuing the assets of four companies, as well as legal issues, delayed the initiative. In December 1998, when it was reported that British Aerospace and DASA were close to merging, Aérospatiale paralysed negotiations on the Airbus conversion; the French company feared the combined BAe/DASA, which would own 57.9% of Airbus, would dominate the company and it insisted on a 50/50 split. However, the issue was resolved in January 1999 when BAe abandoned talks with DASA in favour of merging with Marconi Electronic Systems to become BAE Systems. Then in 2000 three of the four partner

companies (DaimlerChrysler Aerospace, successor to Deutsche Airbus; Aérospatiale-Matra, successor to Sud-Aviation; and CASA) merged to form EADS, simplifying the process. EADS now owned Airbus France, Airbus Deutschland and Airbus España, and thus 80% of Airbus Industrie. BAE Systems and EADS transferred their production assets to the new company, Airbus SAS, in return for shareholdings in that company

Interim developments of the A300, including the A310 and the A300-600, were followed in 1980 by an expansion into the single-aisle, short-haul market with the A320. The diversification helped strengthen the industrial base of Airbus at a grassroots level beyond Europe, and strengthened the manufacturer's reputation across a broad range of airlines and operators.

Airbus based all its wide-body designs on the

Airbus made history with the initial takeoff of its A320 jetliner on 22 February 1987, becoming the first airliner to fly with fully digital, computer-driven fly-by-wire system and sidestick controls. (Photo: Airbus SAS)

same 18 feet 6 inch diameter fuselage cross section of the first A300. The fuselage was circular and provided enough width to accommodate two LD3 containers (the industry standard for cargo shipping) to be housed side-by-side in the lower cargo hold.

Satisfied with the logic of its cross section, which has frequently been identified as the most important specification in any new passenger aircraft design, Airbus intended to stick with this platform for future higher-capacity designs.

Two of these original projects were designated A300139 and A300B11. After the A320 launch, they were renamed TA9 and TA11, respectively, to indicate that they were twin-aisle projects. The TA9 was a stretched A300 with more powerful engines for medium stage lengths, while the TA11 was to be the first Airbus design powered by four engines for long-haul routes. Even at this stage, however, Airbus did not presume to tread on the toes of Boeing and invade the sacred territory of

the 747. The TA11 was aimed at replacing the aging 707 and DC-8 on long, thin routes which were not busy enough to fill an aircraft the size of the 747. Studies into the TA9 and TA11 continued into the 1980s under the leadership of Jean Pierson, but the big question of which one Airbus should launch remained.

The breakthrough came when Roeder, then Airbus chief engineer, hit upon the idea of using the same wing for both designs. The aircraft already shared common fuselages, systems, flight decks, and tails, so the idea of using essentially the same wing became even more appealing to the consortium. Pierson would later recall the debate that raged within Airbus: *'Some people said we should launch a twin, others a quad. Finally, the engineers promised they could do both with a common airframe for half a billion less. So l said, 'Let's go!''*

Adam Brown, vice president for strategic planning during the early years of the A330/A340 and later the A3XX/A380 programs, remembered

Smallest of the A320 family, is the A318, capable of carrying up to 122 passengers (Photo: Airbus SAS)

The A350 - derived from the Airbus TA9 design study. (Photos: Airbus)

that Roeder and his team were '...*able to create a common wing structure, with the quad's outboard engines providing bending relief to counteract the increased weights of the long-range model. The cost savings this presented enabled us to do both aircraft. The idea was really a piece of brilliant insight.*'

Following an Airbus supervisory board meeting in Munich in January 1986, the designations of the TA9 and TA11 became the A330 and A340, respectively. Originally, Airbus intended to launch the four-engine TA11 first, because it was attracting the most immediate interest from airlines. So the plan was to call the TA11 the A330, and the twin-engine TA9 the A340. However, as Brown recalled: '*Our salesman came back and said that airlines would never get their brains around a twin having a four in its name and the quad not, so we reversed the designations.*'

The pair were launched on the eve of the 1987 Paris Air Show, with two versions of the A340 being offered: a 260-seat -200 and a 295-seat -300. At the time, only one version of the A330 was available, the 295-seat -300. The A340 entered service with Lufthansa in March 1993, followed by the A330 with Air Inter in 1994. A later, shorter

version of the A330, the 250-seat -200, was subsequently developed and entered service in 1998. The later variant of the twin would prove to be one of the most popular members of the family eventually outselling Boeing's 767.

Airbus were considering how to get more passengers into the A340 as it saw the possibility of taking a slice of the Classic 747 replacement market. The epithet 'Classic' had not yet come into vogue, but by the late 1980s it was obvious that the improvements in the then newly developed 747-400 would spark a replacement race for the older generation 747-100, -200, and -300 variants.

In September 1989, even before assembly of the first 295-passenger A340-300 had begun, Airbus revealed studies of a double-deck modification that would seat up to 60 passengers in a converted forward belly hold.

It was intended to counter the MD-11 rather than take orders from the 747, and soon morphed into a stretch derivative with greater market appeal - the A340-400X. However, the study ran into problems because of the limited power of the CFM56 engines.

The -400X stretched the fuselage by 20 feet, 7 inches, providing capacity for 340 passengers in three classes. But without changing engines and

The TA11 study, which emerged in 1980 out of earlier A300B11 derivative work, was intended as a 707/DC-8 replacement market.

Renamed the A340 in January 1986, the four-engined jetliner entered service in March 1993 with Lufthansa and provided the platform from which Airbus would launch the long-range and higher-capacity derivatives, the A340-500 (Photos: both Airbus)

wing design, the range capability was penalized by about 1,500 nautical miles compared to the baseline A340-300, thus rendering the -400X a non-starter.

The -400X exercise was not a wasted effort. Airbus had seen a vision of the future and was intrigued by the possibilities of this emerging market opportunity, so it canvassed engine manufacturers for a larger powerplant for its stretched A340. In 1991, Airbus Engineering Vice President Bernard Ziegler prophesied: '...*one day, for sure, we'll have new-generation engines for this aircraft.*'

It took six years of torturous negotiation, redesign, indecision, market uncertainty and posturing before the project emerged as a qualified challenger to the Classic 747. By now it had again evolved, this time into a two-member family renamed the A340-500 and -600. In another break with tradition for Airbus, which had used General Electric and Pratt &Whitney engines for all its wide-bodies up to the A330, it signed a deal with British manufacturer Rolls-Royce for their Trent 500 engine.

The new A340 design, coupled with a larger wing and more powerful engines, could carry 378 passengers and their luggage across ranges of up to 7,300 nautical miles, or right in the middle of the Classic 747 replacement frame. Furthermore, by trading airframe weight for range, the shorter -500 sibling could carry 313 passengers over the great distance of 8,300 nautical miles. At 247 feet, 1 inch, in length, the A340-600 became the longest airliner ever built, while the A340-500, at 222 feet, 7 inches, became the longest range airliner ever built. From the moment these aircraft entered service in 2002, both helped confirm the credibility of Airbus in the long-haul jetliner market, while at the same time securing a precious foothold on the virtually untapped ultra-long nonstop routes between the United States and Asia.

It was the inherent flexibility of the basic A340 fuselage that Roeder seized on for the new UHCA project in late 1988. '...*the purpose was to try and do something at the lowest possible cost by using as much as we could from the existing products. When I presented the original project to Pierson, it was all based on what we could afford.*'

Wolf-Dieter Wissel, appointed to lead the UHCA study project and who would ultimately become the director of configuration integration for the A380, said: *'lt all came from first ideas on a piece of paper, almost on the back of an envelope, if you like. To be honest, it was all a bit like a dream, there was nothing available from which to start. But one of Roeder's brilliant ideas was to use the A340 design elements to create this horizontal double-bubble [HDB] concept. We took the A340 fuselage and sort of stretched the fuselage laterally and put the A340 wings on it and used slightly larger versions of the HTP [horizontal tailplane] and both vertical tails.'*

The bisarre-looking concept was sized to be about 20% larger than the 747-400, and could therefore seat up to 517 in a three-class configuration.

A flight deck was located on top of the fuselage. The Airbus technical director at the time, Bernard Ziegler, was also keen to emphasize the

possibilities of a clean-sheet design. *'We've got to think about a wider fuselage. We get no lift at all from the fuselage today'* he said when details of the design began to emerge.

Pierson and Heribert Flosdorff gave Roeder the go-ahead to continue with studies, and the Airbus supervisory board gave its approval for further evaluations after Roeder's first formal presentation to them in June 1990. Airbus decided to test the market with the concept at the 1990 Farnborough Air Show having set a goal of having direct operating costs that were at least 15% lower than the operating costs of the 747-400, though Jean Pierson told *Flight International* in May 1991 that the development would take account of *'...the improvements they* [Boeing] *will make to the 747 by the year 2000... our obligation is to offer something to the market that is far better than that.'*

There was a need to focus on specific new

The most important design decision in the life of an airliner is what cross-section to use. Double-bubble, cloverleaf or oval - Airbus studied everything for their UHCA, from a giant circular section, which limited the upper deck seating configuration options, to a clover leaf design that provided optimum space but was less aerodynamically and structurally efficient. The A340-derived horizontal double-bubble section is seen centre left, while the ovoid cross section finally adopted. (Airbus)

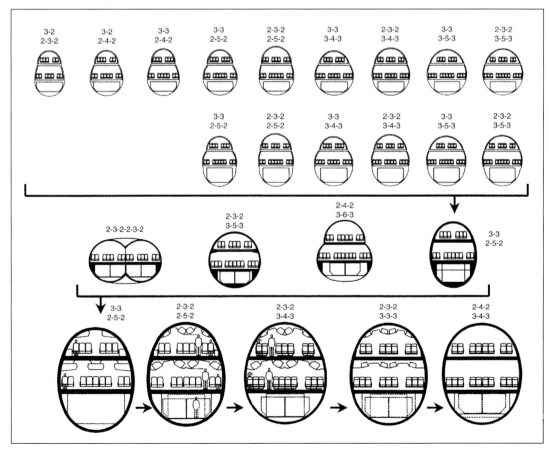

46

Airbus' first publicly revealed UHCA concept was an unusually configured aircraft with a 'double-width' fuselage made up of two A340 fuselages merged together side by side. It was the brainchild of Roeder, who believed the use of existing A340 components, including wings, tails, and other systems, was the only way to afford such an ambitious project. The concept got as far as the wind tunnel stage but did not produce encouraging results. (Airbus)

support technologies for a UHCA, Airbus and its four partners launched a joint technology programme. This new partnership was formed under the auspices of the European 3E - environment, economy, energy - technology effort originally organized by Airbus, its partners, and the European governments in the late 1980s to coordinate and rationalise research efforts.

The initiative was directed at defining three new technology demonstration platforms: one for the single-aisle A320-size class; one for the A340-size category and one in the 500-seat arena.

This approach ensured that Airbus would utilize the best ideas and technologies from throughout Europe by organising four pre-project teams from its partners-Aérospatiale, DASA, British Aerospace, and CASA. The plan directed the four teams to effectively compete with different designs to be presented to the Airbus supervisory board by early 1992. The board would then select the most competitive designs, and if

none were sufficiently cost-competitive with the 747 they would have to go back to the drawing board. *'We were expecting we would need new technology to meet the range and weight targets. We knew it could not be done using the existing technology of those days; that was clearly understood'* said Wissel.

Airbus were confident that one or more of the teams would come up with a world-beater, or at least a design that could be merged with features of the other contestants and possibly even those of the in-house concepts. This would then allow the concept to be formally adopted in 1993 in preparation for a launch in 1996 or 1997. At this stage, Airbus planned to begin searching for risk-sharing partners and estimated that the overall development cost would be in the $4 to $5 billion range - an enormous amount of money that would eventually form less than half of the new airliner's final cost.

Bernard Ziegler is the former Airbus senior vice president for engineering. For his efforts in advancing the fly-by-wire cause, he was honoured by the Flight Safety Foundation in 1998. He retired from Airbus after 25 years of service in 1997. (Photo: Airbus)

Chapter Four

'SuperJumbo'

Airbus had been making all the noise about UHCAs, but that was to change. In June 1991, United Airlines chairman Stephen Wolf revealed that they had asked Boeing to study a requirement for a 650-seat trans-Pacific aircraft. Called the N650, it spurred Boeing into action so they began to sketch three concepts: a stretched 747, a full double-deck variant of the 747, and a clean-sheet design. Details of Boeing's response came at the Paris Air Show, where the company's executive vice president, Phil Condit, said: *'We fully intend to compete in that double-deck version market.'*

Jürgen Thomas is frequently referred to as the father of the A380. He was European project director of the VLCT study with Boeing and immediately afterward took the helm of the A3XX programme by running the Airbus large aircraft division when it was formed in 1996.

entry into service some time after 2000. Then Deutsche Aerospace unveiled details of proposals to meet the new UHCA - a leviathan that was of a conventional configuration designated the A2000. It was 255 feet long, with a wingspan of 262 feet, an overall height of 75 feet, a wing area of 8,180 square feet, and a maximum takeoff weight of 1.16 million pounds. It was designed to seat 615 passengers on three decks, with economy passengers on the upper deck, business travelers on the main deck, and first-class passengers, for whom beds would be available, on the lower deck.

John Hayhurst, a former marketing vice president, was appointed as Boeing's vice president for large aircraft development. He saw a clear need for a UHCA, particularly when Boeing forecast that 54% of the commercial market up to 2005, was for 350-seaters and above. *'...we believe we can fulfill that by a combination of 747- and 777-sized aircraft as well as a requirement for an aircraft larger than the 747-400.'*

'We have had a number of product developments aimed at this, ranging from stretches of the 747-400 to all-new aircraft. What we're doing is bringing together all the efforts we've had up to now and focusing them to find out what the market needs are for this segment and then to design it.'

The joint United/Boeing move impacted on Airbus, who announced an accelerated schedule for its own jumbo effort, calling for launch in 1995 and

DASA proposed a suite of high tech features to achieve a 15% fuel burn improvement over the 747-400 - that included a fly-by-wire flight-control system to help offset weight by creating a smaller empennage. They also proposed the use of laminar-flow control on the wing and tail, but ruled out the use of carbon-fibre in the primary structure of the wing.

DASA knew that such a large aircraft would present a psychological barrier to overall acceptance but added that it would be built nonetheless. The company's executive vice president for design and technology, Professor Uwe Ganzer: *'...we're seeing such an increase in traffic that it is inevitable.'*

Boeing saw something similar. In September 1991 at the UK Institution of Civil Engineers, Boeing Product Strategy Analysis Manager Richard Bateman said that a 600-seater could take a large part of a

The A2000 concept began to make appearances on the Airbus stands at air shows in the early 1990s and offered a glimpse of the ovoid cross section and overall layout that would one day be adopted for the A3XX. The best features of the A2000 were melded with those of the competing Aerospatiale ASX 500/600 and BAe AC14, to produce the Airbus 3E P500-100/200 family. The A3XX and the A380 were therefore direct descendents of this triple-decker design. (Photo: Airbus SAS)

market forecast to be worth $617 billion through to 2005.

When 767 sales began to weaken in the face of competition from the A330-200 in the late 1990s, Boeing were forced to consider a replacement. As the 747-400 was also starting to slow down in sales terms, the company began to think about two new projects: the Sonic Cruiser and the 747X.

The Boeing Sonic Cruiser was born from numerous research and development projects with the goal to look at potential designs for a possible new near-sonic or supersonic airliner. The strongest of these concepts was unveiled on 29 March 2001. It was intended to achieve speeds of Mach 0.98 while burning fuel at the same rate as the existing 767 and A330.

The 747X would stretch the 747-400 and have a composite supercritical wing to improve efficiency, but market interest in the 747X was lukewarm; the

Sonic Cruiser had brighter prospects - several major airlines, primarily in the United States, voiced their optimism for the concept, for by decreasing travel time, they would be able to increase aircraft utilisation and customer satisfaction.

Instead of the high capacity of the 'superjumbo' – that requires a hub and spoke model of operation, where a passenger flies in an aircraft the size of the 747 or larger for the long haul part of the flight, then changes to a short haul airliner to reach their final destination - the Sonic Cruiser was designed for rapid point-to-point connections for 200 to 250 passengers. With a delta wing and canard arrangement, and flying just under the speed of sound, the Sonic Cruiser promised a faster speed than conventional airliners, without the noise pollution caused by the sonic boom from pure supersonic travel. The aircraft was to fly at altitudes in excess of 40,000

The much-vaunted Boeing Sonic Cruiser with which Boeing suddenly tried to convince the airlines that rapid point-to-point connections were the way forward. This was after spending thirty years of pushing the high-capacity hub and spoke concept with their 747 - which they were still trying to do with the 747X Stretch.

The airlines never bought into the concept.

ft, with a range between 6,000 and 10,000 nautical miles. Boeing estimated the Sonic Cruiser's fuel efficiency to be comparable to current wide body twin-engine airliners.

However, most airlines were not able to justify large capital expenditures, and due to increased fuel prices, were more interested in efficiency than speed. Boeing offered airlines the option of using the airframe for either higher speed or increased efficiency, but due to high projected costs, the potential market continued to evaporate.

Boeing considered larger-capacity versions of the 747 during the 1990s and 2000s. The 747-500X and −600X, proposed at the 1996 Farnborough Airshow, would have stretched the 747 and used a 777-derived wing, but did not attract enough interest to proceed with development. In 2000, Boeing offered the 747X and 747X Stretch derivatives as alternatives to the Airbus A3XX. This was a more modest proposal than the previous −500X and −600X. The 747X increased the 747's wingspan to 229 feet by adding a segment at the root. The 747X was to carry 430 passengers up to 8,700 nautical miles. The 747X Stretch would be extended to 263 feet long, allowing it to carry 500 passengers up to 7,800 nautical miles. However, the 747X family was unable to attract enough interest to enter production, so Boeing then decided to offer an alternative project, cancelling the 747X.

Boeing now claimed, after thirty years or so pushing the hub-and-spoke model, that passengers suddenly wanted the convenience of flying point-to-point and that smaller, long-haul aircraft made it economic to do so.

As evidence to this, they pointed to the drying-up of orders for passenger versions of the 747. Airbus has some equally persuasive counter-arguments. John Leahy dismissed the claims as not just wrong but irresponsible: *'It's ridiculous. Boeing's answer means burning more fuel per passenger, putting more strain on overloaded air trafic control systems and creating more congestion at airports that are already finding it difficult to cope.'*

Boeing's replacement for the Sonic Cruiser project was dubbed the 7E7. The 'E' was said to stand for various things, depending upon the audience. To some, it stood for 'efficiency', 'environmentally friendly'... In the end, Boeing claimed it merely stood for 'Eight', after the aircraft was eventually rechristened '787' when several Chinese airlines ordered the product, as eight is a lucky number in Chinese numerology.

The 787 used the technology proposed for the Sonic Cruiser - including carbon fibre composites for a series of fuselage 'barrels' and wings, bleedless engines, cockpit and avionics design - but in a more conventional airframe configuration. Boeing claimed that the 787 would be up to 20% more fuel-efficient than comparable aircraft.

Boeing claimed that the 787, '*...could be in service by the end of the century if the market wants it'*.

Teams from both aircraft manufacturers headed to the headquarters of the world's biggest airlines, most of them in the Asia-Pacific region, to see if they wanted it. Airbus marketers visited about a dozen carriers. Speaking in Singapore in September 1991, Airbus Marketing Vice President David Jennings said: '*...We are at the stage where we think it is technically feasible. We think that Airbus could produce such an aircraft, and we are testing some of our assumptions about the market.*'

Boeing visited QANTAS, learning that they were desperate for a shorter-term 747 stretch solution. But after hearing encouraging news at an operators conference in Hawaii, Boeing set up a customer advisory committee like it had for the 767-X, which led to the 777.

Speaking in South Korea after the November 1991 handover of the first 747-400 to Asiana, a new Seoul-based airline, Boeing's Everett division vice president, James Johnson, said: '*The decision must be made for a stretch of the 747-400 or a new aircraft or both - 1we're actually considering both. There is active interest in a new, large 650- to 680-seat airplane, and there are a number of customers who'd like us to do it real soon.*'

Johnson believed that a new design was the best option, if they made use of 777 technologies: '*...We could go to a circular double-deck cross section, which is lighter and more efficient and which obviates the cargo capability...*' he added. In addition, Johnson said that the effort would '*...probably be financed by ourselves, with a sort of co-manufacturing arrangement with someone like the Japanese on the 777, though not necessarily the Japanese.*'

At the same meeting was Boeing's vice president for international sales, James Chorlton, who, like his equals within Airbus, was aware of the market opportunities of the Asia-Pacific region. '*This is big aircraft country. For people like JAL, ANA, and Thai, the bigger the airplane the better. They keep saying: Are you going to build it, and when, and how big?*'

When it came to China, Chorlton pulled no punches: '*China's traffic is growing by 20% a year internally and 10-12% internationally. They have a whole warehouse of Russian junk that has to be done away with, and it's a big market for aircraft. China Southeast wants the biggest airplanes we can build.'*

Boeing's challenge was whether to take advantage of the established 747 family, or whether go for an all-new design. The two 747 studies included a 280 inch stretch that would add 84 seats, taking typical three- class seating to 484, and a more radical modification that extended the hump of the upper deck aft along the entire length of the main-deck cabin. But, as with any derivatives, both 747s suffered from being sub-optimized designs. Range was the big issue, with the stretch machine being capable of only 80% of the -400's range, while the upper-deck stretch would only have 73% of the range.

Enter McDonnell Douglas

It was neither Airbus nor Boeing who emerged first with a firm new double-decker design, that honour fell to the Douglas Aircraft Division of the McDonnell Douglas Corporation. The Long Beach, California-based manufacturer had not even registered on the radar screen as far as the UHCA race was concerned, but had been busy for several years attempting to bolster its product line with a stretched version of the MD-11 - itself an update of the DC-10 - and

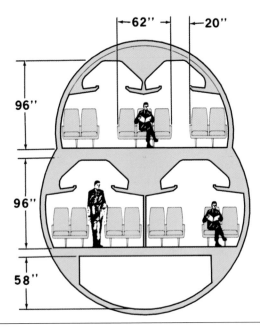

A PROGRESS REPORT ON THE DOUGLAS DC-10

RECEIVED
17 JAN 1966
GENERAL MANAGER
ENGINEERING

PR66 D-950-327

The MD-12 was not the first time the Douglas company had suggested a double-deck design. Back in the mid 1960s they came up with a four engined twin-deck DC-10

The cross section of the DC-10-D952 design from the 1960s - a similar concept would surface again from the company in 1992.

dubbed the MD-12X. In early 1992 the airlines that were involved with the MD-12X studies began pressing for a more efficient four-engine design with greater growth potential.

Estimated costs climbed to $4.5 billion by mid-1991, forcing McDonnell Douglas into a rethink. Instead of digging into its own dwindling coffers for development dollars, why not invite partners to share in the development? In return for taking this risk, the partners would be entitled to part of the profit. Douglas could benefit by sharing its own risk and by bringing in partners who could perform work at relatively low cost.

Casting its net wide to talk with companies in Japan, South Korea, Taiwan, and elsewhere, Douglas hoped to offset more than 60% of its costs through the concept of risk-sharing partnerships. To further encourage the move, which was pivotal to the launch of the MD-12X and with it the long-term survival of the company itself Douglas offered equity in exchange for investment in the effort.

The first came in November 1991 when they signed a MoU covering equity investment by Taiwan Aerospace Corporation and the possible creation of what was dubbed an 'Asian Airbus'.

Douglas President Robert Hood claimed that the big jet was '...bold and visionary', and had '...leapfrogged our competition and is, in short, an aircraft for the twenty-first century'. Hood believed the MD-12 would capture a share of the 2,500 aircraft worth $300 billion that Douglas had forecast would be needed in the long-range market over the next 20 years.

It was clear that the Douglas design had more in common with the new double-deckers Airbus had shown at the previous year's Paris Air Show than with anything Boeing had shown until then. The driving force behind the design, according to MD-12 Vice President Walt Orlowski, was the goal of beating the seat-mile costs of the 747-400 while at the same time meeting the payload/range goals its

target airline group had established.

The new wing supporting the big double-decker was a key part of the design, which was meant for stretching from the start. The wing was designed with a divergent trailing-edge drag-reduction feature that Douglas had patented. It produced an effect similar to the variable-camber concept Airbus had studied for the A340, and gave the MD-12 wing both significant inverse camber and a blunt trailing edge almost 1.5 inches deep. The divergent trailing edge was optimized for a Mach 0.85 cruise and promised a 3 to 4% improvement in overall aerodynamic efficiency.

Desperate attempts to prop up the MD-12 continued as 1992 wore on. The autumn issue of McDs *Spirit* magazine that year proudly announced that the super-sized airliner '...will be the biggest-and the best-jetliner ever built.' predicting that the MD-12 '...could be the revenue earner that puts McDonnell Douglas on top in the commercial aircraft industry'. It also said that the '...introduction of the MD-12 gives McDonnell Douglas a head start over its competitors. Boeing is studying the concept of a 750-passenger wide-body, and an 800-passenger superjumbo is said to be under development at Airbus. But no such aircraft have yet been offered to customers.'

What McDonnell Douglas failed to realize most was that the MD-12 dream - and the Taiwan deal - were already dead and the MD-12 quietly died.

Airbus smelled blood, and despite McDonnell Douglas's subsequent attempts to reinvigorate the MD-11 with studies of a long-range variant, possible plans to develop new-generation twins, and the launch of the MD-95 100-seater, most airlines recognized that the end was not far off for McDonnell Douglas.

Boeing's VLCT concept followed many of the company's hallmark features, particulalrly flightdeck, wing fairing and empennage.

Unperturbed by the Long Beach fiasco, Airbus spent much of 1992 further defining its approach to the UHCA market and continuing its dialogue with 10 selected airlines. By October, the consortium revealed that it was focusing on a two-family design approach with a smaller version seating between 600 and 800, and a larger UHCA seating between 800 and 1,050.

Still loosely designated the A350, the baseline UHCA had a huge wing with an area of 8,020 square feet, compared with 3,900 square feet for the A330/A340. Span was set at 255 feet, and the mean aerodynamic chord was a full 63% longer than on the A340 wing. The design continued to be centred around two A340 fuselages married laterally to form a flattened ovoid cross section. Overall, the UHCA was to be about 260 feet long with a 51-foot-tall tail.

The smaller 600-seater had a planned payload of about 163,000 pounds, of which 30% was to be made up of belly freight. In a single-class high-density 800-seat layout of the type the Japanese airlines used on the domestic 747SR variants, the aircraft would have a payload of about 167,400 pounds but no capacity for freight. The larger family versions were similarly configured, with payload limits of up to 407,490 pounds and seating for as many as 1,050 in a single-class layout.

Other weird and wonderful configurations were considered, including the cloverleaf cross section that combined the fuselage of the A340 with an A320 on top, or a larger version with a new cross section on the main deck and an A340 on top.

Supporting studies to help answer all the other questions about developing the world's biggest airliner were under way. Questions about how to deal with the levels of mass and stiffness distribution within such a huge flexible structure; how to spread the weight of a one-million-plus-pound aircraft on the wheels; how to steer the aircraft around existing airports and their taxiways; how to handle the flying controls; the noise it might create; and how to evacuate all the passengers in an emergency.

Meanwhile, Boeing's future large aircraft studies, now being led by Chief Project Engineer John Roundhill, showed an all-new design that bore an even closer resemblance to the MD-12 than the first double-deck shapes revealed the year before. Roundhill said the designs were '...a lot different in detail. In general terms, one of the designs is short and fat. A circular cross section is our baseline, but there are variations.'

The new design could seat up to 750 and was based on three different cross-sectional arcs in a triple-bubble configuration for added strength at reduced weight. The design also avoided most of the structural problems Boeing encountered with the upper-deck fairing of the 747's nose section, while allowing the incorporation of an extremely wide main deck. For most configurations, this was 12 abreast, with 14 abreast studied for short-range domestic Japanese routes.

The wing provided a 6% gain in cruise efficiency over the 747-400, with another 3% from the use of state-of-the-art engines. The use of hybrid laminar-flow techniques for drag reduction was studied as a way of achieving a Mach 0.86 cruise speed with low drag.

Like Airbus, the Boeing study included aspects of the infrastructure, including runways and ground handling. After reviewing 70 runways at likely destinations around the world, the study estimated that 17 would require strengthening. Intriguingly, the study also recommended the use of closed-circuit TV cameras mounted in the empennage and belly to help prevent the crew from taxiing over the edges of runways and taxiways.

The study group split into two parts - one focused on the 747X derivatives and the other on the all-new design. No timetable was discussed, but Boeing Executive Vice President Phil Condit suggested that 1994 to 1995 would be prime time for launch. 'Our thinking has to be five years out, in terms of delivering at the end of the century.'

What Condit did not reveal was that secret transatlantic talks had started over the future of the UHCA. The revelation would equally shock and confound the industry for several years to come, and the ultimate outcome of these talks would alter the destiny of both Airbus and Boeing.

Back in 1992 Daimler-Benz and British Aerospace, two of the partners in the Airbus consortium as it then was, pushed for co-operation with Boeing on what came to be known as a new Very Large Commercial Transport (VLCT).

Jürgen Thomas, a veteran German engineer appointed to lead the project, was convinced that Boeing was serious about the partnership, but others were less sure. The prevailing view within Airbus - particularly with its French chief executive Jean Pierson - was that the Americans wanted to string the talks out for as long as possible for nefarious ends.

The main reason behind this thinking was that Boeing was insistent on producing an aircraft substantially bigger than the 747, which would complement rather than replace it. Another was that for as long as there was no agreement on how to build the VLCT, Boeing could continue to milk its 747 monopoly, which at that time it had held for around 25 years. It is said to have used its estimated $30m profit per 747 to cut the price of its other jets like the 737, which faced direct competition from Airbus with its A320 family.

A marriage is announced...

On 5 January 1993 Boeing's UHCA project manager John Hayhurst and DASA chairman Jürgen Schrempp announced that the two were joining forces on a UHCA or very large commercial transport (VLCT) feasibility study. Acting on contacts first made at the Farnborough Air Show the previous September, Schrempp and DASA aircraft group leader Hartmut Mehdorn followed up the contact with a visit to Boeing in late 1992. But the announcement posed far more questions than answers, the biggest being whether or not Airbus itself was involved in the feasibility study.

As far as Jean Pierson was concerned, the European consortium had already played a direct role. Speaking at the annual Airbus results conference in Paris he declared that initial discussions had taken place at Farnborough between himself, Schrempp, and Hayhurst, and that at the end of the month the Airbus board was due to review a discussion document that the meeting had generated.

Journalists at the meeting had also listened to the Boeing/DASA press briefing only a few days before and asked why Hayhurst had made no reference to Airbus. Pierson replied '...*either he does not remember me, which is impolite, or he has a short memory, which disqualifies him from being a project manager, or he's having second thoughts. I think it's more likely he's having second thoughts.*'

Pierson indirectly admitted that Airbus had not been invited to participate in the VLCT study, even though one and possibly more of its members had. Pierson was adamant, however, that the move did not threaten to undermine Airbus or the consortium's continuing aircraft studies or those being conducted with the consortium's members. '...*There has been no betrayal by an Airbus member. This is not the end of the Airbus system*'.

The Boeing line was equally strong. '*We are open to working with member companies of Airbus, rather than Airbus itself. We think we will always compete with Airbus head to head. We will be just as vigorous in our competition as we expect them to be.*'

Boeing denied the move was intended as anything other than studying the UHCA and also denied that it was subterfuge aimed at destabilising Airbus or was driving a wedge between the partners in the consortium. What they could not deny that the link with DASA was extraordinary - the primary reason of course was the $10 billion plus development costs Boeing estimated would be needed to see the new design through development.

Then there was the issue of market size. After its first rush of enthusiasm, and the painful post-Gulf War period for the airlines, Boeing's view of the size of the superjumbo market had changed. It now predicted a near- to mid-term demand from only a handful of international customers, nowhere near the market size that would be required to support competing designs.

Then there were other, less direct reasons

Boeing's New Large Airplane (NLA) appeared in many versions to fulfill the UHCA requirement. Most were designed around an all-new wing with 777 aerodynamic heritage and 777-derivative engines. This version could seat up to 750 passengers in a 'triple-bubble' fuselage cross section to incorporate an extra-wide main deck.

Artwork of the Boeing 747X Stretch design.

related to the ever-changing tactical and strategic struggle for market share. For Boeing, faced with the task of getting the 777 through certification and into service, the talks with DASA would be extremely beneficial. It would gain a clearer and broader view of the true state of the market as well as the market's technical requirements, and of course it would delay rather than speed up the entry into service of a 747 competitor. Boeing was not in a position to make a commitment to develop a new super-jumbo, but by engaging DASA in this dialogue, it could slow Airbus' progress toward deciding on a competitive programme of its own.

Boeing pointed out that the study could not involve Airbus, even if Boeing wanted it to. Boeing Corporate Vice President of Planning and International Development Larry Clarkson pointed out that as a GIE (Groupe d'Interet Economique) Airbus did not control the financial or physical assets of its member companies. The US manufacturer, therefore, had no choice but to deal with these 'real' companies instead. DASA would be first, but there would soon be more. As Boeing explained; *'We have left open the possibility of bringing in others to the study. These include our Japanese friends, Kawasaki, Mitsubishi, and Fuji, as well as Aerospatiale, British Aerospace, McDonnell Douglas, and the Russians. It's a pretty wide-open ball game. The reason we're talking to DASA is that it is like Boeing: very diversified. Airbus is only one segment of their business. We can see ourselves doing business with them.'*

It was true that as a GIE, Airbus represented a group of independent companies with a joint family of products rather than a single company. The structure of the GIE, a uniquely French business concept, had been the perfect platform on which to float Airbus into the market. It allowed the companies to work closely together toward a common goal with a set of joint products, without having to operate under the tight legal and financial ties of a partnership.

The Boeing manoeuvre appeared to have left Airbus vulnerable and exposed. All the consortium's member companies remained free to work individually on aircraft outside the 100- to 350-seat range already covered by the existing Airbus product line, and there was nothing Airbus could do to prevent it. In the long run, however, Boeing's move would prove to be a double-edged sword. By delaying the ultimate super-jumbo development, Boeing unwittingly gave Airbus more time to make important design changes to accommodate new noise legislation. The initiative would also help accelerate Airbus toward a radical restructuring into a single entity that enabled it to launch a superjumbo and carry it forward into the twenty-first century Boeing, DASA, and the other main Airbus partners, Aerospatiale, British Aerospace, and CASA, signed a MoU on 22 January 1993, that covered the start of the first phase of the VLCT study. Part of the agreement included the creation of 'firewalls' within each organisation to prevent the crossover of sensitive information between the Airbus and Boeing large-aircraft project camps. John Hayhurst admitted that the arrangement was like tightrope walking.

Hayhurst knew that all parties would be forced to share their newly refined knowledge of large aircraft from their respective UHCA studies. If the study was viewed as positive by the end of 1993, the plan was to look at details of joint manufacturing, but *'...for the moment it's going to take time to figure out how to work together.'*

While the transatlantic VLCT team got down to work, both Airbus and Boeing continued to go their own ways. Within days of Boeing's VLCT move, Airbus made an offer to the Japanese aerospace industry for an equal, risk-sharing partnership of up to 30% of the UHCA. Airbus were anxious to outflank Boeing in Japan, where they a very close relationship with the aerospace industry and airlines.

Loyal 747 users such as JAL and ANA were

One of the fuselage barrel sections of the A380 before being joined together. This 'cross section' view gives and idea as to the floor positions and the composite upper deck beams (Photo: Airbus)

targets for the future UHCA, and increasing the Japanese work share was seen as crucial to winning the hearts of the airlines. Although Airbus had been sowing the seeds of a Japanese campaign for over a year, the VLCT manoeuvre injected fresh urgency into its efforts.

In late January 1993, Pierson presided over a series of meetings with the three main Japanese aerospace companies: Fuji, Kawasaki, and Mitsubishi Heavy Industries. *'They would be offered a decision-making partnership in the UHCA program and be treated as equal partners throughout.'* Then, taking a swipe at Boeing, which had contracted large structural elements of several civil programmes such as the 767 to the big three Japanese manufacturers, Airbus added: *'We will not simply present them with a design which they will then be expected to build.'*

Airbus refined its market predictions, which showed a need for up to 727 UHCAs between 2001 and 2011. *'Our forecasts indicate that 25% of the seats in as-yet-unordered aircraft in the next 20 years will be in UHCA-type aircraft. That's too*

important to leave in the hands of a Boeing monopoly.'

The studies revealed that the average requirement was for an aircraft with 759 mixed-class seats. And perhaps not surprisingly, in a region where the 747 was referred to as a regional jet, the studies identified the Asia-Pacific region as the key market, forecasting that 11 of the airlines in the region would need more than 30 UHCAs each, which together would account for 66% of the total demand for the aircraft.

Five of those airlines were also working with Boeing, who spent much of 1993 attempting to define a New Large Airplane (NLA), or 747X. ANA, Cathay Pacific, JAL, Singapore Airlines (SIA), and QANTAS were involved, as were Air France, British Airways, and Lufthansa. It was a sign of the times that United Airlines was the sole US representative.

The plan was to reduce the five concepts to two by July 1993, and to a single configuration by the end of the year. The studies gave birth to a variety of shapes and sizes, with seating between 550 and 630 passengers, and stretch capacity up to 750.

Only one of the five finalists was a 747 derivative, a massive 282 feet in length, allowing it to seat up to 550 in three classes. Although it was by far the longest aircraft, it was also the smallest in capacity. Two of the other finalists were double-deckers, one was a model that looked like a 747 with an all-new cross section, and the fourth was a 244-foot-long single-deck machine.

The new baseline was designed to take up to 624 passengers in three classes, with 18 abreast in economy. The aircraft was about 18 feet longer than a 747 and weighed in at about 1.4 million pounds. Other designs included an alternative double-deck seating for 584 and a single-deck design based on a 777-style fuselage.

While Boeing's concepts were headline grabbing at the 1993 Paris Air Show, Airbus was approaching a critical juncture in its history. Determined not to lose the initiative to Boeing and, spurred on by the challenge the VLCT conundrum posed, they consolidated the results of the UHCA studies it had originally commissioned from the three main consortium members: Aerospatiale, British Aerospace, and DASA.

They were all similar double-deck designs that included Aerospatiale's ASX 500/600, which was aimed at satisfying both the 500- and 600-plus-seat markets. BAe came up with a concept dubbed the AC14, while DASA's P502/P602 had by now become as familiar a shape as the A2000 on every Airbus show display. Airbus took the best characteristics of each of the three designs in June 1993 and blended them into an group called Family 1.

The concept was called 3E P500 to reflect both its 3E technology-demonstrator designation and its capacity of more than 500 seats. The family consisted of two major versions, the 3E P500-100 and a stretch -200 variant.

Clearly the Family 1 group favoured a conventional double-deck vertical design, but some believed that the unusual design of the HDB held merit. The solution was to take it to the next stage and compete the concepts against one another, and it was to this end that in October 1993 Airbus announced the formation of the A3XX integration team that were tasked with comparing the ovoid with the HDB. This raised the intensity of the UHCA/VLCT debate to a new level. The designation provided a sharper focus for the design teams and, by bestowing it a pseudo-official Airbus identity it spoke volumes to the market about the seriousness of Airbus' intentions.

The 3E P500-derived Family 1 aircraft was renamed the A3XX-V600, with an ovoid cross section carrying 10 abreast on the main deck and seven on the upper deck. The original Airbus UHCA HDB was renamed the A3-H600, but this was soon rejected in favour of the V600 alternative.

The HDB was limited in the length to which it

could be stretched, and had tie rods in the middle for load carrying that were a problem as far as the interior was concerned. The advantages of the horizontal layout, especially in terms of fuselage commonality with the then current models, were not as great as first thought, and worse still, wind tunnel tests showed that the hoped for lift contribution from the wide fuselage was not there, so the concept was discarded.

In January 1994, Airbus emerged with a single concept that would form the basis for its talks with airlines and that would eventually become the A380. The initial A3XX was divided into two main versions, the -100, provisionally seating about 500, and the -200 seating about 600. Airbus designers were determined to focus on keeping cost, complexity, and weight to a minimum from the outset, and as a result began the A3XX design with just three main gear legs in the tradition of the A340. But it soon became obvious that for system redundancy and pavement loading considerations, Airbus would have to follow the 747's lead and spread the weight over four main gears.

By March 1994, these changes were incorporated into a wider package of design updates that included moving the entire wing slightly aft to achieve a better centre of gravity, stretching both the -100 and -200 by two fuselage frames, and increasing the cabin volume by

Looking significantly different than today's A380-800, the early A3XX concept in this artwork had a smaller area wing of reduced span and a smaller belly fairing than the final design. The forward fuselage and nose shaping was also different, as was the vertical fin that, although the same overall height as the current design, was almost twice the chord. Note also the additional forward upper deck exit, which was later deleted, and the blunt tips of both the horizontal tailplanes and the wings which have no endplates. (Airbus)

shifting the aft pressure bulkhead, or rear dome, rearwards. The space created sufficient room for up to 530 seats in the -100 and 630 in the -200.

As the A3XX concept gained momentum, cracks began to appear in the VLCT team. Jürgen Thomas, then DASA's executive vice president of preliminary design and technology, conceded in January 1994 that, although it was established Airbus policy to allow both the VLCT and A3XX studies to go ahead in parallel, there would be no possibility of both projects going ahead, because the market simply was not big enough.

Airbus added that it *'...would be difficult to see how we could cooperate with Boeing on a large aircraft and be at loggerheads with them on everything else. We do not believe they would want to do something that would damage their interests in Airbus Industrie. There is no intention for Airbus to do one aircraft and the partners to do another.'*

There was an increasing atmosphere of uncertainty and suspicion between the US and European camps. Aerospatiale made little secret of its misgivings, while senior Boeing figures within the study were questioning who was gaining the most out of the project.

Although the VLCT teams were separated by firewalls from their respective NLA and A3XX project teams, news of each others projects leaked through. Details of Boeing's stretched 747X plan told the Europeans that they were studying an aircraft with a maximum takeoff weight of some 420 tons and a range of up to 7,700 nautical rniles. The variant was based around an all-new wing using 777-style aerodynamics.

Speaking to *Flight International* in June 1994, Aerospatiale's director of aircraft programs, Claude Terrazoni, suggested it indicated a hidden Boeing agenda. *'...If Boeing launches the 777B this will be*

Engine efficiency was a key part of the Airbus strategy to win a major operating cost advantage over the 747, yet ironically the A3XX/A380 would build on a new generation of engines originally launched for the 747-500X/600X. The A380 is available with two types of turbofan engines, the Rolls-Royce Trent 900 (variants A380-841, −842 and −843F) or the Engine Alliance GP7000 (A380-861 and −863F). The Trent 900 is a derivative of the Trent 800, and the GP7000 has roots from the GE90 and PW4000. Noise reduction was an important requirement in the A380 design, and affected engine design. Both engine types allow the aircraft to achieve well under the QC/2 departure and QC/0.5 arrival noise limits under the Quota Count system set by London Heathrow Airport, which became a key destination for the A380. (Photo: author)

in direct competition with the 747-400. Boeing will therefore be obliged, in order not to kill its 747 market, to push the 747 toward a bigger aircraft. It's what Boeing is actually doing now. We have proof. They're studying a new wing for the 747'.

Boeing countered that, like Airbus, it was within its rights to study options to the VLCT, which had moved onto phase two, with an agreed agenda covering a refined market forecast, first steps toward a joint business arrangement, and key technical issues.

What was not widely known outside the project was that the VLCT team had decided to shrink the aircraft slightly. Phase two was to examine the arrangements of a European-inspired 500- to 550-seat design versus the Boeing-led 600-plus seater studied in phase one.

Then in March 1994 American Airlines' influential chairman Robert 'Bob' Crandall dropped a bombshell: *'We just don't think that bigger airplanes are the way to go. Smaller aircraft with longer ranges are the way to go.'* These few words were to reverberate around Boeing's leadership and help nudge it toward a shift in strategy that would doom the company's VLCT and NLA while giving Airbus a free hand in the so-called superjumbo market of the twenty-first century.

By January 1995, planning was under way on where to take the VLCT study beyond the end of phase two, with evaluations of a common configuration starting later that year. Targets included discussions about launch criteria, putting

a joint venture together, financial viability, common product development standards, laying out of key milestones, programme integration, and sorting out the value of work packages in the event of a go-ahead.

But it would not happen. While phase two was getting into its stride, Boeing's independent re-winged 747X study had meanwhile mutated into a two-family double-stretch pair dubbed the -500X and -600X. The new wing had a broader chord than the existing design, and just fitting it to the fuselage created a slight stretch that would create space for between 500 and 600 passengers. Based on the same wing, Boeing believed it could also develop a larger stretch variant capable of seating as many as 800, if the market needed it - which Boeing doubted.

Even as Boeing's NLA team reported encouraging figures from its 747-500X/600X studies, the strategic thinkers within the company continued to echo the thoughts of Crandall. As Ron Woodard, the president of the Boeing Commercial Airplane Group, said in May 1995: *'The challenge is: will the Pacific marketplace fragment? History has shown that the Atlantic fragmented when the twinjets appeared - nearly all of them 767s.'*

Boeing was busy developing longer-range variants of the 777 with exactly this phenomenon in mind. They were also beginning to baulk at the risk. A stretched, re-winged 747 would cost about $4 billion to develop and this seemed a lot less risky and costly than the European partnership and its estimated $10 to $12 billion price tag. As Woodard said, *'We are convinced a company the size of Boeing would be threatened, even if we were in a partnership, if the marketplace wasn't there. We remain convinced that there is only room for one aircraft the size of a VLCT and we will pursue this development only if it makes economic sense.'*

The VLCT was falling by the wayside, and, in July 1995, the final meeting of the teams at a hotel in Long Island, New York, brought this chapter of the superjumbo story to a close. It was back to the bitter cut and thrust of competitive warfare between the commercial giants that was about to get far more brutal.

A change of Corporate Structure

Airbus had learned a very useful lesson out of the joint project with Boeing - it was impossible for a project of that scale could be managed under the existing Airbus GIE structural arrangement.

Airbus had grown and prospered under the GIE structure, but as it became larger and more

Around the world there is an accepted standard of runway weight limitations that is defined as so much weight per wheel. Aircraft manufacturers accepted and followed these rules while developing aircraft that greatly exceeded this limit by adding sufficient wheels to the landing gears. For instance, the Boeing 747 has a takeoff weight of as much as 870,000 pounds and the Airbus 380 weighs up to 1,340,000 pounds before takeoff. For both of these aircraft, the undercarriage - or landing gear - has sufficient wheels with the proper spacing to prevent excessive pavement stress. Aircraft live load distributions recognize much heavier aircraft takeoff weights, so that existing runway designs are not overloaded.

In Airbus' case, this was done by spreading the load over multiple wheels - 12 under the belly, four under each wing and two nosewheels. (Photos: all author)

successful, the limitations of the business model was starting to hamper growth. Under the GIE, Airbus was effectively a coordination and sales operation, not a manufacturer - exactly the excuse Boeing used to justify not inviting it to participate in the VLCT. As much of the design and manufacturing of the Airbus aircraft was carried out by the partners, any savings that came out of improvements in cost or design were enjoyed by the partners and their subcontractors rather than by Airbus itself. As a result, the savings could not be passed on to the airlines.

Due to the same restrictions, Airbus had far less ability to negotiate price reductions with its suppliers and partners than did Boeing. The bottom line was that Airbus was unable to take a lead on price, and this too would have to change before any A3XX launch was possible. In addition, Airbus' ability to raise money for big projects or forge new relationships outside the traditional partnership was very limited.

In view of this long-term losing proposition, the UK and German governments began to put pressure on the partners to set up a more independent corporate structure. They believed that such a change would allow Airbus to take

tighter control of costs as well as gain access to funds on its own account.

Airbus laid out plans for a large aircraft division that would bring together personnel from the partner companies and from Airbus itself - the combined team would be led by an A3XX programme director and marked the beginning of a process that would culminate with the total restructuring of Airbus and the launch of what would become the A380. Announcing the new division in March 1996, Airbus Strategic Planning Vice President Adam Brown said the organisation would also '...*work closely with key potential customers to define the aircraft.*'

Although the chairman of Aerospatiale, Louis Gallois, remained cautious over moving too quickly on a re-jigging of Airbus, French transport minister Bernard Pons added to calls for action on the basis that the existing structure was making Airbus uncompetitive.

Then British Aerospace's Chief Executive Dick Evans added his voice, saying that there was little prospect that the UK manufacturer would lend approval to the A3XX plan '...*unless there is a satisfactory restructuring running in parallel.*'

Under the GIE structure, the four consortium

To help airports cope with the massive span of the superjumbo, Airbus considered options such as a folding wingtips. To save weight and make the wingtip fold function more practical, the primary structure of the wing outboard of the number one and four engines was intended to be made from carbon composites, but this never made it into production. Wing folding, it was decided was both an unnecessary expense and complication in view of airport expansion programmes, and the composite outboard structure was dropped after studies showed an all-metal structure would weigh slightly less! (Photo: author)

companies took responsibility for funding on their own balance sheets, and BAe simply could not see any easy way to raise finance in its own right at interest rates in excess of 10% for an $8 billion project with a long-term payback like the A3XX. Under its launch plan, Airbus had told the partners that it expected to raise up to 30% of the money internally, 33% from refundable government loans and subsidies, and 40% from the risk-sharing partners and associates.

The restructuring panel completed its report and presented its findings to the Airbus supervisory board, who on 8 July 1996, gave its approval to the proposal under which it would become a full-fledged company by the end of the decade.

The partners agreed on 13 January 1997, to reorganize the consortium amid pressure from the German government, which tied the transition to a single company and the launch of the A3XX to further research and development funding in aerospace. This restructuring as a precondition for A3XX research funding was dubbed unrealistic by the German Aerospace Industries Association (BDLI), whose president, Manfred Bischoff said: *'To avoid unfair competition, we need a deliberate innovation policy for aviation in the future.'*

In the design office, Airbus made fundamental changes to the all-important cross section, increasing the overall width to allow 10-abreast seating on the main deck, while adding extra width to the upper part of the ovoid to provide space for up to eight across on the top deck. The move represented a return to the main-deck size recommended by the original vertical DB studies of the A3XX-V600 in late 1993 but added considerably to the capacity of the upper deck.

Airbus had now studied more than forty cross sections and was intent on meeting the demands of as many airlines as it could. The latest widening allowed Airbus to configure the main deck with four seats in the middle and three on each side to avoid what Airbus famously referred to as the 'prisoner' middle seats in the five-abreast arrangements found on US wide-bodies.

Airbus briefed 13 airlines on the progress of the superjumbo at a meeting held that summer. Boeing was briefing the same airlines about the 520-seat 747-600X, which they were quoting with a 2000 delivery target date - three years ahead of the A3XX, so it was vital that Airbus drove home the advantages it claimed for an all-new design. Top of the list was an estimated 17% lower seat-mile operating cost with the initial A3XX-100, and up to a 23% lower cost

with the -200.

The growth of the A3XX, and particularly the -200, forced the abandonment of plans to use A330 engines. The aircraft's 72,000-80,000-pound thrust requirement overlapped the A330 engines at its lower end, but they ran out of steam at the higher end. Airbus already knew that options would be available from Rolls-Royce, which was discussing a new Trent 800 called the Trent 900, and from the General Electric/Pratt &. Whitney Engine Alliance, which had already embarked on the similarly sized GP7000 engine for the 747X derivatives.

The larger wing, which was increased from 7,804 square feet to 8,396 square feet, provided capacity for up to 639,000 pounds of fuel for both models.

With an aspect ratio of eight, the wing was designed to give the aircraft a range of 7,450 nautical miles and was approximately 40% larger than that of the 747-400. At this stage the wing did not have winglets, though Airbus said that folding wingtips were still being considered as a serious option.

Since Airbus pioneered the use of large-scale composites, it was no surprise that even the wing design incorporated carbon-fibre composites in the primary structure outboard of the engines, as well as in the fin and horizontal tailplane.

Other key features included the decision to adopt a cockpit common with the A320/A330/A340 to give operators the benefit of cross-crew qualification among all modern Airbus types. For operators concerned about the ability of the design to meet the 90-second evacuation rule from one side of the aircraft, the -200 form - which could seat a staggering 966 passengers in a single-class layout - Airbus reassured them with details of new solutions from slide and life raft manufacturers. The studies covered several accident scenarios, including nose wheel collapses that left aft-seated passengers 50 feet above ground level!

The preliminary design freeze was set for the third quarter of 1997, with the final design freeze set for the following year. At this stage, Airbus still targeted full go-ahead in the third quarter of 1999 and initial deliveries in 2003. Some airlines, faced with a dilemma of whether to opt for the earlier option of the new 747 or wait for the all-new A3XX, had asked if it could speed up delivery.

This was one thing that Airbus did not want to do, for a number of reasons. It did not want to be exposed to the sort of low production rates it faced in the early days of the A300, and it wanted

UPPER DECK - BUSINESS CLASS 6 ABREAST

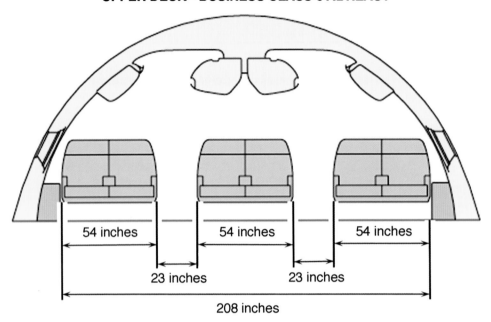

54 inches   54 inches   54 inches

23 inches   23 inches

208 inches

While design engineers worked out the technical solutions, the Airbus marketers worked on ways to beat Boeing's 30-year dominance with the 747. The heart of the matter, they finally concluded, was cabin cross section and the ability to offer more space and comfort, regardless of deck or class of seating. With the basic ovoid sufficiently large to absorb containers below the main deck, the designers were free to explore interesting possibilities. The A380 ended up with a maximum main deck width of 259 inches at about window height - or 21 feet, 7 inches, compared to the 747's 20 feet, 1 inch. This gave a 248 inch width for seating while the upper deck not surprisingly was 46% wider with a width of 233 inches at floor level. or 19 feet, 5 inches. It gave 208 inch width for seating. One positive effect of the ovoid cross section was that on the main deck, the 'walls' were hardly curved at all and gave plenty of headroom for the window-seat!

MAIN DECK - TOURIST CLASS 10 ABREAST

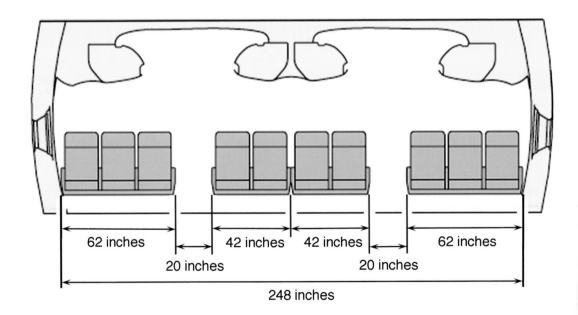

62 inches   42 inches   42 inches   62 inches

20 inches   20 inches

248 inches

guarantees of 40 to 50 aircraft per year at launch. It was also eager to get it right the first time rather than put an immature product into the market. Airbus had suffered initial problems of this sort with the early A340 and was anxious to avoid a repeat.

The pressure however was intense, and some within Airbus saw this as a glorious opportunity to derail the Boeing plan, which was using the earlier in-service target as its major trump card. The decision to switch to a faster track was made, and news emerged in mid-September 1996 when the engine makers were asked to prepare more detailed specifications, which indicated an overall programme acceleration of about one year.

Airbus also decided to undercut the expected $200 million-plus price tag of the new 747 derivatives by offering the A3XX at '...*no more than $198 million,*' according to Airbus Senior Vice President John Leahy.

Plans covered three family variants, including a base 555-seat (three-class) A3XX-100 with a slightly increased range of 7,500 nautical miles; the stretched 656-seat -200; and a longer range, higher gross weight derivative of the -100, the -100R, that would be capable of flying 8,520 nautical miles.

This appeared to outflank Boeing, who had seemed certain to launch the first stretch of the 747 since its crreation three decades earlier. It seemed only a matter of time before the two machines were unleashed on the market, with entry into service of the first variant-the 546-passenger, 7,500-nautical mile-range 747-600X - expected to be about December 2000. The smaller -500X, carrying 487 passengers over longer ranges up to 8,150 nautical miles, would follow six months later.

Boeing was so confident that the new models would be launched and would succeed the -400, that new 747-400 contracts signed that year with British Airways and United included clauses allowing them to convert later delivery slots to -500Xs or -600Xs.

The design was well advanced and revolved around a 777-style wing that reduced the 747`s wing sweep from the almost 40-degree angle of the -400 to 36.5 degrees. The wing was also a massive 248.6 feet in span with an area of 7,540 square feet, but it was set to grow again to 255 feet in span and 8,100 square feet before its final completion.

Other design aspects included 777-style technology for the fly-by-wire flight control system, high-lift system, flight deck, power distribution, electrical and hydraulic systems, as well as the undercarriage. But the adoption of so much 777 technology was a calculated gamble for Boeing, which was torn between sticking to 747 systems and flight decks for commonality and moving to the newer technology for longer-term operating-cost benefits and faster development times.

In the short term, the wholesale adoption of new technology forced Boeing to virtually double its development cost estimates for the new derivatives to about $7 billion. To amortize this cost, Boeing also increased the price tag for the larger -600X version to $230 million in projected 2001 dollars compared to the then-list price of $165 million for the -400.

Despite the hurdles, Boeing held a final airline advisory group meeting at the end of August, on the eve of the 1996 Farnborough Air Show. The hopes were that Boeing would use it to announce the go-ahead of the project, stealing the limelight and maybe even the life out of the A3XX. Seven key carriers were in the frame to launch the 747X programme, , but Lufthansa, a loyal Boeing 747 operator and launch customer for the 737, was not among them. The airline's chief executive of operations, Klaus Nittinger, openly criticized the move away from commonality with the -400, saying that rather than improving the chances of launching the programme, the lack of commonality was damaging it. He argued that costs had been driven up, which meant Boeing was forced to increase seating capacity to keep seat-mile costs down. The extended fuselage of the -600X was, as a result, 16 feet, 5 inches longer than the 262-foot 'box' it was generally agreed that future large aircraft would have to fit inside to be operationally feasible within existing airport infrastructures.

With a root chord of 39 feet, 6 inches and a height of 79 feet 1 inch, the impressively tall tail of the A380 towers above everything else. The rudder is split into two for yaw control, with each part controlled by a pair of electric backup hydraulic actuators from independent hydraulic and electrical systems. These are normally active and driven by the flight control computers. If a hydraulic system failure occurs, the affected actuators automatically revert to electrical mode. These operate at a slightly slower speed but still provide maximum rudder deflection of plus or minus 30 degrees. (Photo: author)

Airbus evaluated fuselage-mounted canards for both the A340 and A3XX as a way of aerodynamically off-loading the horizontal tailplane, thereby enabling these control surfaces to be reduced in size. The foreplanes were mounted above the crown of the fuselage above the flight deck. Although the wind tunnel tests showed the potential for reducing the size of the empennage, the structural complications and weight of the foreplane wiped out the slim advantage. It also made 'docking' even harder at the double-deck jet bridges being planned for the A3XX. (Photo: BAe)

Boeing Pulls The Plug..

Things started to go sour for Boeing's planners, who were hoping to make the headlines at Farnborough. One reason for this negative turn was that the airlines did not want to be pressured into making decisions before they were ready. British Airways Chief Executive Robert Ayling said that it was '...*important not to go rushing into orders just because of meeting the deadline of some air show somewhere.*'

Without a consensus or even orders, other than outline 'accepted proposals' for up to 15 aircraft from MAS and Thai, the planned December 1996 launch decision came and went. Over the company's year-end break, senior officers faced the decision of whether or not to abandon the 747 growth plan. By now the -500X/600X project already employed more than 1,000 design and system engineers and was allegedly costing Boeing $3 million a day!

Boeing officially pulled the plug on the stretch plan at a board meeting in mid-January 1997, and announced it on January 20. Boeing's product strategy and marketing vice president, Mike Bair, admitted: '*We just could not make a business case for it. The small size of the market meant the money we'd have to spend on it, with or without the affect of fragmentation, just did not make sense.*'

Market reaction was subdued for several reasons, although Boeing continued to claim that the aircraft itself was a good one, with the 10% reduction in direct operating costs relative to those

The shape of the A3XX underwent extensive wind-tunnel testing, with many evolutionary stages investigated.

of the -400. What killed it was a number of factors, not the least being the Airbus decision to accelerate the A3XX, thereby upsetting Boeing's calculations.

Wall Street reacted enthusiastically, with Boeing stock moving up by 157 points, or about 6.9%, on the news. After all, mused the pundits and 'aerospace analysts', not only would the $7 billion be better spent on long-range developments of the 777, but the move would also prolong the life of the 747-400, which had just brought in 75 orders in 1996. Boeing, they argued, had bigger fish to fry. It was into the throes of taking over arch rival McDonnell Douglas and had just bought big chunks of Rockwell as part of a concerted effort to grow its defence and space businesses. Besides, they trumpeted, there was always time later to develop better versions of the 747-400 when the market called for it. Who needs a superjumbo anyway?

Airbus Forges On
Airbus continued to refine the A3XX and work toward an initial design freeze that was scheduled for the end of 1997.

Airbus has always been innovative, and in its fight for market share against Boeing and McDonnell Douglas it had often used technology as a trump card in new designs such as the fly-by-wire A320. But now Airbus faced an embarrassment of riches as it surveyed the next-generation possibilities for the A3XX which included everything from avionics and in-flight entertainment to advanced design and assembly techniques.

Anticipating the research and development (R&D) needs of the massive project, Airbus had created an initiative involving the four main partners in 1996, aimed at identifying where the main focus should be. Called the 3E Plan (environment, economy, and energy), it was seen as a vital tool to keep development costs under control.

By coordinating R&D efforts, Airbus planned to eliminate duplication between programmes across the consortium and, at the same time, promote a cross-fertilisation of ideas and solutions. Part of the 3E Plan was aimed at reducing the

weight and maintenance cost of aircraft systems and included making less do more, including making fewer avionics computers to serve multiple roles.

Other ideas included extending the use of aluminum electrical cable, designing servo controls to actuate the A3XX's horizontal tail surfaces, and harmonisation of aluminum welding procedures. There were also studies into using titanium in the landing gear, carbon-composite primary structure in the outboard sections of the wing, and laminar-flow control around the engine nacelles.

Configuration issues ranging from the location of the engines on the wing to the possible use of fuselage-mounted 'canard wings' mounted on the upper fuselage crown area aft of the flight deck This had appeared in April 1996 in the artist's impressions of the A340-600, and was tested as an option for aerodynamically off-loading the horizontal tailplane. BAC Airbus conducted wind tunnel tests at its Filton site near Bristol. The concept was dropped from the A340-600 because

Wingtip fences function in different manners, but the intended effect is always to reduce the aircraft's drag by partial recovery of the tip vortex energy. They are designed to improve aircraft handling characteristics and enhance safety for following aircraft. Needless to say, that although the A380 wing-fence was based on the A320 design, it was considerably larger!
(Photo: author)

The belly fairing grew in size to help reduce aerodynamic drag - it was also a good place to store the huge fuselage undercarriage units. (Photo: author)

of worries that the canard would interfere with the operation of jet bridges, and also because their effect was relatively minimal. Initial results from the A3XX were, on the other hand, more positive. The idea was soon dropped as being impractical for as with the -600 study, the benefits did not justify the complications.

The engine location change came as part of the Status 9b update when both engines were moved outboard, the outermost being relocated to about 60% of the span. This reduced the structural weight of the wing by allowing the designers to take advantage of the bending moment relief provided by the mass of the outboard engine. This let the weight of the outboard engine oppose the upward lifting force on the wing structure, thereby reducing the need for excessive structural stiffening.

Airbus revised the fuselage frame pitch aft of the nose section 11/12. Compared with its other designs, which had 21-inch frame spacing, Airbus made the frame spacing proportional to the aircraft's size, with frames approximately every 25 inches.

The Status 9b changes coincided with concerns that development costs were heading toward an estimated $9 to $10 billion. There were several factors at play, especially the growing R&D investment that would be needed to support technological developments to meet the cost-performance goals. This was becoming increasingly complex with potential market opportunities falling out of Boeing's axing of the 747-500X.

In mid-1997 Airbus began to study a reduced-capacity 480-seat aircraft that would have been a new member of the family joining the initial 7,500-nautical mile-range, 550-seat A3XX-100 and the longer range -100R version, along with the larger 656-seat A3XX-200. The new variant, the A3XX-50, was shortened by about 16 feet, and was to be offered with derated engines and lower takeoff weights.

This fitted in with Airbus plans for a family of derivate models, including a freighter called the the -100E and multi-role cargo/passenger combis called the 100C. US package freight company FedEx pushed along studies of the -100E and told Airbus that it needed capacity earlier than it expected.

Further Refinements

Airbus was coming to the realisation that the performance figures from wind tunnel tests and other work were simply not good enough. Airbus knew that if it could not meet the cost savings target of 15 to 20% over the 747-400, it could not launch the A3XX.

68

The preliminary design freeze was accomplished on 22 January 1998, about a month later than planned according to Philippe Jarry, vice president of market development at the large aircraft division.

Officially the Asian economic crisis was not to blame. Unofficially, Airbus was still looking for risk-sharing partners, particularly in Asia, and the financial meltdown of the region's so-called 'Tiger' economies had not only impacted fleet expansion plans, but dampened investment across all industries.

The real reason behind the move, however, was that the new design was not yet achieving the vital 15 to 20% cost reductions. Airbus knew that there was no way the new aircraft could be launched by the target date of late 1998. Even worse, Airbus had to acknowledge that a plan to reach those cost savings had still not been resolved.

Pierson's tenure at Airbus was ending and, at his final press conference before departing, he used the Asian show to spell out Airbus' determination not to rush into the A3XX. Numerous areas still needed to be addressed, including aerodynamics, cost-effectiveness, and

aero-elasticity. The teams had been given another nine months to come up with the goods. And if they didn't, Pierson said that he would recommend a further delay.

Meanwhile engineers at the large aircraft division were working on Status 10a, the stage of incorporating the shorter-bodied A3XX-50 into the Airbus family and the preliminary configuration freeze. This phase saw some changes, one of the most dramatic being the decision to increase the wing size from 8,395 to 8,794 square feet. The cross section was also improved, with a variation introduced into the size of the ovoid from forward to aft. This was needed to increase the internal height of the aft lower cargo hold to allow for an additional pair of LD3 containers. Further revisions were also made to the main gear, while the layout of the nose area was further improved to allow for a seventh freight pallet in the forward hold.

The flight deck was designed from almost the start as a 'mezzanine' placed between the two main-deck levels. Together with the lower cargo hold deck, this formed a four-floor arrangement that was considered best from an aerodynamic perspective, but presented a set of unusual

While discussions and decisions were being made about the politics and engineering regarding the A3XX, designers and 'concept artists' were working hard on flights of fantasy to make use of the massive amount of interior space they saw being made available, like this upper deck lounge area aft of the flight deck. (Lufthansa Technik)

configuration issues.

The revised nose layout cross section had the look of two aircraft merged into one. The upper aircraft resembled the standard Airbus profile, and included the flight deck and crew rest areas. The lower aircraft was a massive unpressurized area, which occupied an underhang area beneath and forward of the flight deck containing the large nose undercarriage bay and the radome. The area was enclosed with a simple reinforced fairing providing easy access for maintenance.

Continuing efforts were made to reduce the area of the horizontal tailplane and vertical fin. Although necessarily very large structures, Airbus hoped to reduce their size, and therefore drag, by use of a digital fly-by-wire (FBW) flight control system derived from the A320 - the first FBW production airliner in the world. This allowed Airbus to design some critical flight control surfaces smaller and lighter than in a conventionally controlled aircraft.

By May 1998 weight issues were being dealt with through a series of materials changes, while the marketing team was paving the way to launch the A3XX. The team had reset its sights on getting airlines on board for a programme launch in the last quarter of 1999. This would enable entry into service about October 2004.

Airbus began seeking letters of intent from airlines in which they would formally state their requirement for an aircraft in the A3XX category. These would then be used as a form of collateral to secure a full programme launch by the Airbus supervisory board in the fourth quarter of 1999.

But before then, Airbus faced the design freeze, which was needed to launch the parallel industrialisation effort to actually build the aircraft. Up to 40% of the programme was on offer to outside partners beyond the usual Airbus family and by mid-1998 only half of this was still up for grabs. Alenia, Belairbus, Fokker Aviation, Saab Aircraft, and Finavitec had all taken early slots, being joined later in 1998 by GKN Westland Aerospace Structures and Eurocopter. Talks also continued with Aerostructures, as well as a group of East Asian companies.

Towards the end of 1998, there were further revisions to the landing gear and rear fuselage as well as the layout of the main-deck floor. The profile of the flap track fairings were modified for further drag reduction, while each wingtip sprouted A320-style fences.

The belly fairing, until now a relatively minor feature, increased in size to help drag reduction. Stretching from just forward of frame 33 all the way aft to beyond frame 81, the fairing ended up being over 100 feet long, or just under half the length of the fuselage. This was part of Status 10d in October 1998 and incorporated more alterations to the landing gear. Two months later, Status 11, saw the overall dihedral, reduced to about 5.6 degrees as a result of the earlier engine position change and other decisions, while the plumbing arrangements for the outer engine fuel feed tank (No. 4) were also revised.

Another cost- and weight-saving change discussed with the airlines involved reducing or eliminating the use of engine thrust reversers. Cutting wear and tear on brakes was a major cost saver, and the decision to eliminate some or even all the reversers was not to be taken lightly.

Eventually the reversers were dropped on the outside engine pair only, since most airlines agreed that the increased braking thrust from the improved-efficiency engines to be used on the A3XX would help achieve a predicted stopping distance similar to, or better than, the A340, or even the 747.

The combined changes of Status 10a, b, c, and d and Status 11, meant that the performance target had narrowed to within a few points.

Now, after more than a year of frantic work, the teams could return to the airlines with a much more attractive design - but they were in for a disappointment - the prospective airline customers had been taking a financial beating.

The new Airbus president, Noel Forgeard, admitted that the Asian market forecast had now shrunk slightly, but he still believed an overall requirement existed for about 1,300 aircraft with a seating capacity over 400 through 2017. Of this, Airbus believed it would take a minimum of 700 orders in the category.

Forgeard's words were full of foreboding for those hoping for a 1999 launch. It was not only in the market where the omens had begun to look bleak, but also in the painfully slow establishment of the new Airbus upon which the A3XX was so dependent.

Talks between the partners lagged so far behind schedule that Airbus had made the decision to officially separate the two issues. But everyone knew that, being realistic, there could be no full-scale launch of the A3XX without the formation of what was termed the single corporate entity (SCE).

The Boeing takeover of McDonnell Douglas in 1997 created mounting political pressure to speed up the process, the agreement had been held up by the ongoing restructuring of the aerospace industry in Europe.

Friction between the partners continued into 1998, with a proposed merger between BAe and DASA that Aerospatiale viewed as a dangerously destabilising alliance. Despite reassurances that this was not the case, Noel Forgeard later confirmed that the restructuring was not likely until the end of 1999. But speaking at a French aviation press club meeting on November 10, he once again stated the vital need for the SCE process to go forward. '...*Boeing has just finished reorganising and will seize the initiative. We must advance at a forced march.*' The SCE was the only way to reduce production costs even more, and he confirmed the consortium's determination to continue. '*We told the shareholders in 1996 that it would be done by 1999. We are redoubling our efforts to achieve that.*'

The performance figures Airbus revealed in April 1999 once again pointed to the vital need for the SCE, although it had achieved record sales of $13.3 billion in 1998,

Corporate confusion continued throughout Europe in early 1999 as BAe and GEC-Marconi announced a surprise merger, just as the UK Airbus partner was closing in on its long-negotiated deal with DASA and the formation of a European Aerospace and Defence Company. The Marconi deal sparked bitterness between the prospective Anglo-German partners and diverted DASA into the welcoming arms of newly privatized Spanish Airbus partner CASA.

A restructured European aerospace and defence industry was emerging, and with it some hope that progress toward the SCE might follow.

The twin-track move to restructure Airbus and launch the A3XX gained momentum from 1999 onward. The Paris Air Show that year once again provided the stage to act out the latest drama - this time the players were the transport and industry ministers from France, Germany, Spain, and the United Kingdom, who met to issue what was probably the nearest thing to an ultimatum the Airbus consortium partner companies had yet experienced. The deal was simple: come up with firm plans to transform into an SCE or risk a clear path to research and development aid for the A3XX.

Although hidden in diplomatic language, the implicit threat warned that unless Airbus made rapid progress, it might yet be caught by Boeing. French transport minister Jean-Claude Gayssot said that '...*determination was expressed very*

strongly' on the need '...*to move forward very quickly and set up the SCE for Airbus.*' Gayssot revealed that the French government had set aside Fr200 million (US $31 million) in R&D funding for the A3XX for the year.

The German government position, on the other hand, remained hard-line. The German minister, Siegmar Mosdori, said that Berlin would not budget any money for the programme without the guaranteed formation of the SCE.

Airbus knew the frenzied rounds of mergers and privatisations throughout Europe were now all but complete. Said Forgeard: '*The privatisation of Aerospatiale is finished, and CASA is also going into the private sector, where the main focus is on shareholder value. That can only be good for the Airbus SCE process.*' Forgeard's words were prophetic: within months, the formation of the union between DaimlerChrysler Aerospace, CASA, and Aerospatiale Matra broke down the last hurdles, the Anglo-German EADC dream was converted to a larger pan-European juggernaut dubbed the European Aeronautic Defence and Space Company (EADS), and with it the task of setting up the planned integrated company suddenly became a lot easier. Instead of four partners, there were now only two - EADS and the newly strengthened, renamed, BAE Systems.

Could a new Airbus now finally emerge, and with it the long-awaited A3XX?

The White Heat of Technology...

Airbus had elbowed its way into the commercial aircraft market using advanced technology as one of its trump cards. Innovation was key to putting its products into a marketplace already crowded by the American giants.

The design team working on creating the A3XX enjoyed what had become a proud heritage of technological advances. With the first Airbus A300, they had introduced the world's first twin-engine, twin-aisle wide-body. It featured several then-new technologies, including automatic wind-shear protection, a full-flight-regime autopilot, an aft-loaded wing design, and triplex power and control systems.

Airbus followed it up in the early 1980s by introducing a raft of new flight-deck technologies that would become the standard for all future cockpits on both sides of the Atlantic. The A300FF (forward-facing) cockpit was the first to automate the flight engineer's tasks and to introduce a computer-based digital flight management system (FMS) to reduce pilot workload.

Airbus took this philosophy to the next logical step with the A310 in 1983, when it introduced cathode ray tube-based flight instruments and an electronic centralized aircraft monitor display. The same aircraft was also used as the platform for two other hallmark Airbus technological innovations: large-scale composites and fly-by-wire flight control. Although the A310 was just a stepping stone toward much fuller implementation of these advances in later aircraft, it was the first to have carbon-fibre-reinforced plastic (CFRP) used in aerodynamic fairings, and the first to use electrically signaled flaps, slats, and spoilers.

§The A310-300 in 1985 took these on another great leap when CFRP was used for the first time in a major primary structure - the fin box. Taking cue from Concorde, the -300 introduced the subsonic world to the use of tailplane trim tanks for controlling the centre of gravity.

It was with the A320 that Airbus gained its global reputation as an innovator. The consortium's first narrow-body faced the best-selling 737 and MD-80 families, and was packed with new game-changing technology - for the first time on any commercial airliner, the A320 featured digital fly-by-wire flight controls and active ailerons. On the flight deck it had side stick controllers that seemed more familiar to F-16 pilots and computer game players than to commercial air crew.

The side sticks controlled pitch and roll, with an automatic system for pitch trim. Structurally the A320 was highly advanced, with a greater proportion of composites than anything before it. Combining previous lessons from developing the A310, the A320 not only used CFRP in the ailerons, spoilers, and elevators, but in the tailplane and fin as well.

Similar evolutionary developments emerged on the A330/A340, which in most cases saw their use on a much larger scale. From an innovation perspective, however, the larger quad and twin family were most important for having a common cockpit, which not only enabled crews to fly either the A330 or A340, but also the A320 series. This so-called 'cross-crew-qualification' feature proved to be a winning formula in the battle for sales, and a vital weapon in the war with Boeing for market share.

While management, accountants, and lawyers struggled through the complexities of forming the SCE, the team of engineers and designers

Airbus made use of advanced, automated laser beam welding techniques to produce a number of sections on the A380. (Photo: Airbus)

continued to battle the challenges of weight and cost targets for the A3XX as the final design freeze came closer. It was becoming clearer which key innovations would be at the forefront.

By early 2000, an estimated 40 % of the A3XX structure and components were to be made from carbon composites and advanced metal alloys. The design by now incorporated a one-piece wing structure with a carbon-fibre wing box, the first in any commercial aircraft. The use of composites saved up to a ton and a half compared to using the most advanced aluminum alloys, said Airbus. A monolithic CFRP design was also adopted for the fin box and rudder, as well as the massive horizontal tailplane and elevators.

Inside the fuselage, the upper-deck floor beams and pressure bulkheads were also to be made of CFRP. At this stage the wing skins were still expected to be made of advanced aluminum alloys, though here again composites soon took over. The fixed-wing leading edges, on the other hand, were to be made from thermo-plastics, while the secondary support structure holding the interior furnishing and cabin trim in place were expected to be made from the same materials.

Further potential applications of thermoplastics included ribs in the fixed leading edges of the vertical and horizontal tailplanes.

To save weight, a material called GLARE (glass-fibre-reinforced aluminum laminate) was chosen for the upper fuselage shell of the A3XX. This had been tested as early as 1990 by Delft University and the Netherlands National Aerospace Laboratory, along with Aerospatiale, Deutsche Airbus, and original GLARE maker AKZO. The material consisted of alternating layers of four or more 0.015-inch aluminum sheets and glass-fibre-reinforced bond film and was 10 % less dense than aluminum. The material thickness could be changed by adding sheets to match the local load requirements, while the glass fibre served as both a load path and crack-stopper between the aluminum sheets. Offering a weight saving of 15 to 30 % over aluminum, the material was tested on an A330/A340 fuselage barrel and had been considered for possible use in the A321.

Flight tests were also conducted from the second half of 1999 onward on a German Air Force A310 multi-role transport, which was fitted with a 12-foot- by-4-foot,-11-inch panel between frames 35 and 40 and stringers 5 and 13 on the right forward fuselage. The modification was completed by Lufthansa Technik with DaimlerChrysler Aerospace Airbus and was

Other interior suggestions saw lounge areas more in line with hotel lobbies. (npk industrial design)

The forward fuselage and flight deck mock-up at Toulouse.

certified by Germany's civil aviation authority. By mid-2000, Airbus estimated that it would save about 1,760 pounds on the ASXX, as well as having better corrosion, fatigue-, and damage-resistance properties.

Another advanced manufacturing process developed to speed up assembly as well as reduce weight was laser-beam welding (LBW), which would be used to attach the stringers of the lower fuselage shell skins. The same process, which could weld up to 26 feet of stringers per minute, cut weight by reducing the amount of weld material used and included a built-in automated inspection unit. It also eliminated fasteners, which for many years were a major source of corrosion and fatigue cracks. So promising was the process that it was introduced into the assembly line as early as 2001 to make the fuselage lower skin panels of the A318, with other applications to follow. LBW was also proposed for use on the curved, pressurized bulkhead below the flight deck floor.

Tests showed that empty weight could be trimmed by about 1 metric ton by using a new higher-pressure hydraulic system running at 5,000 psi or about one-third higher than contemporary conventional aircraft systems. The final design was a partially decentralized system that included a local hydraulic reservoir for a series of electro-hydraulic actuators and saved an estimated 2,200 pounds overall. The final design would incorporate a remarkable network of tubes and pipes stretching over 3,300 feet.

Faced with maintaining just the right cabin atmosphere for a space that could accommodate up to 840 passengers, Airbus scoured the industry for the most powerful environmental control system (ECS) ever conceived. The chosen system, which Hamilton Sundstrand eventually selected for development was a double-spool, air-generating system that promised better thermodynamic efficiency, occupied less volume, and offered more redundancy. The A3XX was to have two innovative double-packs, each containing four air cycle machines of four stages each, and were 85% more powerful than any previous ECS developed by the company. Each unit performed separate functions within the overall cycle.

By June 1999, flight tests had begun of an

A340 that was fitted with a reduced-stability configuration as part of efforts to validate the technology for the A3XX. Natural stability was reduced by transferring fuel between tanks so the aircraft's centre of gravity was moved aft. This meant that the aircraft was more finely balanced and required less downward force to be applied by the horizontal tailplane for stability. By using a high-fidelity FBW flight control system, Airbus believed it could take maximum benefit from the move by reducing the size of the 2,580-square-foot tailplane by up to 10% to approximately 2,153 square feet. This could reduce trim drag by about 0.5% and save 1,500 pounds in weight, directly contributing to overall operating cost reduction.

Up to this point everyone involved in the A3XX had been forced to use their imagination to judge the true scale of what they were involved in, be they engineers, designers, suppliers, or airlines. Now, as the winter of 1999-2000 approached, this was about to change as the first huge ABXX

mockup sections started to arrive at Toulouse. Made by a local supplier, Sefca-Qieutelot, the initial mockup was the upper-deck section only but would later be extended to provide a full-length, full-diameter representative cross section, including main deck and lower cargo hold.

The section, installed in a new mockup centre adjacent to the Airbus headquarters building at Toulouse, gave airline customers in particular a real-life impression of what they were being offered or what they had already bought. Various interiors and features, some of them future options not yet finalized, would also be displayed among the mockup collection.

Aware of the need to keep the momentum going, the supervisory board meanwhile met across the road from the mockup centre at an extraordinary meeting in early December. The board authorized Managing Director Noel Forgeard to begin touring airlines to ask them to sign letters of

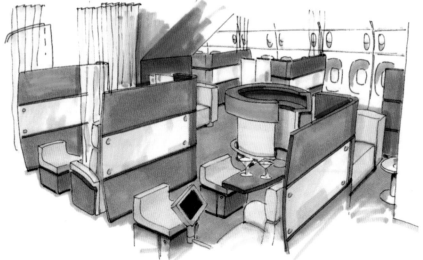

support to gauge
market demand.
Assuming that
sufficient commitments
could be obtained, the
outline plan was to
expedite the delayed
A3XX schedule and
target mid-2000 for the
commercial launch.

Although the 1990s
had turned out to be a
difficult time to launch
the double-decker, the
culmination of the decade was a watershed time
for Airbus and its dream of market parity with
Boeing. As the 1999 numbers were tallied, it
became clear that Airbus had not only completely
outsold its rival, but had also ended the year with
a massive 48% of the total number of undelivered
new airliners held in the firm order backlog. What
better omens could there be as Forgeard headed
out on his quest for signed letters of support?

The airline response to the first major sales
foray was certainly encouraging, but SIA and
QANTAS were adamant about needing an

additional range of 300 to 400 nautical miles.
Airbus Marketing Vice President Colin Stuart:
*'SIA needed to reach London, of course, and
QANTAS wanted transpacific range. SIA also
wanted QC/2 - the emerging new tough nighttime-
noise requirement at London Heathrow. Until then
we weren't guaranteeing QC/2. We targeted it, but
SIA wanted it guaranteed. It therefore became a
directive from Forgeard that we had to have these
things in order to launch.'*

Stuart recalled that at that meeting both the
range improvement and the requirement to meet
QC/2 rules became
pivotal conditions for
launch.

Tests and predictions
increasingly showed
that the A3XX was
marginal at best to meet
the noise requirements,
so Airbus decided that it
had to bite the bullet and
immediately build in
greater takeoff noise
margin.

The changes included
a significant series of
engine modifications to
increase bypass ratio
and reduce noise

One of the 'star areas' of the interior that features in most designer's plans was the forward stairs from the main to the upper deck.

treatments resulted in an overall weight increase of about 6,600 pounds and led to the further extension in the use of advanced alloys, composites, and thermoplastics in the wings.

Many of these changes were still being finalized at the time of the 2000 Asian Aerospace show in Singapore, where Airbus vice president for A3XX market development, Philippe Jarry, was telling airlines that the aircraft would still be a great performer. *'You have airlines that have a policy of replacing their aircraft early so we believe 2005 is in line with market requirements.'* He did add, however, that airlines had shown zero interest in the proposed 480-seat A3XX-50R shrink. It also emerged that hopes remained high of launching both the base-line -100 passenger and -100F freighter variants simultaneously at the end of the year, even though the cargo version would not enter service until 2007.

Outline proposals were handed out to the airlines, with Cathay Pacific, MAS, and SIA being offered deals of between 12 and 15 aircraft each. Discussions were also underway on the A3XX-100F with Emirates, United, and Virgin Atlantic, as well as with the big cargo carriers, including Atlas Air, Cargolux, Lufthansa Cargo, and FedEx.

Mike Turner, chief operating officer of BAE Systems, clearly thought that it was more important to secure a range of major airline customers covering all the major global alliances than it was to rack up a specific tally of aircraft orders. Penetration of the four major alliances was vital. *'If we can secure a first wave of major customers, we would expect other airlines to follow'*. Significant discounts were offered as an incentive to the first takers and, depending on options and interior configurations, the official list price for the A3XX-100 varied from $218 to $240 million, while the stretched -200 was priced

emissions, as well as the knock-on effects of drag and weight.

To improve the lift/ drag ratio by 5%, the wing design was changed to incorporate a droop-nose device by the inboard leading edge. This variable-position device, similar in design to one developed for the de Havilland DH.121 Trident, was used instead of a more conventional Kruger flap because of the sheer depth of the giant wing root. The droop device was a masterpiece of design to solve a difficult problem, according to Frank Ogilvie, A380 aerodynamics director and deputy head of the overall aircraft design.

'One of the thoughts was to go to a completely sealed slat system, but we couldn't do that because Boeing has the design rights. Also, the wing was still stalling between the engines and not near the root, so the question was, how could we do a sealed slat that wasn't sealed? In the end, British Aerospace at Filton came up with the drooped nose idea. The beauty about the design is that it is always sealed as the rotating part is within the profile of the wing. In high-lift configuration, it meets the requirement for maximum lift but has substantially better drag. It also allows the wing to stall inboard, because it does not have a slot.

The ailerons were also rigged to droop at takeoff; adding to the overall lift. The FMS was optimized for improved takeoff and noise abatement procedures. The changes, added to the range increase, resulted in a total weight impact of about 26,000 pounds, which was reflected in a decision to increase the highest maximum takeoff weight option from 1.207 to 1.233 million pounds. The increases in engine size and acoustic between $244 and $253 million.

The airline response to the first major sales foray was encouraging and was enough for Airbus to pencil in 26 May as the date for a decision on the commercial launch of the A3XX, which, should it come, meant that a full industrial launch would follow in December, with delivery of the first aircraft toward the end of 2005.

Rumours started to circulate that despite all the focus on the big-name airlines such as Cathay Pacific, QANTAS, SIA, United, and Virgin as being the launch customer, it was the rapidly growing Dubai-based airline Emirates that first emerged as a potential buyer.

Emirates would only say it had officially notified the manufacturer of its intent to order five A3XXs and place five options should the programme be launched.

Two further A3XX-100Fs were also tentatively added to the mix. Then, within weeks of the planned critical May meeting, SIA quietly followed Emirates by signing a letter expressing interest in up to ten A3XXs.

Airbus confirmed SIA was in discussion for ten firm and six option A3XXs for delivery from 2005, although the final deal announced at the end of that September for up to 25 aircraft was bigger than anyone at Airbus could have hoped for.

The air of secrecy existed, for SIA was traditionally a cautious, conservative carrier and was considering its options, which still included a potential 747X offering from Boeing. The airline had gained massive strength in its global network on the back of the 747 and had even taken delivery of the 1,000th aircraft produced by Boeing. SIA was also a major 777 customer and enjoyed close links with the US manufacturer, which had offered it a deal covering six firm -

400X and nine options as a possible bridge to a stretched 747X variant.

Boeing had stepped up efforts to promote the higher gross weight 910,000-pound takeoff -400X, and planned a seminar for potential customers in June. The -400X was a vital part of a revised Boeing strategy to try and counter the A3XX with a renewed attempt to develop a stretched 747. This time, Boeing was trying a building-block approach, with the first step on the ladder being the -400IGW (increased gross weight) variant, which was first proposed in 1997. The -400IGW was later renamed the -400X and ultimately became the -400ER when launched with an order by QANTAS for six passenger versions in November 2000.

The airlines remained cool to the Boeing plan, so a more radical revamp was designed, but still using the -400X as a foundation. The stretched version again featured a wing root insert that extended wing span to 230 feet and increased fuselage length by 31.5 feet. Maximum takeoff weight was increased to 1.043 million pounds, and up to 100 more seats could be fitted. The aircraft would have up to 545 nautical miles more range and about 10% lower seat-mile costs and was also to be offered with derivatives of the Engine Alliance GP7000 engines in development for the A3XX, or a new variant of the Rolls-Royce Trent family dubbed the 600.

By using the bigger wing, improved aerodynamics, and engines of the larger stretch, the new 747X would become the world's longest-range aircraft, capable of flying up to 442 passengers across a range of 8,975 nautical miles.

Armed with performance data that said the 747X Stretch would beat the projected operating costs of the A3XX-100, a high-powered Boeing

The launch customer was to be Dubai-based Emirates. (Photo: author)

team hit the board-rooms of the major Asia-Pacific carriers in the crucial few weeks before the Airbus meeting in May The team included the experienced Boeing Product Strategy and Development Vice President John Roundhill and Joe Sutter, the mercurial father of the 747. To prepare the airlines for their visit, Boeing Chairman and Chief Executive Phil Condit sent each a letter advising the airlines not to commit to the big Airbus until they could be fully briefed on the final performance estimates of the 747X.

This somewhat desperate effort did succeed in establishing the launch of the -400ER, which went on to be ordered as both a passenger and a freight aircraft, but it could not stop the inexorable progress of the ASXX toward launch.

The first state-aid grant for the 3XX programme, now valued at about $12 billion, was announced by the U.K. government, which approved an £530 million loan to BAE Systems. The move inevitably sparked complaints from Boeing that, over the subsequent years, would eventually reignite the furious transatlantic dispute over subsidies that had only been grudgingly settled under the provisions of a 1992 trade agreement.

News of the loan came as the Airbus partners reached agreement to house the A3XX final assembly line in Toulouse, France. The rumors leaking out of Airbus suggested that the agreement covered an overall rationalisation of the production setup, with Toulouse taking the lead on all wide-body production, and Hamburg assuming final assembly of all single-aisle aircraft.

Customer momentum was simultaneously building, with Air France becoming the next airline to join the potential launch group with a requirement of up to 10 new aircraft. In early June, Air France's president, Jean-Cyril Spinetta, said that the A3XX, '...could constitute the appropriate solution for Air France in the very-large-capacity market, meeting our needs in terms of capacity for the projected growth in air traffic, but also in terms of range, operational efficiency passenger comfort, and environmental friendliness.'

A week later, Emirates Chief Maurice Flanagan was more vocal in his support when he wrote a letter to London's Evening Standard newspaper saying, 'With world passenger numbers growing at 5% a year, I don't know what other airlines are waiting for.

Takeoff and landing slots at major airports will continue to be tight and we will need bigger aircraft.'

Meanwhile, talks to create the new Airbus, now dubbed the Airbus Integrated Company (AIC), went ahead between BAE and the soon-to-be-formed EADS companies, though a number of issues remained to be solved, including financial share and corporate governance. Although the issues of the AIC and the A3XX launch were officially separated, the two were inevitably linked, and by June 2000 the partners agreed to sort out both issues at the same time. In theory, the AIC and ASXX could not be tied directly because talks over the formation of the 'new' Airbus were going on at partner level, while authority to offer the A3XX rested with the Airbus supervisory board.

The building blocks of the AIC were completed when the last hurdles were cleared for the formation of EADS with the merger of Aerospatiale Matra CASA, and DaimlerChrysler Aerospace.

The basic framework of the AIC divided ownership between EADS, with 80%, and BAE Systems, with 20%. The company was to be registered in France and was expected to produce savings by allowing the partners to streamline procurement, eliminate duplication, and reduce production overheads. Overall, EADS predicted savings of up to €350 million (US. $407 million) by 2004. Employing about 41,500 people, the AIC was to be governed by a seven-member shareholder committee, with five representatives from EADS and two from BAE. Rainer Hertrich, co-chief executive of EADS, would be chairman while the day-to-day management would be headed by Forgeard.

In an interview with the French newspaper Le Monde on 14 June 2000, Forgeard described the talks between BAE Systems and the newly created EADS as going well. As for the commercial launch decision, which now seemed to be subject to one embarrassing holdup after another, he said, '...there is no reason to delay further. From now on, Airbus' credibility as well as my own is at stake.'

Chapter Five

The A380

Finally, on 9 December 2000, the news the industry was waiting for broke - the Airbus supervisory board had voted to launch the A380, the new name for the A3XX.

Manfred Bischoff, the chairman of the Airbus supervisory board and EADS co-chairman, announced that '...*Airbus has a new flagship. This is a major breakthrough for Airbus as a full-range competitor on world markets. We are convinced that this aircraft will have a bright and extremely successful future. It will be proof of the outstanding capabilities and skills of Europe's aerospace industry and represents a completely new generation of technology in the field of aircraft manufacturing and air travel. I am personally very proud and happy to give the go-ahead for a project that I fought for since 1989.'*

But why A380, when the A350 or A360 were the next logical designations in the Airbus numbering system? Although the use of the numeral 8 was already believed to be good luck to many Asian cultures, and therefore a consideration toward the large customer base of the region, Forgeard said the final designation was selected because an '...*8 suggests double-decks, one on top of the other.'*

The first variant was the A380-800, replacing the A3XX-100, while the reduced-capacity 480-seater variant previously dubbed the A3XX-50R was renamed the A380-700. The stretched A3XX-200 was now known as the A380-900, While a longer-range derivative of the baseline A3XX-100 was to be called the A380-800R, and the freighter version the -800F. Then there was the question of using the

higher-end -700/-800/-900 designations for the derivatives straight out of the box. Airbus Chief Commercial Officer John Leahy said that this approach was taken because the three versions were fully developed aircraft and the -100/-200/-300 designations would be subject to earlier obsolescence and therefore lower residual values.

Forgeard – now with the credibility of Airbus and himself secure - was also happy. '*This decision crowns the efforts of all those who have worked so hard on the project for the last four years, and in particular the 20 airlines and 50 airports, the airworthiness authorities, engine manufacturers, suppliers, industrial partners, and not least, our share-holders and all the Airbus staff whose dedication helped shape the programme and bring it to fruition.'*

The group included SIA, Emirates, the leasing giant International Lease Finance Company (ILFC), QANTAS, Air France, and Virgin - the latter's $3.8 billion order for six in December being the final breakthrough needed to achieve Airbus's 50 order target. The Virgin deal, announced just four days before the final go-ahead, included initial deliveries from 2006 and was part of the airline's strategy to expand its existing trunk routes as well as add new services. The airline's chairman, Sir Richard Branson, said, '*I am incredibly excited about the opportunities these aircraft will bring - our reputation has been built on innovation and the A3XX will give us the opportunity to create a new flying experience for our passengers.'*

The new interiors of its recently ordered A340-600s, featuring

Sir Timothy Charles Clark KBE, President of Emirates.

Founder of the Virgin Group of Companies, Sir Richard Branson was quick to describe what many in the industry saw as flights of fantasy interiors he had in mind for the A380 when it was first launched: bars, massage stations, libraries, casinos, showers... Remarkably many came to fruition.

At the time of the A380 reveal in January 2005, Sir Richard Branson stated, 'It is a proud moment for Airbus to unveil the first A380, a momentous day in aviation's history and an exciting opportunity to create new ways of flying for our passengers. Virgin Atlantic's A380s are going to be bigger and better than any aircraft which has preceded them, with bigger and better cabins for all our passengers.' Later, changes in corporate ownership and other 'delays' meant that it is unlikely that Virgin Atlantic will take delivery of its first machine until 2018.

stand-up bars and the provision for some massage stations on its 747s, underlined the willingness of Virgin to think outside the box, with the A380 providing scope for never-before-seen features on modern aircraft. Although Airbus was keen to market the potential for bars, libraries, gyms, and even showers, it wasn't clear how many if any of these would actually become reality.

Cheong Choong Kong, deputy chairman and chief executive of SIA, which was a 49% stakeholder in Virgin preferred a note of restraint, saying that the A380 had great potential for '...*service innovations and unprecedented levels of comfort*', but that the airline would be reluctant to give up revenue-earning seats for what he called 'flights of fantasy' features.

QANTAS added force to the prelaunch momentum in December 2000 by placing orders and options for up to 24 aircraft. The deal, worth $4.6 billion, also included A330s and the launch order for the 747-400ER, although the latter was widely considered something of a consolation prize to Boeing, which had worked hard on the Australian campaign as hopes of finding a strong 747X Stretch candidate in the Asia-Pacific market.

Like other launch customers, QANTAS benefited from a discount on the A380 list price of $230 million. Philippe Jarry commented that follow-on customers lining up to sign on the dotted line early in 2001 would benefit from a similar offer.

Airbus took the opportunity during the industrial launch of the A380 to make changes within its management team, just as the company began its official transition to AIC. The biggest

was the appointment of Charles Champion as senior vice president of the A380 programme. An aerospace engineer with a master's degree from Stanford University who had begun with Aerospatiale's Airbus division in 1979, Champion came from the single-aisle A320-family programme where he had led the effort to ramp up production to an unprecedented 23 aircraft per month. He had also done tours of duty with sales for southeast Europe and the CIS, as well as managing director of the Airbus Military Company which was being set up to develop the A400M airlifter. Champion led the A400M through the ups and downs of five years of prelaunch development, and had taken over from Jürgen Thomas, who had stepped down from the project to become special advisor to Forgeard. Almost immediately, Champion invoked changes in the structure to see the A380 into production.

Aircraft component management teams (ACMTs), tasked with engineering, manufacturing, and product support, were co-located at Airbus sites around Europe. ACMTs were devised for the wing, nose, centre fuselage, forward and aft fuselage, propulsion, empennage, landing gear, systems, interior, and final assembly line (FAL).

Each ACMT acted like a mini-programme of its own, with a head overseeing programme management, engineering, industrial, procurement, quality and customer services.

Within each ACMT were several combined design build teams (CDBTs) with responsibility for sub-elements. ACMT allocation was related to the traditional Airbus centre-of-excellence philosophy, with responsibility for the nose and centre fuselage being taken by Airbus France, the forward and aft fuselage by Airbus Germany the wings by Airbus UK, tail cone and empennage by Airbus Spain, and wing leading edges by Belairbus of Belgium.

Even though suppliers and risk-sharing partners were being selected, some key design decisions were still undecided. One of these was the decision to build an all-metallic wing. Although the composite wing offered a weight saving of up to 3,080 pounds per ship set, a more detailed analysis showed that the final weight saving would have been eroded by the need for a massive structural join between the two sections where the inboard metal structure attached to the carbon-fibre-reinforced plastic outer third of the wing. Added weight would have also been incurred through the need to strengthen the wing to counter the loss of bending relief moment from the lighter structure. Added together, the 'plastic' wing ended up bringing in a weight savings of less than 1,500 pounds, which was simply not worth the higher manufacturing costs.

Sales appeared to be on a roll during the first year and were forecast by John Leahy to break the 100 barrier by the end of 2001. In particular, talks with freight operators were well advanced, he said, and it was a deal with parcel carrier FedEx for 10

A380-800Fs that took the tally to 97, along with 59 options, by the end of December 2001.

In late February 2001, Qatar Airways became a surprise ninth firm customer and the third freighter operator after FedEx and Emirates (which had ordered two) with an order for two plus two options. The order came as part of a bigger deal including A330s.

Others placing orders in 2001 included Lufthansa, which signed for fifteen. The aircraft '....could be used for daily flights from Frankfurt to New Delhi, New York, Tokyo, and Singapore,' said Lufthansa, which, despite officially opting for the A380, still kept the door open for a 747X purchase.

As the programme entered its first full year as the A380, major suppliers began to line up for work. The US based undercarriage maker BF Goodrich was selected early in 2001 to supply the body and wing gear in a deal worth $2 to $3 billion over the first 20 years. Goodrich, which also provided the gear for the 747 and 777, beat off competition from Messier-Dowty, which nonetheless won the contract for the hefty forward landing gear.

The massive six-wheel body gear, similar in overall appearance to the 777 main gear, weighed in at more than 8,970 pounds compared to about 3,000 pounds for the stockier four-wheel body gear on the 747. The four-wheeled wing gear, by contrast, was expected to weigh about 5,100 pounds compared to the 3,890-pound 747 gear. Under the deal, which was its first main gear contract for any Airbus aircraft, Goodrich agreed to supply completed landing gear

Malaysia Airlines A380. By the time the aircraft was to go into service, the colours had changed.

Queensland and Northern Territories Air Service A380

from a former Rohr engine nacelle facility in Toulouse.

In May 2001, Airbus selected Rockwell Collins to supply an avionics full duplex (AFDX) Ethernet switch for the A380, the first sole source selection for the aircraft's avionics suite. The switch provided the electronic backbone for the communications infrastructure to connect various aircraft systems, including displays, radios, and navigation sensors. The 100 megabit-per-second Ethernet network was designed to be a thousand times faster than the ARINC 429 avionics databus used in other Airbus designs. The broadband design, which was selected over a competing offer

Lufthansa Chief Wolfgang Mayrhuber with Chancellor Angela Merkel at the Berlin Air Show. (Photos: Airbus SAS)

Above: Left: Etihad Airways A380.

Right: Sheikh Ahmed bin Saif Al Nayhan, founder and Chairman of Etihad Airways.

Below:Thai Airways A380. (Photos: Airbus SAS)

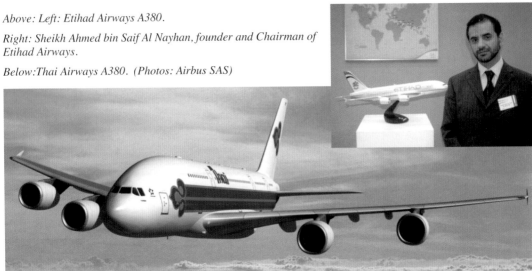

Computer renderings allow different colour schemes to be 'painted' on the same basic illustration. Left: Air France. below, a Singapore Airlines A.380. (Photos: Airbus SAS)

from Thales Avionics, was based on a limited 10 megabit - per - second system used on the 767-400ER, but was much larger and had enormous capacity for growth.

Thales soon rebounded with its selection by Airbus to provide the integrated modular avionics (IMA). Teamed with Diehl Avionik Systeme of Germany, Thales offered a systems

architecture in which avionics functions were distributed among generic computing modules slotted into cabinets placed throughout the aircraft. The modules were to be linked via Ethernet. To ensure safety and redundancy, other suppliers were to develop the software for avionics functions ranging from display processing to communications routing to utilities management.

Perception and Certification

Safety - both aircraft and passenger - was the driving force behind the basic structural and systems redundancy of the design A380. Yet, as the A3XX became the A380, it became as much about public perception as it was certification. As the design became finalized, was clear that there would be fewer certification issues with the new double-decker than with the pioneering fly-by-wire A320 of the previous decade.

Airbus wanted to demonstrate to the travelling public, operators and regulatory authorities that the A380 was no different from anything before it. In terms of scale, the 35-40% capacity increase of the 550-seat A380 over the 747 was insignificant compared with the 100% increase seen with the

introduction of the first 375-seat jumbos over the 150-seat 707.

In order to satisfy certification requirements, Airbus still faced the task of proving that the double-decker could be evacuated within 90 seconds using only half the available exits. To enable the certification basis to cover the higher-capacity versions with up to almost 900 seats, Airbus decided that an evacuation demonstration would be performed with 873 people - 20 crew and 853 passengers.

For the trial, more than 320 people would have to be evacuated through only three of the six doors on the upper deck. These escapees faced a descent of 27 feet to the ground. The balance, more than 550 people, had to make their escape through five of the ten main deck exits.

Airbus tested this in Hamburg, where the 'passengers' - all volunteers from local sports and social clubs - represented the required mix of age and gender as laid down by the European Aviation Safety Agency (EASA) and the US Federal Aviation Administration (FAA). These rules called for a minimum of 40% females, of whom 15% had to be over 50 years old - indeed, 35% of the total

84

Cho Yang Ho, the chairman and chief executive officer of Korean Air, chairman of the Hanjin Group, and a founding member of SkyTeam alliance.

Right: Qatar Airways CEO Akbar al Baker.

Al-Baker became Chief Executive Officer of Qatar Airways in 1997. Prior to his appointment he worked at the Civil Aviation Directorate of Qatar. He is also the former Chairman of the Qatar Tourism Authority.

Below: China Southern Airlines came into being in 1998, following the government's decision to split the operating divisions of Civil Aviation Administration of China (CAAC) into separate airlines.

participants had to be over 50.

For the test, conducted in a darkened hangar at Finkenwerder, the passengers slid to the ground on Goodrich-developed dual-lane slides, each of which could handle up to 70 passengers per minute. To help overcome the chances of hesitancy by passengers at the top of the slide - particularly the upper deck - the slides were extra wide and projected farther out from the sides, making them appear less steep. Higher sidewalls and built-in illumination were also added to reassure the passengers, while also improved the sea-worthiness of the slides as rafts in case an aircraft needed to be ditched at sea.

Production of these slides had been awarded in July 2001to Goodrich who were to supply up to 18 evacuation slides per aircraft. These slides were and are the largest ever developed, each equipped with a survival kit, integrated lighting system and radio beacon. The multi-role inflatables double up as liferafts - on the upper deck they are housed in stowage bays below the door sills, on the main deck in the doors in a more conventional manner.

The slides were a major feat of design engineering in their own

right, being built to fully inflate in 6 seconds and to remain stable in a 25-knot wind from any direction, with all engines running at idle. Not only did they have to avoid the 'twisting' effect seen on earlier wide-body escape slides, including the upper-deck escape system of the original 747, but they had to be long enough to reach the ground even if the aircraft ended nose up or down. In the case of the A380, this made a big difference. For example, the main-deck forward door sill height was only nine feet above ground if the A380 nose gear collapsed, but was thirty-two feet above ground if it rocked back on its tail!

To help plan for the optimum location of exits,

Above: the upper and lower deck Type A doors on an Emirates A380. Each door has a clear opening width of 42 inches and a height of 76 inches. They are fitted with a double-glazed window to allow the crew to monitor the area below the door before deploying the slide. Note the upper deck door has the slide fitted behind the blow-out panel under the door sill, whereas the main deck door has the slide as part of the door structure. (Photo: author)

Left: Goodrich test an early prototype of an upper deck A380 escape slide (Photo: Goodrich).

The evacuation trials conducted in Hamburg on MSN007/F-WWSD. These had to be successfully completed with only half the doors and slides in use and, in one test, in the pitch dark! (Photo: Airbus SAS)

These two photographs show the steps taken by Airbus to ensure the rapid evacuation of passengers from the A380. Passageway widths between fixed items of equipment such as galley items was set at 30 inches, not the mandatory 20 inches, which gives wider routes to the Type A doors, used here to replenish the galley supplies.

Also visible, but not that noticable, are the designed in 'grab holds' - mostly high up on equipment, but also lower down in bulkheads - for use by the crew in the event of turbulence. (both author)

Airbus commissioned Professor Edward Galea of the UKs Greenwich University, a leading aircraft evacuation safety expert, who specialized in developing computer-based models that allowed the study the impact on safety of various design options. Data from the models, derived in part from live evacuation trials at Cranfield University near Milton Keynes, helped prove that the final exit and cabin configurations would satisfy the 90-second rule.

The work at Cranfield demonstrated that the best way to guarantee the safest passenger flow toward an exit on any airliner - not just the A380 - was to increase the space between the galley or lavatory bulkheads. Often stationed as 'monuments' by an exit, the research showed that the optimum width between these units was the 30 inches already used in the A380, against the required minimum of 20 inches. Overall, the aircraft boasted 16 emergency exits, with eight each side. The main deck had four double-width slides, a single overwing slide that deployed aft, and three wide upper-deck slides.

New York-based Parker Aerospace's Electronic Systems Division was picked to provide the fuel measurement and management systems. The system would measure fuel quantity in the massive tanks held within the wings, fuselage, and horizontal tailplane, while the management system, controlled by the IMA suite, was designed to monitor the distribution of fuel while commanding pumps and valves to transfer fuel, handle refueling, and control centre of gravity. Another big-ticket item decided in 2001 included the air generation system, the biggest environmental control system ever built for a commercial aircraft. Awarded to Hamilton Sundstrand, the system was closely linked to the operation of the auxiliary power unit (APU), which was to be developed by sister United Technologies Company Pratt & Whitney Canada (P&WC).

Airbus was happy to see the US and Canadian content of the A380 grow. In late 2001, a new dimension to the US growth strategy came with the announcement of plans to develop a wing design centre in Wichita, Kansas. Employing about 60 people, mainly structural and stress engineers, the centre was established as a satellite office of the wing design centre at Airbus UK in Filton, and allowed design work to continue around the clock. Although several other US sites had been considered, Airbus selected Wichita because of the large number of skilled engineers already based there. Boeing, Bombardier, Cessna, and Raytheon were all local employers, but the constant ups and downs of business and general aviation, and commercial and defence markets, meant that a pool of highly trained engineers was readily available.

The US content was further expanded in December with the selection of Honeywell as the supplier of the flight management system. Based on the company's Pegasus FMS, as used on the Boeing 717 and MD-11, the A380 system was expanded with new hardware for greater speed and more memory. It also featured a graphical user interface with pop-up menus and a cursor control device, rather than the more usual text-based interface. Although Honeywell's FMS had become standard on every new Airbus since 1984, the preceding series of nonstandard equipment selections for the A380 meant that nothing could be taken for granted.

Honeywell's win over stiff competition against a combined Thales/Smiths team was therefore seen as a major victory, which estimated its overall potential value at $200 million over the next 15 years.

Meanwhile, Eaton, based in Cleveland, Ohio, was selected in October 2001 to provide the high-pressure hydraulic system, and a few months later the company's aerospace unit in Michigan was chosen to provide its Aeroquip-brand Rynglok and high-pressure hoses as well. The A380 would be the first commercial aircraft to use 5,000-psi hydraulics. Using the higher-pressure system produced weight savings of about 2,200 pounds, or about 30% less than an equivalent 3,000-psi pressure system that would have been standard on other commercial aircraft. The weight savings came from reduced actuator size and smaller-diameter lines.

While the North American partners and supplier base were consolidating swiftly, the picture in Asia was considerably more fluid. Japan remained the prime target for Airbus, both as a source of skilled potential partners and as an untapped market.

Changes to Airports?

It was Boeing, rather than Airbus, who warned the airports to prepare for the advent of very large aircraft when it addressed the Airports Council International (ACI) meeting in Switzerland in 1994. Boeing forecast that airports such as Tokyo, Hong Kong, Taipei, and Osaka would need to handle thousands of high-capacity transports per year from about 2010 onward.

Airbus surveyed airports around the world where they expected the A380 to see service – a survey based on route structures or regular destinations of the key carriers that had either ordered the A380 or had made expressions of interest. By 2003, the tally reached 86, including 32 Asia-Pacific airports, 15 in Europe, 18 in the USA, and a spread of 21 in destinations as varied as Argentina, Brazil, Canada, India, Mexico, the Middle East, Pakistan, Sri Lanka and South Africa.

Priority went to the airports where the first wave of A380s would begin operation in 2006 and 2007. These included Bangkok, Paris Charles de Gaulle, Dubai, Frankfurt, Hong Kong, Jeddah, New York JFK, Kuala Lumpur, Los Angeles, London's Heathrow and Gatwick, Melbourne, Montreal, Tokyo Narita, San Francisco, Singapore and Sydney. The next wave, from 2008 to 2009, was expected to include the big cargo hubs at Anchorage, Indianapolis, Memphis, Ontario and California as well as Kansai, Shanghai, and Taipei. Other potential early destinations beyond phase two included

Auckland, Amsterdam, Beijing, Minneapolis/St. Paul, Nice, Paris Orly, Toronto, Vancouver, and Zurich.

In working so closely with the airports, Airbus was promoting the high-capacity, high-efficiency value equation that formed the foundation of the A380 concept. The message was simply that the A380 was part of the solution to the growing congestion, rather than the problem itself. Airbus argued that adapting to the ultra-high-capacity aircraft was a more efficient use of ramp and runway space than developing extra runways and gates to handle a larger number of smaller aircraft.

Airbus also determined that the cost of adapting to the A380 would be relatively small compared to the roughly $20 billion per year airports of the world spend on general upgrades.

Using data from a group of 30 airports originally surveyed by ACI, Airbus predicted that adaptation costs would be about $100 million each for taxiway and apron improvements, strengthening of taxiway and culvert bridges and terminal upgrades, including the development of double-deck air bridges. Airbus said that, '...*about 200 airports accept the 747 today As aircraft capacity has not changed for more than three decades, it is time to prepare for the future.*'

Not all agreed with this analysis, particularly in the USA, where the General Accounting Office (GAO), estimated that the 14 airports most likely to handle the A380 would have to spend about $2.1 billion.

Airbus challenged the findings, saying they were '...*not the result of detailed analysis, but rather reflect extremely rough and inconsistent estimating.*' Airbus calculated that US airports would need to spend about $520 million, or just under a quarter of the GAO's estimates. Part of this 'error' was because Airbus identified costs in the GAO's estimates that would have been spent on modernisation and capacity improvement anyway!

Most of the estimated costs were due to wider taxiways and runways that the GAO said were required for the A380, which the FAA classed as a Group VI aircraft. This included extending the width of runways to 200 feet and taxiways to 98 feet, the latter only being required to be 75 feet wide for Group V aircraft such as the 747. However, as Airbus pointed out, the landing gear footprint of the A380 was less than 46 feet, meaning that it would still be able to use the standard Code E (75-foot-wide) taxiway as long as the shoulders were extended by 61 feet on each

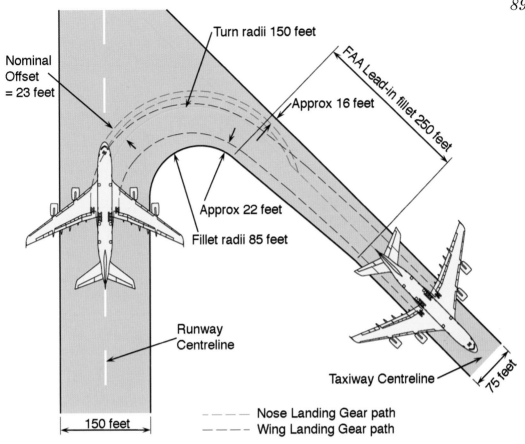

Turn radii 150 feet

Nominal
Offset
= 23 feet

FAA Lead-in fillet 250 feet

Approx 16 feet

Approx 22 feet

Fillet radii 85 feet

Runway
Centreline

Taxiway Centreline

75 feet

150 feet

— — — — Nose Landing Gear path
— — — — Wing Landing Gear path

A 135° Turn - from Runway to Taxiwayusing the Judgemental Oversteer Method

side. This would take overall taxiway width to 197 feet, compared to the minimum 144 feet typically required for the 747.

The distance between the nose gear and the aftermost main gear - the six-wheel body-mounted undercarriage units - was just over 104 feet, or roughly 20 feet longer than the 747. However, when measured to the steering point around which the A380 turned, the axis was just over 97 feet, making it slightly less than the 100-foot steering axis of the 777-300 and the 108 feet of the A340-600. Airports had already adapted to these aircraft by adding fillets to runway access taxiways and other areas where maneuvers could be limited, so Airbus was sure that this would not be a problem.

To work out how the enormous weight of the A380, and particularly that of the 1.3-million-pound freighter version, would impact runway and taxiway surfaces, Airbus built a curious contraption called the landing gear configuration test vehicle. Loaded with heavy weights, the skeletal vehicle rolled along on 20 wheels to simulate the pavement loading of the

A380. As well as maneuvering around, the vehicle was rolled over a special flexible pavement area that was laid down at Toulouse with weight-sensing instruments built into the concrete and asphalt. Using the data, Airbus discovered that the A380's ACN (Aircraft Classification Number - an ICAO method of calculating the load-bearing value of an aircraft - was between 66 and 72, compared to 69 for the 747, as much as 75 for the A340-600, 83 for the 777-300ER and 69 for the 767-400ER.

The use of a static load on a slowly moving trolley-like device to simulate the aircraft was sometimes questioned but was perfectly valid. A popular misconception was that the greatest load applied to a runway surface was when an aircraft lands. But the actual impact weight is about 50% of the total weight, as the aircraft wing is still producing lift, and the weight is gradually transferred to the wheels as the aircraft slows down. Conversely, the weight on takeoff gradually decreases as the aircraft accelerates and lift increases. The most critical

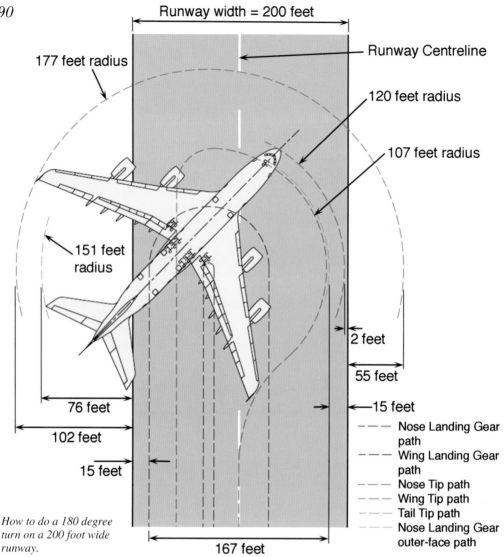

Runway width = 200 feet

177 feet radius

Runway Centreline

120 feet radius

107 feet radius

151 feet radius

2 feet

55 feet

76 feet

102 feet

15 feet

15 feet

--- Nose Landing Gear path
--- Wing Landing Gear path
--- Nose Tip path
--- Wing Tip path
--- Tail Tip path
--- Nose Landing Gear outer-face path

How to do a 180 degree turn on a 200 foot wide runway.

167 feet

weight situation is when the aircraft is fully loaded and static on the ramp, or when it is slowly moving toward takeoff.

Turnaround time, or the period needed to offload the passengers, service the aircraft, and board the next passenger load, was also a critical concern. Airbus believed that the fundamental design of the A380 cabin architecture would be the key to smooth operations and quick turnaround times and placed its faith in the positioning of the two forward main deck doors and the stairway to the upper deck. *'This results in a more balanced door utilisation in comparison to the 747 where, although there are two doors, the majority of passengers board through door 2'*. The design caused congestion because, Airbus said, most airlines used door 1

for first and business class only on the 747, and even in the unrestricted use of door 1,

Airbus said the design caused delays as *'...flow to the aft of the cabin is choked by congestion in the door 2 area due to back-queuing of passengers on the narrow stairs to the upper deck.'*

With the A380, passengers on the upper deck and first-class main deck area were expected to load through door 1, while the bulk of main deck passengers would load through door 2. Referenced against a typical 747-400 turnaround time of 85 minutes with 417 passengers and two bridges, the A380 was expected to be turned around in about 90 minutes with 555 passengers and two bridges, plus a trolley lift at door 2 to help with upper deck catering. If main-deck-only catering and other services were used, the time was extended to 126 minutes. The time was shortened considerably to 80 to 85 minutes if the airport was using three bridges and upper deck servicing via the upper deck door 1 on the right side.

The airports themselves ramped up steadily to prepare for the aircraft on services from 2006 onward. Airports such as New York, San Francisco, and Los Angeles were in the forefront of the major group of eleven phase one US destinations that declared themselves ready for the aircraft by 2005. In Europe, ten airports were ready by the same time, while a further thirty spread across the Middle East, Asia, and the Pacific region also declared themselves prepared for the giant aircraft by the middle of 2005.

In Europe, Eryl Smith, the planning and development director for British Airports Authority (BAA) Heathrow, told the press in July 2004 that, '...the Airbus A380 is critical for us - it will change the face of Heathrow and the face of long-haul travel. Building for the A380 is the right thing to do.' The airport completely rebuilt Terminal 3's pier six to provide four double-deck A380 stands under a $180 million scheme, with an additional four stands and three gates planned for Terminal 4 from mid-2006, and five additional A380 stands designed for the new Terminal 5 by 2011.

Overall, the airport expected to have 14 A380-capable stands by 2016, when it expected that A380s would operate one in every eight long-range flights.

Munich Airport in Germany became the first in Europe to gain formal ICAO Category F classification to handle the A380 in early 2004.

To prepare for the A380 in New York, the JFK board of commissioners authorized $179 million worth of upgrades in April 2004. Bill DeCota, aviation director of JFK's operating group, the Port Authority of New York and New Jersey, said the investment was worthwhile because '...the arrival of the A380 is as important to JFK International Airport as the Boeing 747 was when it was introduced. There's a huge economic benefit to seeing an aircraft like that in a market like ours.'

On the West Coast, San Francisco took the lead in making preparations, becoming one of the first airports in the United States to obtain full FAA certification for its A380-adapted terminal and airfield changes. The airport's director, John Martin, said, 'We planned for the future by designing the new international terminal to accommodate the new large aircraft, such as the A380, and that just makes sense, given we have 50 daily nonstop flights to 27 international cities, many of which will be served by the A380.'

Hong Kong was always expected to be a priority destination for the A380. Luckily the old Kai Tak airport closed and operations switched to the new Chek Lap Kok Airport before it entered service. (Simon Peters Collection

...unlike London Heathrow who made sure that not only their Terminal Five was A380 compatible, but also Terminal Three had a number of stands capable of accepting the aircraft, even if it meant installing an extra jetway ourt of the end of a finger.
(Photos: author)

Los Angeles Airport, which was expected to handle up to nine A380s a day by 2008, dragged its heels because of budget problems and political infighting within the governing city council. In late 2003, Virgin Atlantic Chairman Sir Richard Branson said, *'Los Angeles has been the slowest of all the early A380 airports to get its act together. I have written to Arnold Schwarzenegger (who was the Governor of California) to ask him to intervene.'*

Virgin Atlantic later delayed its A380 deliveries because of worries over interior configurations and concerns over preparations at LAX, one of its key destinations. LAX meanwhile stepped up its plans, which included modifying two gates at the Tom Bradley International Terminal as well as double-bridge jet bridges at multiple remote gates at the west end of the airfield where it intended to develop a mini-terminal for A380s by 2010-2011.

Weighty Matters

Like all aircraft manufacturers, Airbus waged a constant battle with weight in all its new aircraft, and so it was with the A380. However, the sheer scale of the aircraft meant that apparently minor changes such as over-designed parts or inaccurate sensors could have massive downstream effect on weight. A 1% fuel calculation error for example, equated to the weight of 30 passengers.

Following the design changes implemented for QC/2 and the longer range requirements of Singapore Airlines and QANTAS, the maximum takeoff weight grew to 1.23 million pounds, an increase of 35,000 pounds. This came from the weight of the larger re-fanned engines, the add-on wing weight to carry them, the additional fuel volume, changes to the control surfaces for improved take off performance, and structural enhancement for the added weight in the fuselage and undercarriage.

Weight adds weight, and very soon the situation threatened to get out of hand. Speaking in 2003, Charles Champion recalled the problems when he said that, '...*we had the idea to put the whole company in a crisis mode two years ago, and the pressure is still on.*' So-called 'Tiger Teams' pursued a series of weight-reduction initiatives.

Suppliers were asked to cut weight in areas such as interior fittings, where they were tasked with taking out up to 30%. The weight reduction target was set at 22,000 pounds.

Most observers used operating empty weight (OEW) as the baseline against which to judge the overall weight problem of the project, which grew from 588,000 pounds in early 2000 to almost 608,000 pounds in 2004. In late 2004 estimates showed that the OEW would be a little below 639,000 pounds by the time the interior was completely fitted out.

Structurally, Airbus kept its sights on the maximum weight empty (MWE), which was the baseline weight of the completed airframe, engines, painted structure, systems, and undercarriage. The company was convinced that its Tiger Teams could drag back the OEW specification to 596,000 pounds and that the launch customers would be comfortable with the OEW of the first aircraft.

But there were other things to consider: operator's items adding to the weight included 1,600 pounds of unusable fuel, 460 pounds of oil for the engines and APU, 3,750 pounds of water for the galleys and lavatories, plus 160 pounds of waste-tank treatment chemicals, 100 pounds of aircraft documents and tool kit, 19,700 pounds for seats, around 17,500 pounds of catering, another 7,700 pounds for the galley and other structures, plus 4,390 for the escape slides and other emergency equipment. The crew, including two pilots and 20 attendants and their luggage, added a further 3,700 pounds.

This amounted to almost 60,000 pounds and, when subtracted from the OEW, gave an estimated MWE of just over 536,000 pounds. This was the key figure, because it meant that Airbus would still be able to meet its contractual specified empty weight even if it did not meet its target OEW. Additionally, the weight equated to payload and

Despite its size and location in probably the wealthiest city in the USA, Los Angeles Airport (LAX) dragged its heels in getting ready for the arrival of the A380.

To help make the A380 more maneuverable on the ground, the rear axles of the six-wheel body landing gear were designed to be steerable in a similar manner to those on the Boeing 777. The feature is active during taxiing and push back, and during towing only if electrical power is applied, generated by the aircraft or the tow truck. (Photo: author)

range and performance. Despite the weight issues, Airbus remained confident that it would meet performance guarantees from the start, including the ability to reach 35,000 feet within 200 nautical miles and 30 minutes of brake release.

Better news began to energe during early 2004 with the start of subassembly production and the advent of additional weight-saving initiatives. Although too late for incorporation into the first three aircraft, several were built into the fourth airframe - Manufacturers Serial Number (MSN)007 - which would also be refitted for eventual sale to SIA. These changes included the use of GLARE for leading edges of the tail and would later be retrofitted to the MSN002 and -004.

The changes meant that the higher weight option was no longer vital to meet guarantees, making it an extra-cost option.

The battle for Asian customers became intense early in 2001, when Boeing upped the ante by offering Japanese industry up to 20% of the proposed 747X, including the entire wing. Undaunted, Airbus pressed on with talks with Japan's big three, Fuji Heavy Industries (FHI), Kawasaki Heavy Industries (KHI), and Mitsubishi Heavy Industries (MHI), as well as Japan Aircraft Manufacturing and ShinMaywa. While risk-

sharing was the goal, Airbus acknowledged that simple subcontracting would help sell the A380 in prime ultra-high-capacity territory.

Internationally the risk-and-revenue programme was filling up, but it continued to fall short of the 40% of the $10.7 billion launch budget. Risk-sharing partners outside the main partners included Saab, with up to 5%; Hurel Dubois, with up to 2%; as well as AIDC (of Taiwan), Belairbus, Eurocopter, Finavitec, GKN Aerospace, Latecoere, and Stork. Italy`s Finmeccanica-Alenia was also set to join (through Alenia Aerospazio) as a 4% risk-sharing partner with fuselage work, while Aermacchi would also become involved by the end of 2001 in the design and production of carbon-fibre nacelle parts.

Although Airbus could not match the Boeing wing offer, it discussed a substantial work package worth about 10%, including wing spoilers and ribs, cargo doors, and panels. The Airbus argument was that it, not Boeing, was the commercial powerhouse of the future, and that forging new links with Europe would provide an opening for greater quantities of commercial aviation business in the twenty-first century

The Japanese manufacturers were caught between a rock and a hard place. Boeing raised concerns that its old industrial partners could risk infringing agreements with them should they invest in the A380. Furthermore, Boeing was busy pushing its recently revealed Sonic Cruiser concept, and had expressed confidence that Japanese industry would feature prominently in its development. Airbus gave FHI, KHI, and MHI until June to decide on whether or not to become risk-sharing partners, though by the end of the month it had already become clear that it was not going to happen.

After reports in the Japan Industrial journal pointed to '...*doubts over the project's viability*' from undisclosed sources, it came as no surprise when FHI, KHI, and MHI reaffirmed loyalty to Boeing and rejected the full risk-sharing offer from Airbus. From here on out, Airbus' focus widened to attract second- and third-tier Japanese suppliers, which quickly began to join forces with Airbus. JAMCO, developer of the non-slamming toilet lid for the 777 and a traditional Airbus fin part producer, was named as supplier of the upper-deck-floor carbon crossbeams, as well as stiffeners and stringers for the fin centre box, at its Mitaki site in Tokyo.

Others included Toray and Toho Tenax, which were signed up to supply intermediate carbon-fibre filaments for several airframe structures,

while Sumitomo Metal Industries was contracted to supply titanium sheets. Some involvement from the heavies then followed when FHI, MHI, and Japan Aircraft Manufacturing all became involved as simple subcontractors. FHI was contracted to provide leading and trailing edges for the vertical stabilizer, plus the fin tip and aerodynamic fairings. The parts would be produced at FHI's Utsunomiya site. MHI, working through EADS subsidiary Eurocopter, was meanwhile contracted to supply forward and aft lower cargo doors at its factory at Oye in Nagoya. Japan Aircraft Manufacturing signed up to produce horizontal tailplane tips at its Yokohama factory Later in 2002, new deals were also struck with a further group of Japanese companies, taking the island nation's potential total revenue in the A380 to well over $1.75 billion in the years to come.

The new deals included Kobe-based ShinMaywa Industries, which was signed up for the very large main wing root fillet fairing, and the Yokohama Rubber Company, which was contracted to make composite water and waste tanks at its Hiratsuka factory in Kanagawa. Nikkiso was also signed up to provide composite cascades for the thrust reversers, which were to be

Weight gain was the enemy of every new aircraft project, and threatened to overwhelm the A380, particularly when the design changed to meet the OC/2 noise rules and operators asked for additional range performance in 2000. Airbus attacked the problem with Tiger Teams that addressed every aspect of the design. The engine makers worked on the issues themselves, while tackling the challenges of increasing power without badly impacting noise and weight. Note the noise-absorbing inlet honeycomb forward of the main fan. (Photo: author)

fabricated at its Shizuoka plant in Haibara.

Over the following years, the potential Japanese revenue share increased to over $3 billion, according to Airbus, which later awarded a second contract to ShinMaywa for composite wing ramp surfaces. It also signed a deal with Mitsubishi Rayon for advanced composites for various A380 parts.

Australian, Korean, and Chinese manufacturers also became involved, with Korean Aerospace Industries (KAI) becoming the first Asian-based risk-and-revenue-sharing partner with a 1.5% share. Its initial contract covered the supply of 21-by-10-foot aluminum lower outer wing skin panels to be made at its Changwon factory. Australia`s Hawker de Havilland company was selected to build the large A380 wingtip fences and was already a manufacturer of similar devices for the A330/A340. Hawker de Havilland was owned by Boeing, making it the first time the US company had directly contributed to an Airbus programme. Not counting, of course, the heavily modified Boeing Super Guppy transports that had formed the backbone of the Airbus transport system since the 1970s.

China's AVIC I - China Aviation Industry Corporation I - a Chinese consortium of aircraft manufacturers that was created on 1 July 1999 by splitting the state-owned consortium China Aviation Industry Corporation (AVIC) into AVIC I and AVIC II - was later added to the subcontractor list with a deal to make the upper and lateral panels of the A380 nose landing gear bay. The work was subcontracted via the French company Latecoere, and represented the first direct involvement by a Chinese manufacturer in the A380. It seemed that the world itself was now involved in assembling the planet's largest airliner.

Subtle changes in aerodynamics helped improve takeoff performance to help meet the QC/2 noise targets, and for the first time on any new large commercial transport, advanced computational fluid dynamics optimisation programmes were used to refine wing geometry in the presence of the fuselage, wing-body fairing, and engine installation. As a result, Airbus saved a 'significant' amount of structural weight without a drag penalty (Photos: Author

Chapter Six

Where To Build The Beast?

Designing the world's largest airliner would only be equalled by the challenges as to where and how to build it. The assembly site would become home to one of the greatest engineering accomplishments of the century and a towering symbol of European industrial success. There was also a very great danger that the selection process would become mired in politics. Jürgen Thomas was at the forefront of the decision-making process when the study to find an assembly site was launched in mid-1996.

There were two options: since its first aircraft was assembled in the 1970s, Airbus had relied on its unique air transport system to bring together sub-assemblies from all the partner sites around Europe using a pair of Super Guppy transporters. Originally developed in the USA by Aero SpaceLines so that NASA could move rocket sections around, Airbus used them to move A300Bs and later A310s.

The first, the Super Guppy was built directly from the fuselage of a C-97J Turbo Stratocruiser, the military cargo version of the 1950s Boeing 377 Stratocruiser passenger aircraft, itself derived from the wartime B-29 bomber. The fuselage was lengthened to 141 feet and ballooned out to a maximum inside diameter of 25 feet, the length of the cargo compartment being 94 feet 6 inches. The floor of the cargo compartment was still only 8 feet 9 inches wide, as necessitated by the use of the Stratocruiser fuselage.

In addition to the fuselage modifications, the Super Guppy used Pratt & Whitney T-34-P-7 turboprop engines for increased power and range, and modified wing and tail surfaces. It could carry a load of 54,000 pounds and cruise at 300 mph.

The second version was known as the Super Guppy Turbine (SGT), although it used turboprop engines like the first Super Guppy. This variant used Allison 501-D22C turboprops.

Super Guppy F-GDSG '3' rests between ferrying Airbus components around Europe. (Photo: Simon Peters Collection)

The turbo-prop Super Guppy was hinged aft of the cockpit to allow the cargo to be loaded and unloaded. (Photo: Simon Peters Collection)

The A310 Beluga - originally named 'Super Transporter' got it's nickname from the beluga or white whale. Unlike the Super Guppy the cargo was loaded through an upward opening 'door' over the top of the flight deck. (Photo: Klaus Fingler)

Unlike the previous Guppy, the main portion of its fuselage was constructed from scratch. By building from scratch, Aero Spacelines was able to widen the floor of the cargo compartment to 13 ft. The overall cargo compartment length was increased to 111 feet 6 inches, and the improved fuselage and engines allowed for a maximum load of 52,500 lb. These design improvements, combined with a pressurized crew cabin that allowed for higher-altitude cruising, allowed the SGT to transport more cargo than its predecessors.

The SGT retained only the cockpit, wings, tail, and main landing gear of the 377. The nose gear was taken from a Boeing 707 and rotated 180 degrees. This dropped the front of the aircraft slightly, leveling the cargo bay floor and simplifying loading operations.

In 1982 and 1983, two additional Super Guppies were built by UTA Industries in France after Airbus bought the right to produce the aircraft. The first-generation Super Guppy fleet was gradually phased out in favour of the faster jet-powered 'Beluga' Airbus Super Transports derived from the A300-600 airliner and capable of carrying twice as much cargo by weight.

But even though the planned A3XX sub-assemblies far exceeded the capacity of the larger Beluga, the air link was still considered. The A340 became the focus for a piggyback wing-delivery vehicle with various options considered for building the wings as either single or two-part units. Splitting the fuselage sections lengthwise was also considered. Other advantages of the air transport system over the land/ sea alternative included the obvious time

savings, as well as the reduced vulnerability of the supply system to industrial problems such as strike action by truck drivers or dock workers.

However, given that the horizontal tailplane was roughly equal in size to the wing of the A310, and that the double-deck fuselage sections and the individual wings were each over 100 feet long, it was obvious that the existing airborne transport system would not do. Thus a land and sea transport network was considered, the Airbus study looking at both inland and coastal locations. *'We have to consider the relative advantages of transporting smaller components by aircraft to a potential inshore site, against the ability to carry complete sub-assemblies by ship to a coastal location,'* Thomas told *Flight International* in late 1996.

With so many potential options worth studying, it was little wonder that uncertainty raged for years over the site of the final assembly line that would be the last stop in either a light- or a heavy-assembly process. The light method, modeled on the traditional Airbus system of bolting together virtually complete sub-assemblies on the line, was obviously a problem because of the size of the assemblies. The heavy system, on the other hand, would require the establishment of a Boeing-like system that threatened to disrupt the anticipated

work-share arrangements of the A3XX partners.

By late 1997, six potential locations, with one in Spain, two in France, and up to three in Germany were being considered. The Spanish contender was Seville - home to the assembly lines of CASA aircraft, but it did not make the cut, losing out to the more experienced commercial lines in more northern regions.

It was between Toulouse and Hamburg that the true battle would rage. In the meantime, other sites remained briefly in the chase. They were Saint-Nazaire on the Brest peninsula of western France and two sites in Germany: Rostock, close to the shores of the Baltic Sea by Germany's northern coast, and a remote site farther to the east by Peenemunde, on the island of Usedom. Both areas had been in the former East Germany and were undeveloped, with open land and a relatively low-cost workforce. Peenemunde had a large Luftwaffe-era airfield, having been built to help service and defend the adjacent German rocket research site.

The choice of sites was a political hot potato, particularly as DASA Airbus'prime bid for its Hamburg Finkenwerder site had sparked an environmental controversy. To accommodate the A3XX, the Hamburg site would require a massive expansion and, after several alternatives had been examined, included levelling an old submarine factory to the east of the site. But the

The CASA site in Seville was considered, but eventually was used for Airbus Military. (Photo: Airbus SAS)

only realistic option was filling in part of the Muhlenberger Loch, a area of wetland by the Elbe River and also Europe's largest freshwater tidal mudflat.

Remarkably, the Social Democrat party and the Green Party, supported the choice, despite the fact that the loch was home to a rare species of wildfowl. This was largely because developers were planning to reclaim only a fifth of the water and were creating a new habitat for the ducks that was twice the size of the area being filled just a few yards away The head of the Christian Democrat party, Ole von Beust, voiced his support for the Rostock option, stating Hamburg's site limitations and the expansive possibilities of the windswept north German plain.

While the debate raged over the final assembly site, another erupted over where the enormous wings would be built. Wing building was traditionally the United Kingdom's specialty, but Germany had long held ambitions

to break the British wing monopoly that had existed since Hawker Siddeley's initial contract to make the A300 wing. DASA had fought hard for responsibility for the future large aircraft wing, that created a serious disagreement between the United Kingdom and German camps in 1995. DASA had signalled its intent to make a bid to lead development of a next-generation wing for the A380.

To help back DASAs bid, the West German government allocated DM 600 million (US $327 million) for an A3XX-focused research project in 1996 under a four-year programme, about half of which was for advanced wing work. To counter this, British Aerospace, along with Shorts, Dowty Aerospace, and Rolls-Royce, among others, requested £230 million (US $380 million) to help support an equivalent wing, engine, and landing gear R&D effort.

Known as the integrated powered wing programme, it was one of a number of R&D efforts the Society of British Aerospace

Hamburg's Finkenwerder site was dramatically expanded to accommodate the A380 interiors installation, major component assembly building, and paint hall, which were essentially completed by early 2005. The new A380 buildings are on the right side of the photo, while the new paint hall is in the distance by the River Elbe. The site also contains the interiors test site close to the water's edge. (Photo: Airbus SAS)

Activities at Airbus' facility in Broughton, UK include wing skin milling, stringer manufacture, full wing equipping and wing box assembly. The River Dee, used for the delivery of A380 wings to Mostyn can be seen beyond the airfield. (Photo: Airbus SAS)

Companies (SBAC) supported that lobbied the UK government on behalf of the disparate manufacturing group. The critical importance of the A3XX was widely recognized at high government levels throughout the continent, and the European Commission had earmarked aerospace for key action as part of its newly ratified Fifth Framework €16.3 billion (US $18.9 billion) research-and-development initiative.

By mid-1999, the complex assembly jigsaw puzzle was starting to fall into place. Wing work was allocated to British Aerospace in Broughton near Chester, but the fuselage detail remained undecided. DASA, which made the forward and aft fuselage sections of the A330/A340, argued more strongly than ever for Hamburg. Gerhard Puttfarcken, DASA Airbus vice president of product management for the A3XX, supported a ship-borne system that would support existing centres of excellence, and suggested a single roll-on, roll-off ship that would make a weekly round-trip voyage among Aerospatiale's Saint-Nazaire factory, Chester in the United Kingdom, and Hamburg, delivering the sub-assemblies to support a rate of four aircraft per month.

To support its bid, DASA would construct a 345-acre factory on the site of land reclaimed from the filled-in lake.

Aerospatiale countered with a proposal to help set up a huge aeronautical park in Toulouse and to use Belugas to transport the top and bottom halves of the double-deck fuselage sections. To simplify mating, these would be assembled as full-length sections and joined to create the entire fuselage. The wings, Aerospatiale argued, would be carried atop the modified A340 one at a time, requiring two rotations a week.

Airbus looked all the options, but when considering the lowest cost option in 2000, it finally opted for a compromise that put ASXX assembly in Toulouse but used Hamburg's Ro-Ro sea transport scheme as the transportation method. In order to satisfy German demands for a key role in final production and to relieve some pressure on Toulouse, Hamburg Finkenwerder was allocated the task of completing furnishing, painting, and cabin production test flights. The split also gave Hamburg responsibility for completing aircraft destined for European and Middle Eastern customers, while Toulouse would handle the rest of the World.

The complex production and subassembly transportation system was an incredible logistical and industrial feat of planning, with parts arriving in Europe from all over the world. Once inside Europe's bounds a carefully choreographed ballet of ships, barges, trucks, and aircraft brought together the assemblies in Toulouse using the Airbus multi-modal transport system (MMTS).

With the start of parts manufacturing, the dance began all over Europe at roughly the same time, but the MMTS ballet commences when these parts are assembled into larger sections. The forward and aft fuselage sections are completed in Finkenwerder, where Airbus Germany had built a 300-acre plant expansion, including four huge hangars. The site also includes a cabin furnishing hall and fuselage

production lines, housed in the major component assembly (MCA) hall, as well as two paint shops.

Once assembled with pre-installed electrical, hydraulic, and pneumatic system cables, hoses, and wires, the two sections are prepared for shipping. The sub-assemblies include large sections made at Nordenham and consist of an 82-foot-long aft section (combining the Airbus German-built aft fuselage with the Airbus Spanish-built rear fuselage) and the 46-foot-long forward fuselage barrel. These are loaded onto a specially built 5,200-ton Ro-Ro vessel just over 500 feet long and almost 80 feet broad in the beam. Although the vessel was critical to the A3XX effort, Airbus did not plan to get into the shipping business and chartered it from FRET/Cetam, a subsidiary of Louis Dreyfus Armateurs of France and Leif Hoegh of Norway. This company, in turn, commissioned the building of the ship by Iinling Shipyard in Nanjing, China, in March 2002.

The ship's keel was laid in February 2003, and it was launched from the banks of the Yangtze River just six months later. Christened the *Ville de Bordeaux,* the vessel featured the

The Ville de Bordeaux, *the specialist ship carrier built at the cost of $30 million; it was designed as a roll-on-roll off ferry. Jointly owned by Louis Dreyfus Armateurs of France, and Norwegian ship-owner Leif Höegh & Co, she is operated jointly by their subsidiary companies Fret and CETAM, on a twenty year lease with an option to extend a further ten to Airbus if required. The ship started operations on 10 June 2004. (Photo: Airbus SAS)*

Toulouse Blagnac Airport or Aéroport de Toulouse – Blagnac is located 4.1 miles west of the city of Toulouse.

largest watertight stern door (72 by 46 feet) ever built on such a vessel and had 72,334 square feet of space on the cargo deck. After fitting out, the vessel sailed from Nanjing to Yizheng farther down river in April 2004 before departing China via Shanghai for its long delivery voyage to Europe.

From Hamburg, the *Ville's* first voyage on its regular bus route took it across the North Sea and through the English Channel, around Land's End and into the Irish Sea. Rounding Carmel Head just off the island of Anglesey, it nosed its way into the Dee Estuary, docking at the port of Mostyn. Here it took on the Airbus UK-built wing set, each wing measuring 147.5 feet in length and weighing 72,700 pounds.

The wings were made at an all-new west factory in Broughton, United Kingdom, across the runway from where Hawker Siddeley once assembled the highly successful HS.125 business jet, and from where all the other Airbus wings are made.

As with these structures, the skins, spars, ribs, and stringers were to be brought to the site from Filton, Bristol. The wings for the wide-body aircraft such as the A300 and the A330/A340 are assembled at Broughton before being flown by Beluga to the Airbus Germany site in Bremen for fitting with control surfaces and on to delivery to Toulouse. The narrow body wings for the A320 family are fully equipped at Broughton before delivery to either Hamburg (A318, A319, A321) or Toulouse (A320).

In the case of the A380, about 25% of the wings are fabricated at Broughton; the remainder come from Filton and subcontract suppliers such as Saab, which was to produce the mid and outer fixed leading edges. Each set

The Afon Dyfrdwy, *an Airbus A380 wing transport vessel for use on the River Dee that was completed in February 2004 by McTay Marine Ltd of Bromborough. The vessel is deceptively high tech - powered by a pair of Cummins diesels, each driving Jastram azimuth jet thrusters with a pair of Cummins diesels driving bow thrusters, it has a low level cargo deck with a 300 tonne capacity lift system to lower cargo pallet legs into the hull for low air draft. Electronically controlled ballasting and draught / air draught measurement system to allow it to be ballasted to go under low bridges.*

would comprise 32,000 parts, with additional assemblies from Belairbus (leading edge), Airbus Germany (flaps), and Airbus France (spoilers/ailerons) being added in Toulouse. The west factory houses the main assemblyjigs, where the A380 wing components and sub-assemblies are loaded and assembled into a wing box, and a wing-equipping area, where fuel, pneumatic, and hydraulic systems and wiring are installed and tested. The wings are then loaded one by one on a Dee River Craft

barge for the short journey down the river to Mostyn for transfer to the Ro-Ro vessel.

From here the ship retraces its course as far as Land's End, before heading due south across the channel past Brest and the jutting Finisterre peninsula to Saint-Nazaire, where one forward fuselage is off-loaded so a locally built nose section can be attached. Here Airbus France also incorporates the all-composite centre wing box of the A380 built in Nantes and transported to Saint-Nazaire by road, as well as incorporating the centre part of the Spanish-made belly fairing in the centre fuselage. The two parts of the nose section of the fuselage, which by now also contain the cockpit, are subassembled at Méaulte, nearby in France, and sent by road to Saint-Nazaire. A completed forward/nose assembly is then loaded for the short voyage along the coast and past La Rochelle, down the curving estuary of the Gironde to the Pauillac terminal in Bordeaux harbor.

Having discharged its cargo, the *Ville de Bordeaux* then sets sail on a fourth trip, which takes it west and south beyond Cape Finisterre along the Portuguese coast and past Lisbon and Cape St. Vincent to the Spanish port of Cadiz. Here it takes aboard another immense belly fairing and the Puerto Real-built 89-foot-span horizontal tailplane, the latter weighing seven tons. Airbus Spain's Getafe factory near Madrid produces the aft fuselage, main gear doors, dorsal fin, composite rudder, and belly fairing. Although the latter goes south to join the ship at Cadiz because of its size, the aft fuselage section is flown by Beluga to Finkenwerder for attachment to the German-built rear fuselage. Meanwhile, the rudder is taken by road from

Above: the centre fuselage barrel is loaded onto its transport pallet. Below: The passage under the historic Pont de Pierre bridge at Bordeaux is a matter of good timing for the crews of the river barges taking the A380 sub-assemblies up the River Garonne from the port. Although the barges have special ballast systems to lower their profile, the crews usually aim for a three-hour low-tide window to ensure good clearance. (both Airbus)

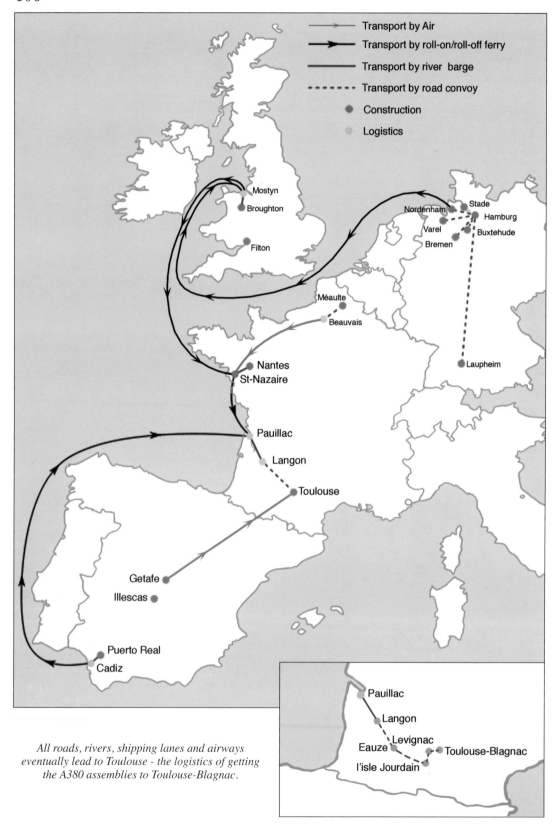

*All roads, rivers, shipping lanes and airways
eventually lead to Toulouse - the logistics of getting
the A380 assemblies to Toulouse-Blagnac.*

To quote Hollywood: 'Looks like we got us a convoy!'
Above: the front, centre and rear fuselage barrels
travel by road from Langon to Toulouse, while a
helicopter hovers overhead checking progress.

Left: The right wing, mounted at an angle on it's
special travelling pallet is followed by the front
fuselage section (both Airbus)

Puerto Real to Stade in Germany for attachment to the fin while the ship turns around at Cadiz and heads back to Bordeaux with its new load.

At the Pauillac terminal, the sub-assemblies, still in their palletised transport fixtures, are off-loaded onto a floating transfer station. Brought to Bordeaux from Gdansk, Poland, the station is almost 495 feet long, 115 feet wide, 25 feet high, and weighs 3,500 tons. The flat-topped station transfers the loads to a pair of specially designed barges that are fitted with a variable ballast system. This allows them to float lower in the water when necessary and enables them to pass under all the bridges on the River Garonne. Made by the Netherlands barge builder De Hoop in 2003, the vessels are operated for Airbus by Socatra.

The vessels travel for twelve hours along the Garonne as far as Langon, the farthest practical point up river for large-scale barge movements, and discharge their cargo at a specially built wet lock in Langon harbor. The parts are then marshalled together into a road convoy that will wind through the pastures, geese farms, and

The centre-section of aircraft No.2 wends its way along French roads to Toulouse. (Airbus)

vineyards of the Landes and Gers regions toward Toulouse.

Organized by the freight company Capelle, the convoy consists of specially developed trailers from Nicolas/Scheuerle pulled by 600-horsepower Mercedes-built tractor units. The trailers have multi-steering capability, height adjustment, leveling compensation, and even their own guidance system.

Including gendarmes on motorcycles, escort and support vehicles, and the tractor-trailers, the convoy consists of forty-three vehicles, twenty-six gendarmes, eight pathfinders, and twenty-nine drivers and operators.

First comes the port wing, followed by the starboard wing, the horizontal tailplane, the aft fuselage, the forward fuselage and finally the centre fuselage. Avoiding the fast Route Nationale A62 between Bordeaux and Toulouse, the convoy makes use of back roads, moving through the countryside by night to avoid disrupting traffic. The journey takes three nights, with up to four en route parking areas available to the convoy before finally arriving at the Aeroconstellation complex. Now the hard work can really begin!

Chapter Seven

Metal, Plastic, Engines...
and Power Politics

All over Europe during the winter of 2001 companies were making a start on manufacturing the first components of the A380. An official 'metal cutting ceremony' took place with great fanfare at Nantes, France on 23 January 2002, with other sites following at later dates.

Parallel with making a start on the actual airliner were a series of massive construction projects to either create or improve the facilities available. By far the largest was at Toulouse, where a huge facility covering more than 123 acres was under way just outside Blagnac Airport. As part of the new Aeroconstellation Park, the site consisted of the static test building and the final assembly hall, which covered an area of 20 soccer fields.

Arranged in a series of adjoining hangars with gently curved roofs, the building was 1,600 feet long, 820 feet wide, and 150 feet tall. It was one of the biggest buildings in the world, incorporating more than 32,000 tons of steel, or the equivalent of four Eiffel Towers.

Preparation for the site, which was to be named Jean-Luc Lagardére, after the co-chairman of EADS at the time of the A380 launch, also started in April 2002.

The final assembly hall roof was raised into place in mid-February 2003, and was all but complete by the end of the year. As well as providing space for final assembly of up to six aircraft simultaneously, the hall also created 365,900 square feet of office space.

Construction work had also been under way since January 2002 of a static test building that covered 129,160 square feet, which became operational by mid-2003 and was ready to house the static airframe that would be a vital part of the A380 certification effort.

A new offlce on the Toulouse St. Martin site carried out the design work and the release of drawings to production. More than 1,000 people worked on eight floors over a total area of almost 182,990 square feet. The process of drawing release, under which final engineering designs were passed on to production, started in a small way at the start of 2002 and passed the 120,000 mark by the end of the year. It soon zoomed to about the 330,000 mark by late 2003. At the programme's peak, more than 5,000 engineers worked on the A380.

Near the St. Martin site, another new building with 204,500 square feet of space was erected to house three A380 flight-deck simulators and a device nicknamed the 'iron bird,' a test rig that replicated all the major systems of the aircraft. The iron bird was used for systems integration and verification and, together with one of the simulators, was so complete that it was dubbed Aircraft Zero. Tests with the iron bird began in December 2003, when the combined Aircraft Zero cockpit and systems rig (flight controls, hydraulic, and electrical) was the same as that in the MSN001.

Pneumatic and cabin systems, including water and waste, were tested in special rigs developed in Hamburg, home of Cabin Zero. The new building also housed a cabin technology device, which was mounted on a moveable platform to simulate a number of effects, including sloping positions and standing impacts. It also housed a virtual-reality lab to assess other cabin redesign alternatives, a full cabin integration rig that enabled the full linking of the AFDX (avionics full duplex) Ethernet network with the cabin systems, and the IMA modules and their applications.

The site also helped evaluate relatively late interior design changes, which saw new manufacturers such as California-based C&D

Fuselage sections in the main assembly building before the 'coming together' Note the fan-shaped safety rails to protect the workers from falling out. (Photo: Airbus SAS)

Aerospace become involved in supplying the crew rest module and other parts of the A380 interior. In-flight entertainment (IFE) tests were performed separately by Thales in a 555-seat laboratory in Irvine, California.

Adjacent to the Cabin Zero area, work was well under- way to complete the new 346-acre site on reclaimed land in Hamburg. Protected from possible coastal and river flooding by a dyke, the site housed the A380 major component assembly hall (MCA Hall). The building was almost 750 feet long, 393 feet wide and 75 feet tall, and was made to house the forward and aft fuselage sections.

Also being built on the site were a cabin furnishing hall, a delivery centre for the formal handover of aircraft to European and Middle Eastern customers, two paint shops, a preflight hangar, and an engine run-up site.

By now, work on the Broughton wing site in the United Kingdom was complete, with a new 226,050-square foot building to make stringers for bottom wing skin panels being completed in mid-2002. Extensions to other existing skin mill and creep forming buildings was completed by the end of the year and well before the official opening of the £350 million UK site by Prime Minister Tony Blair. The new west factory covered an area equal to 12 soccer fields. During the ceremony, the Prime Minister said: *'I am delighted to be asked to officially open the new West Factory and to see for myself the excellent work being done here at Airbus. The order book shows the commercial attraction of the world class product being made here, and is a powerful tribute to the dedication*

and commitment of the highly skilled workforce. I am delighted that the Government has been able to invest in that effort.'

This impressive new factory is creating 1,200 new jobs, in addition to the 5,000 already here, making a strong contribution to the local and national economy. I would like to welcome the long-term commitment Airbus is making to UK manufacturing.'

In Filton, construction of the world's largest landing gear test rig was completed across the runway from the famous Brabazon hangar. By early 2003, work was also under way at the site on a new integrated machining facility for wing ribs. Drop tests in the Filton facility began in July 2004, while extension and retraction tests were completed by the end of November. To make the rig extra realistic, it was integrated with a real aircraft electrical network and associated avionics.

In Spain at Getafe and Puerto Real, new assembly facilities for the horizontal tailplane and the enormous 105-foot-long belly fairing were completed. The facilities covered 204,500 and 161,460 square feet respectively. In Illescas, just outside Madrid, a plant extension housed new fibre placement machines for tape lay-up of parts for several carbon-fibre fuselage sections.

A matter of Power

The engines that were to take the first A380 into the air in 2005 were not the same as were envisaged fifteen years earlier. The early studies revolved around the use of A330-sized engines for improved cost, schedule, and development. But as the size of the UHCA family grew beyond 600 to 800 passengers to include a 1,050-seater, the studies had to include six-engine variants to stay within the thrust capabilities of this engine class.

In 2005 the A380's four engines pumped out 280,000 pounds of thrust, more than any commercial jetliner in history. With heavier future models, such as the freighter, total power was expected to increase to more than 320,000 pounds of thrust. At their ultimate potential, the A380 powerplants have been designed to collectively generate up to 336,000 pounds of thrust, compared with the 260,000 pounds of a current 747!

In 1990 General Electric, Pratt & Whitney and Rolls-Royce were all deeply involved in developing new engines for the Boeing 777. These would prove to be the largest commercial jet engines yet built, and because they were designed for a twin-engine aircraft, they were too big to be used on the multiple-engine UHCA and VLCT designs floating around in the early 1990s.

The major difference between a twin-engine and a four-engine aircraft is that the former are takeoff-thrust limited, while the four-engine designs are climb-thrust limited. The reasoning behind this is simply that a twin must have sufficient power to continue to take off on one engine alone, should it suffer an engine failure on the runway. Individual engine power requirements are therefore not as high in four-engine aircraft, which have more thrust available from the remaining three engines should they suffer a powerplant failure on takeoff. In particular, the focus for a four-or-more-engine superjumbo design was on top-of-climb thrust.

The ratio of take-off thrust to top-of-climb thrust in a big twin and a conceptual UHCA was dramatic. The early 777s, for example, required about 84,000 pounds of thrust per engine for takeoff, and about 16,900 pounds at the top of climb. By contrast, the UHCA would require about 75,000 pounds of thrust for takeoff and close to 20,000 pounds for top of climb.

None of the engine makers were fooling themselves when it came to development costs for the next new generation of powerplants. Stan Todd, director of Trent engines at Rolls-Royce, said in 1994 that, '... *aircraft makers are diligently studying various concepts for VLAs* [Very Large Aircraft], *which, if committed, would be the biggest investment decision the civil aircraft industry has yet taken.*'

Given the scale of the projected designs, it became obvious to everyone that a mega-twin was out of the running. '*A twin-engined VLA is an option in theory, but the required engine size is at least twice the thrust of any engine so far developed, but the investment would be huge and the market base would appear to be too limited to support that level of investment in the foreseeable*

Prototype MSN001 comes together in the assembly hall at Toulouse. (Photo: Airbus SAS)

future,' said Todd.

GE argued that there were advantages in going to the other extreme with as many as six engines in a configuration similar to the Antonov An-225, the largest jet-powered aircraft ever made. *'The advantage with having more than four engines is with redundancy. A six-engine aircraft down to five engines is not going to have a great problem in completing its mission,'* said a GE spokesperson.

Then there was the issue of noise, which from the outset was aimed to be equal to or less than the noise generated by the 747, and well below the limits agreed by the International Civil Aviation Organisation (ICAO) under Annex 16, Chapter 3 (or equivalent US Federal Aviation Regulation (FAR) 36, Stage 3) with environmentally perceived noise decibel (EPNdB) targets of about 100 for flyover, 98 for sideline, and about 100 for approach. To achieve this, the engine makers were concerned that modifying existing engines could incur too great a performance or cost penalty, and began to focus on all-new designs.

Rolls-Royce looked at three concepts for its large aircraft study, all developed from the baseline three-shaft Trent 800 then in test for the 777. The first, dubbed the Trent 895X-119, was an enhanced design for increased top-of-climb performance. The second, the T895X-142, had a considerably larger fan diameter, while the third, the T895X-164, was a more radical departure with a variable-pitch fan and fan-drive gear system. Although all three had similar pressure ratios, temperature limits, and noise performance, they differed in terms of weight, size, specific fuel consumption, and bypass ratio (BPR). The BPR for the standard-configuration engine was 6.5, the larger-fan version's BPR was 10, and the variable-pitch fan had a whopping BPR of 13.5.

By early 1996, both the emergence of the A3XX and the Boeing 747-500X/600X projects had given the engine makers firmer requirements to aim at. Boeing aimed for a service entry target of 2000 to beat Airbus to market, and Rolls-Royce soon adopted a low-risk approach to satisfy the US manufacturers fast-track goal. In July 1996, Rolls-Royce signed an agreement with Boeing to offer a relatively simple derivative of the Trent 800 dubbed the Trent 900.

The heart of this proposal was a scaled-down Trent 800 core attached to a 110-inch-diameter fan, with a slimmer, lighter nacelle. By reducing the core size and yet retaining a large fan, Rolls-Royce was able to increase BPR from about 6.5 on the Trent 800 to nearer 8.5, or fairly close to the target

BPR of the T895X-142 study engine. For the 747X, it was to be offered at thrust levels from 78,000 to 80,000 pounds, putting it slightly higher than the thrust needs of the A3XX, which were then envisaged at between 69,600 and 75,000 pounds.

Internally, the Trent 900 was configured with a scaled core similar in size to what would soon become the Trent 500, the new engine for the A340-500/600. It consisted of scaled-down Trent 895 intermediate-pressure (IP) and high-pressure (HP) compressors, a new five-stage low-pressure (LP) turbine, and reduced-loading IP and HP turbines.

Charles Cuddington became head of the Trent 900 project, which assumed a greater role as Airbus sought a choice of engine for the fledgling A3XX. The engine project was launched formally at that year's Farnborough Air Show, while talks with Airbus reached a new level of intensity after signing the agreement with Boeing. Finally, in November 1996, Rolls-Royce and Airbus signed a MoU to provide an engine in the 72,000- to 79,000-pound thrust range for the A3XX.

Then Boeing dropped its 747-500X/600X plans only a month later. Without the urgency of the 747 derivative, which called for a fast-paced 33-month development effort, the wind suddenly was taken from Rolls-Royce's sails. Instead of aiming for certification in December 1999, the engine maker now viewed a considerably more distant notional in-service date of 2003 at the earliest. The delay saw risk-sharing partners such as Kawasaki Heavy Industries (KHI) opt out of the original programme, which continued to tick along at a relatively slow pace for the next two years or so. With the rising tempo of the A3XX effort, a new team of risk- and revenue-sharing partners began to join the programme. Over the next five years, the team grew to include FiatAvio, Goodrich, Hamilton Sundstrand, Honeywell, Marubeni, and Volvo. Samsung Techwin of Korea and IHI of Japan also participated as programme associates. In June 2003, KHI also rejoined the Trent 900 programme as an associate with responsibility for the IP compressor casing.

The design continued to be refined against the original specifications, but in late 1999, the emergence of tough new quota count (QC) noise laws planned for London Heathrow posed a new threat to the final configuration. It became obvious that under the new QC rules, the A380 operators would be penalized heavily at Heathrow if the airframe and engine design remained as it was.

forward-swept fan that was originally aimed at the 777-200X/300X but which ended up as a technology demonstrator. The eight-stage IP compressor was also Trent 8104-based, and both the LP and IP turbines were scaled up, the former now about the same size as the fan on the RB211-535 engine on the 757. The fan case also had to grow to accommodate the larger bypass requirements.

For the first time on a Rolls-Royce Trent, the HP turbine was designed to counter-rotate, and in tests it had shown a 2% efficiency gain as it optimised the flow entering the IP turbine, requiring fewer nozzle-guide vanes. The vanes that remained were also subject to less stress and were therefore smaller and lighter by design.

At the end of 2000, Rolls-Royce won the first engine competition when SIA selected it to power its ten firm and fifteen option A3XXs. The deal was a strategic victory over the General Electric and Pratt & Whitney Engine Alliance, and gave Rolls-Royce pole position in the

A Rolls-Royce Trent 900 engine is 'turned over' from its vertical build position at Derby in preparation for shipping out to Toulouse and the A380 final assembly (Rolls Royce)

As a result, several late design changes were made, details of which were announced at an Airbus customer symposium held in January 2000. For the engine, it meant some major, last-minute revisions, the biggest being the increase in fan diameter from 110 to 116 inches, making the Trent 900 the biggest engine (in terms of fan size) ever built by Rolls-Royce. *'We had to change the LP system within only a few months, but our design people had lots of options under their belt,'* said Rolls-Royce Marketing Vice President Robert Nuttall.

The larger fan was based on the Trent 8104 configuration, a three-dimensionally designed,

race to gain the lead in the A380 power market. By the time the first Trent 900 fired up at Rolls-Royce's Derby test site on 18 March 2003, the engine had clinched a 57% share of the firm orders, with subsequent wins at QANTAS, Virgin Atlantic, Lufthansa, and International Lease Finance Company By 2 April the test engine had achieved its certification thrust level of 81,000 pounds. On 9 April the engine reached 88,000 pounds thrust, which was *'...not for bravado,'* said Nuttall. *'It was literally to push the engine for data on extreme operating conditions,'* acknowledging that the initial Trent 970 version would be rated at 70,000 pounds thrust for entry into service. The critical blade containment test was passed successfully in August 2003 and was '... even more impressive because it involved the largest fan ever used in a Rolls-Royce engine,' said Ian Kinnear, director of Airbus programmes.

By the end of 2003, five test engines were running in the certification effort and were showing performance that was '...*on spec for weight and fuel consumption and emissions targets. It's now officially the world's lowest emission large fan engine,*' said Cuddington. The only significant problem arose as an engine was passing the 115-hour mark during an endurance test when a nozzle guide vane came loose and hit two LP turbine blades.

Flight tests were undertaken on the well-used A340-300 previously used as an all-purpose testbed for several other tests ranging from flight control system experiments to other engine tests, including the Trent 500. The first flight was made on 17 May 2004, and lasted 3 hours, 40 minutes. With 60 hours of flight tests under its belt, Rolls-Royce completed a final full-scale blade-off test in July and, at the end of October 2004, achieved its European Aviation Safety Agency (EASA) airworthiness certification.

Meanwhile, the aerospace world was stunned when, on the other side of the Atlantic in May 1996, GE Aircraft Engines and Pratt & Whitney jointly announced an agreement to develop a new jet engine for the Boeing 747-500X/600X. The joint engine development programme covered the 72,000- to 84,000-pound thrust range and was agreed between the two archrivals after a standard

Rolls-Royce Fitter Jeremy Galland checks instrumentation on the Trent 900 engine for testing in the Arnold Engineering Development Centre's (AEDC) Aeropropulsion Test Facility at Arnold Air Force Base, Tennessee. The engine, selected as a powerplant for the Airbus A380 passenger aircraft, underwent engine operability and performance and icing testing. (USAF)

prelaunch sparring session earlier in the year. Boeing, said the joint statement, '...*urged the two companies to explore the joint program.*'

GE had been struggling to improve the operability of the GE90, which had become an over-budget expensive development. Boeing was in the thick of certification efforts on three separate and expensive flight-test programmes for the GE, P&W and Rolls-Royce-powered 777, and had been attempting to explore the joint VLCT initiative with the Airbus partners. Boeing considered the market for the new 747 would be too small to cope with the complications and costs of another three-way engine fight, but the cut-and-thrust had already begun with GE offering a CF6-80X, P&W offering a modular

powerplant based on the PW4000, and Rolls-Royce offering either a modified Trent 700 or a de-rated Trent 800.

It was with this in mind that GE and P&W executives began to consider the situation at the Singapore Air Show in February 1996. They agreed that to meet Boeing's timescale, GE and P&W needed new engine designs in the same thrust range and time period. Given that it would be a relatively limited production run, the answer was to team together. GE had the new GE90 core that P&W admired, while P&W had new fan technology enabling a neat technical fit. The idea was proposed to the chief executives of the two companies, Gene Murphy at GE and Carl Krapek at P&W, and following their joint approval, the

An important consideration was designing the engine to fit into the main deck cargo hold of a Boeing 747 freighter. With a fan diameter of 116 inches, the manufacturers realized it would be a tight squeeze so they did everything to try and minimize the overall outer geometry of the engine, particularly the fan case. Based on earlier proof-of-concept rig tests on a Trent 500-sized fan assembly and containment system, Rolls-Royce introduced a revised, smaller design than the standard aluminum/Kevlar containment package. The new system was also lighter, which proved vital in making it easier to transport on a 747.

The Advanced Ground Systems Engineering E131 Basic Roll-Over Stand is specifically designed to be compliant with the Rolls Royce Trent 900 Hi-Bypass jet engines in a height restricted air-ride or truck/trailer shipping mode. The stand with engine is suitable for air transport on the main deck of B747 Freighter Aircraft in both lateral - cover wing position only - and axial orientations. The stand includes a self-contained manual jackscrew for rotating the stand, cradle, and engine at 55° to achieve the minimum height and width to pass through the large side cargo door. Loading demonstrations were successfully conducted on a 747-400F (which has a slightly smaller door than the -200F) at Stansted in the United Kingdom on 28 February 2005. (Photo: Rolls Royce)

Two Trents together! on the left is a Trent 1000 for the Boeing 787. On the right is the Trent 900 for the A380.
(Simon Peters)

venture was launched pending the approval of the European Union which, because of potential antitrust issues, was required to bless the marriage.

Called the GE P&W Engine Alliance, it was unveiled at the Farnborough Air Show that September. Engines were to be assembled at a line at P&W's East Hartford, Connecticut, site using elements from both companies. GE was to supply the GE90-derived high-pressure-core technology with P&W's low-pressure technology based on the PW4000 series. Launch engine was to be the GP7176 for the 747-X, while a second engine, the GP7200, was aimed at the A3XX.

Plans called for a 36-month certification effort to run from the start of 1997 to meet a certification target of December 1999. But it was the Engine Alliances turn to be stunned when, less than four months after the company was founded, the Boeing 747-500X/600X plan was abandoned. Although a proposed GP7100 version was later aimed at the more modest 747-400X and -400ERX studies, the new focus was now firmly on the Airbus superjumbo project.

Despite the Airbus-imposed delay on the A3XX in early 1998, the Alliance's mood remained upbeat. *'All in all the delay is a good thing. It gives us more time to add new things,'* said Hughes. By mid-1999, the Alliance said the final

configuration of the engine was scheduled to be frozen in May 2001, giving a certification target in November 2003.

This timetable was soon open to change again, following the decision to redesign the engine to bring it in line with QC/2 requirements. As with the Trent 900, the Alliance designers were forced to increase fan diameter to 116 inches, raising the fan bypass ratio from 8:1 to 9:1. The changes added stages to the LP compressor and turbine, as well as noise-reduction features, including swept, hollow wide-chord fan blades, contoured exit-guide vanes and re-optimized blade and vane counts in the LP compressor and turbine.

Further core tests got underway in early 2001 under the newly installed president, Lloyd Thompson, with a further revised schedule calling for the first full engine test to run in early 2004. First flight on the A380 was scheduled for January 2006.

May 2001 saw the Engine Alliance clinch its first order when Air France selected the GP7200 to power ten firm A380s, and crowned this with a major win the following February when Emirates chose the engine to power 22 firm and 10 optioned aircraft. The deal, worth about $1.5 billion, pushed the Engine Alliance into the lead over Rolls-Royce. Further orders arrived in July 2002, when FedEx, as long expected, picked the GP7277 version to power its fleet of 10 A380-800Fs.

More re-arranging of the schedule followed in early 2003 when the Engine Alliance decided to bring forward the first planned full GP7200 engine test by two months to mid-February 2004 to give more margin for lessons learned before the expected certification in 2005. Part of the time was allotted to extra tests of the swept-blade design, which was described by P&W GP7200 Vice President Bob Saia: *'The shape gives it efficiency and reduces the shock loss as the flow goes from supersonic to subsonic at the tip.'* The enlarged metallic shape had been selected in March 2002 over an alternative composite-blade design, which had been proposed the year earlier as part of the QC/2 redesign.

December 2003 brought news that Emirates had once again selected the GP7200 for a massive follow-on order of 23 additional A380s, for delivery from 2009 onward. The total meant that Emirates had ordered 199 engines, valued at more than $3 billion, making the GP7200 the best-selling engine on the A380 at that time.

Initial runs of the engine got underway at East Hartford on 10 March 2004, but unexpected surges in the cruise condition caused by compressor vane scheduling problems hampered efforts to quickly demonstrate high thrust levels. These problems were eventually ironed out, and in early April the engine reached 80,000 pounds thrust, eventually topping out at 86,500 pounds thrust in the Airbus configuration (88,000 pounds when adjusted to P&W's measuring conditions), before the first phase of the testing was completed after 45 hours.

Flight tests began on GE's 747-100 flying test-bed at Victorville, California, on 3 December 2004, roughly three months behind the original schedule. Initial work focused on engine operability, but because of the need to add modifications to the HP compressor and HP turbine, the full flight test evaluation was rescheduled for later in 2005.

All testing was wrapped up in the summer of 2005, with the engine's long-awaited certification set for the third quarter. Meanwhile, the first flight of the GP7200-powered A380 was due around November 2005, the first ship set of engines having been delivered to Airbus over the previous three months.

Arguments over Subsidies

As the first flight of the A380 approached a new sort of hurricane proportions over government support loomed on the horizon - an argument that had occasionally raged with varying intensity since the late 1970s.

Until 1980, the US commercial aircraft industry enjoyed a monopolistic position in the world market, despite the European-based Airbus Industrie being created in 1970. The Americans considered Airbus to be inconsequental, but were forced to take notice of the emerging rival following the Eastern Airlines order for 23 A300Bs in in 1978.

The dominant US position, with two US commercial aircraft manufacturers, Boeing and McDonnell Douglas, together accounting for more than two-thirds of the world market share, continued till as late as the mid-1990s. When Boeing acquired McDonnell in the mid-1990s, it was expected that the position would 'improve' even further. Surprisingly, this formidable position came to be challenged by Airbus, who since 1981, and contrary to its initial perception of having been regarded as only a marginal competitor, was progressively eating into the market and increasing its market share.

Urged on by the American manufacturers, Washington trade representatives took up the cause with their European counterparts and finally an agreement was signed to remove trade barriers on civil aircraft. However, this agreement did not limit subsidies, so that by 1989 the issue flared up again when the West German government promised to protect Messerschmitt-Bölkow-Blohm (MBB) from extreme currency fluctuations. Under its plan, the Airbus partner, then owned by Daimler-Benz, would receive a $2.6 billion subsidy if the US dollar exchange rate fell below DM 1.6.

Even the working partnership between Boeing and Airbus proved to be problematic to say the least, with suspicions from many in the Airbus camp that Boeings tactics were that of delay or even worse. The phenomenal success of Airbus was not received well by many in the US who attributed it to the fact that it was mainly due to the huge subsidies it received from European governments. This was followed by a chain sequence of accusations and counter-accusations.

The battle threatened to erupt in an all-out transatlantic trade war which was only averted after long drawn-out negotiations that resulted in a 1992 bilateral agreement on subsidies for the development of large civil aircraft (LCA).

Somehow, after tortuous negotiations, the two sides agreed to make some allowances to each other. The agreement allowed Airbus to receive some launch aid from EU governments and Boeing to benefit from government Research and Development contracts. Under the agreement, direct government subsidies were limited to 33%

Two views of the Engine Alliance powerplant as fitted to an Emirates A380. Designed for low noise, the key features of the GP7200 include the swept-fan blades, extensive acoustic treatment in the fan case, significant axial spacing between the fan blades, and contoured fan exit guide vanes visible in the back of the wide bypass duct. (Photos: Author)

of the total costs of developing a new aircraft, with the condition that such subsidies had to be repaid with interest within 17 years.

The agreement worked well in principle but not in practice, for two main reasons. Firstly, definition was agreed to as to what exactly 'indirect support' meant. Secondly, there were no means of enforcing any of the provisions of the agreement. The agreement also called for a progressive reduction in launch aid, but again this was not clearly defined.

In 1997, the agreement broke down when the European Union decided to challenge the merger between Boeing and McDonnell Douglas on the grounds that it limited competition. Boeing's plea was that the merger was necessary to strengthen its presence in the defence and space side of the aerospace business areas where McDonnell Douglas was traditionally strong. After the two sides listened to each other, the dispute between

Some idea of the massive size of the new-generation high-bypass engines for the A380 can be gathered in this study of the GE 747 flying testbed taken during the engines maiden flight. The GP7200 was initially certified at 76,500 pounds thrust, though subsequent endurance tests cleared the way for certification in 2006 for operations at 81,500 pounds to meet the needs of future growth derivatives of the A380. Prior to service entry with Emirates in late 2006, the nine engines in the test programme were expected to have built up more than 16,000 cycles, or an equivalent time of 30,000 hours in revenue service. (Engine Alliance)

the two appeared to have settled. But soon after, the Airbus executives, who had initially stated that they had no objections to the merger, gradually started opposing the merger again and became increasingly vocal in their pronouncements.

By 2001, with the LCA agreement nearing 10 years old, the A380 launched, Airbus gobbling up a unprecedented amount of market share, and the Sonic Cruiser project emerging, Boeing reviewed the subsidy issue once more. Its research claimed that Airbus had received at least $15 billion in government subsidies since the start of the 1970s, and it believed that the low interest and lenient repayment terms for one-third of the estimated $12 billion A380 development costs had allowed it to make a convincing business case for launching it in the first place.

Boeing questioned whether the launch aid for the A380 even fell within the bounds of the LCA agreement, which it claimed had been violated through state and local infrastructure improvements in France, Germany, Spain, and the United Kingdom.

Boeing claimed that the LCA agreement had been biased in favour of Airbus, which was then a start-up company requiring some sort of protection. When the deal was negotiated, Airbus was delivering just 20 percent of the world's civil aircraft.

By early 2000s, Airbus was consistently garnering a larger share of new orders than Boeing, and in 2003, it even surpassed Boeing for the first time in deliveries of aircraft - 305 deliveries by Airbus as against only 281 by Boeing.

Leading the charge of the rhetoric brigade was Harry Stonecipher, the former chief executive of Boeing. Speaking to *Flight International* in 2004, he said, 'As soon as it came to launching the A380, then all the hosepipes were hooked up to the treasuries of three countries in particular and $4 billion came zooming through. This whole subsidization thing has gone on long enough. They keep trying to turn it into a globalization issue. But this is about transparency and subsidy.'

To this Airbus responded with the accusation that Boeing was still benefiting from subsidies. Boeing was preparing the ground for launch of the 787. All along, Airbus maintained that Boeing (and before the merger, McDonnell Douglas) had benefited directly and indirectly from massive US government aeronautical engineering research-and-development spending with NASA and the Department of Defense (DoD).

Representatives of the European aviation industry believed that Boeing still received indirect government support through reimbursement of independent research and development money by the US Defense Advanced Research Projects Agency (DARPA) and the DoD, and estimated the company had received $18 billion in indirect support since 1992. There was a good case to be made that Boeing had received indirect research help going back to the development phase of the 707 in the early 1950 when that airliner rode on the back of the USAF tanker, the KC-135.

The European Union calculated that Boeing had received $18 billion in indirect support since 1992, while the Chicago-based company had said it took 'hardly any' benefit from these sources. In 2002, the Europeans estimated the benefit accounted for about 8.6% of Boeing's turnover - well above the 4% limit set by the bilateral agreement.

It seemed that there could be no break-through in the dispute. To add fuel to the fire, the British government decided to announce even a fresh dose of aid ($ 700 million) to the Airbus in mid-2005.

The US, dissatisfied with these developments, formally filed a request with the WTO for establishment of a dispute resolution panel. The EU, on its part, quickly reacted and filed a countersuit with the WTO claiming that US aid to Boeing exceeded the terms set out in the 1992 agreement.

The most convincing grievance of Boeing - which was consistently losing its business to Airbus - was that Airbus received huge subsidies, between 1970 and 1990 in the form of loans at below-market interest rates and tax breaks which together amounted to $ 25.9 billion. This benefited Airbus in two major ways. One, its R&D became a highly subsidised, hence, a high-voltage innovative programme with extremely favourable cost and quality implications, and thereby, a competitive edge in the market. Two, it also provided a financial base to Airbus which was strong enough to enable it offer its aircraft to its customers on highly attractive terms of credit.

Airbus reacted by saying that its success was not due to the subsidies it had received, but was due to its state-of-the-art technology and strategic production and marketing vision. It concentrated initially only on market segments not served by new aircraft or not served at all.

Clearly there were major differences between an Airbus subsidy and a Boeing subsidy. The Airbus subsidy was in the form of repayable loans with interest for aircraft development, which is legal according to the World Trade Organisation (WTO). The Boeing subsidy, on the other hand, had been for aircraft production, which is prohibited by the WTO and which is never required to be paid back. This fact was supported by research conducted at the Department of Geography at the Canada-United States Trade Center. If someone was to lose the case on this ground, it would be Boeing. Would they be ready to pay back the subsidies and accept self-financing arrangement to cover for the areas funded by subsidies?

At the 2004 Farnborough Air Show, the dispute about government subsidies became highly volatile with both sides firing salvo after salvo at each other. Airbus Chief Executive Noel Forgeard accused Boeing of having a hidden agenda, and that all the noise over subsidies was deliberately designed to

The reasons for Boeing's 'complaints' to all and sundry about Airbus is plain to see in this graph. Their market share - in light blue - follows an almost inexorable decline since the creation of Airbus in 1970. The Boeing information also includes data from the pre-1997 McDonnell Douglas merger which 'bumps up' their figures and makes the decline even worse. From a zero start, Airbus overtook Boeing in both market share and number of aircraft delivered in the early 2000s.

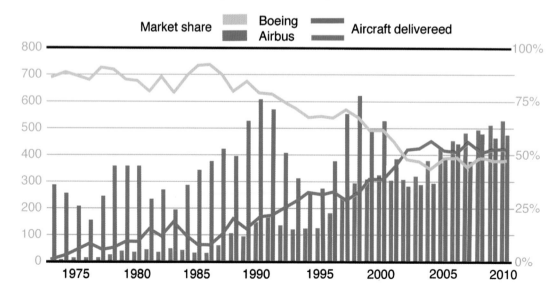

stir popularist anti-Airbus sentiment in the USA ahead of the award of key defence contracts.

By October 2004, the pot boiled over, with Airbus and Boeing both filing complaints to the WTO over alleged abuses of the 1992 agreement. Airbus wanted to see tighter controls on indirect support for Boeing, elimination of the tax breaks that Boeing received from Washington State to secure the location of the 7E7 (later called the 787), and fairer access to the US defence market. Boeing wanted to stop any more government loans to cover A380 cost overruns, and no more launch aid for any new Airbus programmes.

It was this issue from Boeing that caused problems in the talks, particularly after October 2004, when the United States decided to terminate the 1992 bilateral agreement and filed a complaint over illegal subsidies to Airbus with the World Trade Organisation. The European Union responded with an counterclaim alleging that Boeing had been receiving similar illegal subsidies from the US government.

EU Trade Commissioner Pascal Lamy: *'The US move in the WTO concerning European support for Airbus is obviously an attempt to divert attention from Boeing's self-inflicted decline. If this is the path the US has chosen, we accept the challenge, not least because it's high time to put an end to massive illegal US subsidies to Boeing which damage Airbus, in particular those for Boeing's new 7E7 programme.'*

Robert Zoellick, the US trade representative, retorted that the move was merely *'...about fair competition and a level playing field. Some Europeans have justified subsidies to Airbus as necessary to support an industry in its infancy. If that rationalisation were ever valid, its time has long since passed.'*

As the dispute rolled on into 2005, now with EU Trade Commissioner Peter Mandelson at the head of the European delegation, the disagreements threatened to become the most expensive trade dispute in WTO history. It also looked likely to entangle the Japanese government, which had openly subsidised its own manufacturers, who in turn, took large contracts for the new 787 programme. so there was a good case to be made that Boeing was receiving secondary assistance there.

The battle grew more intense with preparations for the launch of the A350, the Airbus countermove to the 787 Dreamliner that Boeing had both expected and feared. At the time of the A380's first flight, it seemed as if a full-blown

A hint of what was to come - a peek through the doors showing the nose of one of the A380s. (Airbus)

trade war could well be looming on the horizon.

Both Boeing and Airbus appeared to roughly agree that the marketplace for the mid-sized A350/Boeing 787 seemed to be around 3,100 aircraft, worth around $400 billion over 20 years. Clearly there were protectionist as nationalistic forces at work here as well and so the arguements rumbled on.

A matter of Engineering

Visually very different from any aircraft before it, the A380 is a blend of high-tech materials, structural advances, and traditional Airbus design know-how.

Wrapped around the ovoid cross section, the aircraft shape was optimized in the presence of all other airframe components using computational fluid dynamics - a first for any Airbus. This process cut drag by 2%, which was vital given the relatively blunt body and stubby nose section.

Apart from the scale and double-deck configuration, the airframe is relatively traditional, but with a wealth of new materials, such as GLARE and reinforced thermoplastics. The aircraft also features carbon-fibre-reinforced plastic frames in the tail cone section and, for the first time, welded stringers in the lower fuselage.

Built to last for a design service goal of 19,000

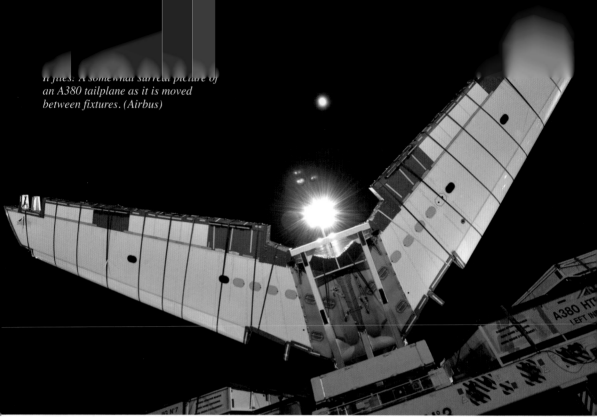

flight cycles, 140,000 flight hours, or 25 years, whichever comes first, the A380 is more ruggedly constructed than any previous Airbus. Advanced aluminum alloys form the semi-monocoque structure of the fuselage, while the skins are chemically milled or machined to reduce the weight.

GLARE is used for the upper and lateral fuselage skins of the forward and aft section above the main-deck level, again mostly for weight reduction, while welded stringer panels are used in the lower fuselage sections below the main deck floor.

The panels for areas in the landing gear bays and other highly loaded sections such as the lower centre fuselage are machined in tandem with integrated stringers for extra strength. The frames that run the length of the aircraft are also heavily loaded.

Where stresses are particularly high - such as near cutout surrounds around doors and hatches, the wing root area, nose and centre fuselage lower shells - critical parts are machined. In less highly loaded areas, such as the upper shell, parts are extruded.

The nose section is another unique Airbus feature, containing a large unpressurized area in the forward lower part for the nose gear bay. The remainder of the nose fuselage, which is called section 11/12, runs aft from the radome to frame

22 and includes the flight deck, crew rest area, electronics bays, and passenger door 1. Locally welded longitudinal stringers stiffen a double-curved panel that forms the internal upper-pressure bulkhead inside and behind the nose gear bay.

Tapering aft from the circular radome, the fuselage is still spherical where it becomes section 13 at frame 22. It remains this way all the way back to frame 31 between the forward cargo bay door and door 2, where it assumes the constant ovoid cross section.

Welded stringers stiffen the skins on the lower side of this section, and GLARE strengthens the upper shell above the main deck door level. The upper-deck crossbeams are made from carbon-fibre-reinforced plastic and are connected to the frames by shear joints and supported by vertical struts, while the main deck beams are made from Al-Li C460/2196 aluminum/lithium alloy. A floor grid sits on top of the beams and supports composite floor panels that are sealed in place for corrosion protection.

A double-width stairway, designed to be passable by two passengers with hand baggage simultaneously and located by door 1, has hand rails that enable its use for in-flight movements. An aft staircase, recessed into the curvature of the rear pressure bulkhead, is reached by door 5 on the main deck and winds up to the upper deck. The stairs are designed to be wide enough for a stretcher to be carried up or down, or for crew members with service equipment.

The middle chunk of the fuselage, section 15/21, runs from frames 38 to 74 and is the largest and most complex fuselage subassembly Airbus has ever made.

The section includes doors 7 and 8 on the upper deck, and door 3 on the main deck, as well as the centre wing box and belly fairing. It also includes the main landing gear bay, which takes up the area between the rear spar of the centre wing box at frames 56 and 72.

The wing gears, each with a four-wheel bogie, stow into the forward area between frames 56 and 63, while the six-wheel body gears stow into the rear area between frames 63 and 72. A traverse wall separates the wing and body gear bays on each side.

The belly fairing is formed from a series of panels made up from Nomex honeycomb and hybrid epoxy skin sandwich. An aluminum substructure supports these panels and helps transfer some of the fuselage loads to the fairing by deformation between the primary structure of the fuselage and the belly fairing support structure.

The aft fuselage, section 18, runs from frames 74 to 95 and includes passenger doors M4 and M5 on the main deck and doors U3 on the upper deck. The fuselage also encompasses a cargo door on the right side and a bulk cargo door on the same side farther aft between frames 87 and 89. At frame 95, the aft section is attached to the unpressurized rear fuselage, which consists of a forward unit and a tail cone. A dome-shaped carbon-fibre-reinforced plastic rear-pressure bulkhead separates the tail section from the rest of the aircraft.

Although a small piece of structure compared to the main fuselage, sections 19 and 19.1 are complex assemblies. The double curvature of the composite panels, which are 'area-ruled' for transonic flow conditions at the root of the horizontal tailplane, are made up by using an automated fibre-placement technique.

Highly loaded frames, which support the attachment for the vertical tailplane, are machined from high-strength aluminum alloys, while weight-saving non- metallic frames made from resin transfer moldings make up several of the less loaded frames. A double row of six lugs and twelve shear bolts attaches the base of the vertical tail fin to the fuselage using the same design concept as the A340.

Forward of the first set of lugs is the large

The core section of one A380 wing is craned around inside the BAe Systems factory ar Broughton. (Airbus)

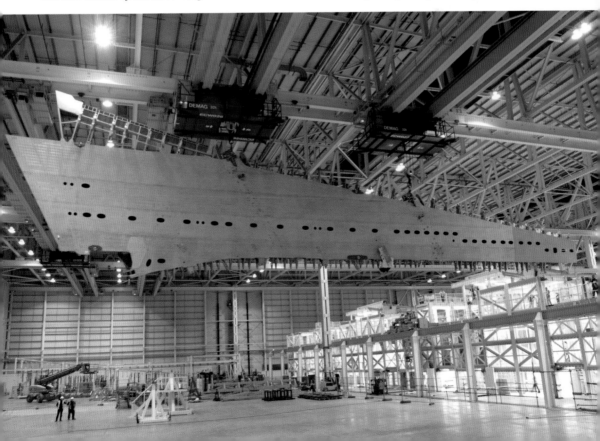

The core section to one wing is fitted out with flap and aileron support brackets. (Airbus)

frame at station 108 supporting the horizontal tailplane pivot points, while a single trim screw is positioned between frames 99 and 100. Aft of this is the tail cone - mainly consisting of carbon-fibre-reinforced plastic skins, frames, and stringers - that houses the auxiliary power unit. A titanium rear fairing encompasses the aft-facing APU exhaust, while the compartment itself is lined with firewalls made from titanium sheets.

The vertical stabilizer is almost 48 feet high, taking the overall tail height to 79 feet 5 inches. The stabilizer has a chord of 39 feet, 6 inches at the root, giving an aspect ratio of 1.74 and a taper ratio of 0.39. The tail is also relatively sharply swept back at 40 degrees, measured at the conventional 25% chord point.

Both the fin and rudder are of a new design that uses a single torsion box and an upper and lower rudder, the latter being just over 16 feet high. The fin box is made up of carbon-fibre-reinforced plastic with two full-span front and rear spars, web and framework ribs and fittings for rudder support made from CFRP, and resin-transfer molding material with aluminum-alloy end fittings.

The horizontal tailplane runs through tailcone section and includes an integral fuel tank between ribs 8 left and right. The fuel level in the tail tank, which can take up to 23,698 liters, is adjustable in flight for trimming purposes. Overall, the baseline

A380-800 fuel-tank capacity is 315,292 litres, most of which is contained in two inner tanks with more than 90,600 litres. Two other mid-tanks hold about 72,000 litres between them, with inner engine 2 and 3 feed tanks containing 28,130 litres each. The outer engine 1 and 4 feed tanks each hold 26,974 litres, while the two outer tanks each hold 9,524 litres.

The screw-driven trim system can adjust the angle of attack of the horizontal tailplane through an angle ranging from plus 3 degrees up to minus 10.5 degrees down. As with the vertical tail, the horizontal unit is an all-new design with CFRP torsion box. The elevator is split into two about midway along the trailing edge, with each part being separately actuated.

Overall, the tail span is just over 99 feet, which is 5 feet longer than one wing of the A340-500/600, or 6 feet wider than the wingspan of a 737-200!

Structurally speaking, two of the most impressive features of the A380 are the enormous 261-foot-6-inch-span wings, which cover an area of 9,104 square feet.

With an aspect ratio of 7.52 and a 33.5-degree sweep angle at the 25% chord mark, the wings have a dihedral of 5.6 degrees at the tip, which has a chord just over 13 feet.

Each wing supports two engine pylons, the

The double-width forward staircase, seen looking down from the upper deck, is 5 feet wide, making it passable simultaneously by two passengers with luggage, and is a fixed installation centrally located on the main deck adjacent to doors 1L and 1R. The stairs are designed to be used in-flight during cruise. (author)

equipped, was delivered by barge from Nantes to the Saint-Nazaire plant at the mouth of the Loire River in August 2003. Within a few weeks, the forward fuselage was ready for fitting out at Meaulte and was joined by the cockpit.

The first landing gear bay was also delivered from Meaulte to Saint-Nazaire, where the job of fitting together the first forward fuselage sub-assembly began with the combination of the German-built forward fuselage and the French-built flight deck.

Meanwhile, the first 75-foot-long centre fuselage sections had been completed and moved out of their jigs at Saint-Nazaire in preparation for the installation of the Spanish-built belly fairing. The rest of the centre fuselage was also coming together with the integration of the structurally complex Meaulte-built main landing gear bays and the Nantes-made centre wing box.

The section also included the Sogerma-produced floor grid and the forward lower shell and part of the upper shell, both made by Alenia at its Turin and Naples sites in Italy. It also

Curving into the recessed aft pressure bulkhead, the 15-step rear staircase joins both decks and provides access to the aft main cabin area. (author)

wing main landing gear, three ailerons for low-speed flight, and eight spoilers for roll control, lift dumping, or gust load alleviation. The leading edge also supports two droop noses and six slat sections, while three single-slotted Fowler flap sections hang off the trailing edge. The inner flap is metallic, while the two outer flaps are made from composites, as are the spoilers and ailerons.

The primary structure is made up of a metallic outer part and a hybrid CFRP/aluminum-alloy centre box consisting of front, centre, and rear spars, upper and lower skin panels, and root rib. Frame fittings attach the centre wing box to the upper fuselage, while the upper fuselage skin is bolted to a large structure called the upper cruciform flange. The inner part of the wing from ribs 1 to 17 has front, centre, and rear aluminum-alloy spars, while outboard of this to rib 49 there is only a front and rear spar. To save weight, 23 of the 49 ribs are fully or partially made from CFRP, most of them occurring mid-span between the engines.

The first centre wing box for flight test aircraft MSN001, weighing in at 25,550 pounds fully

With a root chord of 39 feet 6 inches and a height roughly that of an A320 wing, the tail of the A380 is an increasingly eye-catching sight at airports around the world. The rudder is split into two for yaw control, with each part controlled by a pair of electric backup hydraulic actuators from independent hydraulic and electrical systems, In normal operation, the actuators are active and driven by the flight control computers. In the event of a hydraulic system failure, the affected actuators automatically revert to electrical mode. These operate slightly slower but still provide maximum rudder deflection of plus or minus 30 degrees.

included the 39-foot long central lower fuselage shell, which was supplied by SABCA of Belgium. This formed a load-bearing support between the wings and rear fuselage and also channeled several hydraulic and electrical systems; it was covered in the aft part by double-curved, stretched, and chemically milled skins. The forward skin was mechanically machined from a single piece of aluminum plate.

The first unpressurized two-part aft fuselage, consisting of the largely composite structure supporting the vertical and horizontal tailplanes and the aftermost tail cone housing the auxiliary power unit, was also transported by Beluga to Finkenwerder for attachment to the aft fuselage. In November 2003, the first rear fuselage aluminum ring frame, 24.5 feet in diameter, was delivered from Varel to Hamburg. The ring connected the rear fuselage to the composite rear pressure bulkhead and formed the interface between the rear fuselage section and the Spanish-made aft fuselage. Airbus Germany's Donauworth site also took delivery that month of the first Mitsubishi-built cargo door, which was shipped from Nagoya.

November 2003 also saw Malaysian supplier Composites Technology Resource Malaysia (CTRM) hand over the first set of composite leading-edge wing components from Malacca to Airbus UK, where the first wing set had been removed from its jigs at Broughton. By January 2004, the wing was being fitted out with hydraulic and fuel-system wiring prior to delivery to Toulouse in April. The 66,000-pound structure measured 119 feet root to tip in length, was 36 feet wide and almost 10 feet deep at the root where the wing met the body.

Meanwhile, in the USA, Los Angeles-based Hitco Carbon Composites marked the handover of the first ship set of vertical tail carbon-fibre-reinforced plastic truss structures to Airbus Germany, where the the vertical tail had been

completed for the first static test airframe, termed the *essais statique* (ES).

Assembly of the first two flying aircraft, MSN001 and MSN004, was also under way by January 2004, with the tail for the fatigue test airframe, the *essais fatigue* (EF), started in March. Parts for the MSN001 and ES airframes entered final assembly at Toulouse at virtually the same time, although the static test airframe would be the first to be completed by July 2004.

By May 2004, the first static airframe was coming together in Toulouse in a new process in which it was assembled at a single station, rather than moving it through several assembly stations in the factory. Under the new process, the fuselage sections, wings, and tail were brought to one station before the complete airframe was moved on its own wheels to one of three sites for completion and systems tests. In a full production aircraft, this would entail fitting of the engines, auxiliary power unit, fixed leading edges, and landing gear doors. Once completed, the aircraft was then to be taken to one of ten outside positions for engine and APU runs, pressurisation and fuel system tests, weather radar evaluation and other tests.

On 7 May 2004, French Prime Minister Jean-Pierre Raffarin inaugurated the $425 million Jean-Luc Lagardère Production Complex, and on 27 May the static test airframe was quietly rolled off the production line and into the adjacent test hangar. Work went on to complete assembly of MSN001.

The static test building was an engineering feat in its own right, with a vaulted ceiling height of just over 95 feet under the hook cranes in the roof and standing on concrete reinforced with about 1,000 tons of steel. Mounted inside the test rig the airframe was supported on 306 jacks and connected to 8,000 gauges. For the tests, several structural parts were replaced with dummy parts, including the horizontal and vertical tails, the entire tail cone, the slat and flap tracks, the engines and pylons, and the landing gear.

The tests would be concluded with the gradual bending of the wings to their maximum elastic limit. Engineers predicted these would eventually break with explosive force when they were bent upward at the tip by about 33 feet!

The static and fatigue tests formed the top of what Airbus called a test pyramid. Below the major tests were big-ticket component tests on the empennage, sub-components, details, elements, and down to small parts or 'coupons.' Other component tests included a piece of fuselage made up of GLARE skin, as well as aluminum stringers and frames, and a curved pressurized panel that had been laser welded.

Goodrich and Dowty also conducted separate landing gear static and drop tests, while a further series of tests evaluated the resistance of the

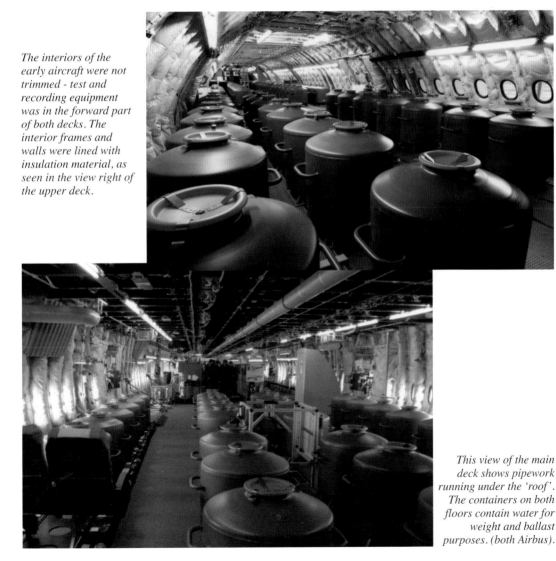

The interiors of the early aircraft were not trimmed - test and recording equipment was in the forward part of both decks. The interior frames and walls were lined with insulation material, as seen in the view right of the upper deck.

This view of the main deck shows pipework running under the 'roof'. The containers on both floors contain water for weight and ballast purposes. (both Airbus).

cockpit windows to bird impacts.

Sub-assemblies for MSN00I came together on the first assembly station in Toulouse on the same day the static airframe rolled out. By 7 July the aircraft was structurally complete and able to move on its own wheels to the next completion station. Work on MSN002 began a few days later, just as the five major sub-assemblies of the next aircraft (MSN004) arrived by convoy.

Further back up the line, parts of aircraft MSN007 and MSN003 were being built in Saint-Nazaire, while assembly of components for MSN015 had already begun at Nantes. In the UK, series production was under way on five ship-sets of wings.

MSN001 was 'powered up' for the first time on 30 July 2004 when the distribution and generation was switched on.

Assembly of the fourth flight test A380, MSN007, began in Toulouse on 18 November. Meanwhile preflight test work was well under way on MSN001, which had spent over two months undergoing checks on the trimming functionality of its large horizontal tailplane, as well as other tests on the flight controls, slats and flaps, undercarriage extension and retraction, brakes and steering, and bleed air system. MSN001 (and MSN004) were also fitted with a representative mini-cabin section in a small area of the upper fuselage, complete with sidewall and ceiling panels, overhead storage bins, and even a galley and toilet.

Following completion of these initial fittings, MSN001 was moved outside for fuel and cabin pressurisation tests before going into the paint hangar for finishing in its new blue Airbus corporate livery. Only MSN001 and MSN004 were to be painted at Toulouse, all others flying to Hamburg for completion at the two new specially built paint hangars at Finkenwerder.

On Show To The World

4,500 guests arrived through winds and driving rain at the enormous final assembly hall in Toulouse on 18 January 2005 to witness the grand reveal of the A380 to the world.

Fireworks, illuminated fountains, music and light shows enthralled the crowd as a the story of the A380 was narrated to the assembled throng by a series of images projected onto giant screens.

Finally, four children pressed a button to raise an enormous blue curtain to reveal the aircraft in its new blue-and-white Airbus livery After the cheers and applause died away, the government leaders of the four partner countries heaped praise on the achievements of the company. French President Jacques Chirac '...It is a technological feat and a great European success... ...when it takes to the skies, it will carry the colours of our continent and our technological ambitions to even greater heights.'

British Prime Minister Tony Blair described the aircraft as '...simply stunning... and praised the '...dedication' of all those involved in the project He went on to say that the A380 was a symbol of European cooperation at its best. ... 'This is the most exciting new aircraft in the world, a symbol of economic strength and technical innovation. Above all, it is a symbol of confidence that we can compete and win in the global market.'

With the recently re-ignited transatlantic subsidies row obviously in mind, German Chancellor Gerhard Schroeder could not resist the temptation to snipe at the United States when he said the multinational project had been accomplished because of the 'tradition of good old Europe.'

Jose Luis Rodriguez Zapatero, the Spanish Prime Minister praised the development project as a pinnacle of European technology. 'When we look at this monument of human achievement, we see that Europe can't be stopped. We're capable of being a leader in science and technology when we are highly determined.'

Also present at the Reveal were a number of heads of airlines and operators. Sheikh Ahmed bin Saeed Al-Maktoum, chairman of Emirates, the largest single A380 customer, confirmed the aircraft was a key element in the future growth of the Dubai-based carrier because of the '...continued constraints on traffic rights and the availability of landing slots.' Despite the incredible size of the Emirates A380 fleet growth plan, which included up to 45 aircraft, Sheikh Ahmed added that '...every single one of the A380s we have ordered has been carefully prepared for and supports present and future network needs.'

ILFC's Steve Udvar-Hazy hailed the A380 as the '... beginning of a new era in civil aviation,' saying that it represented '....the direction the airline industry is going: mass transportation on a global scale.'

FedEx Chairman, President, and Chief Executive Fred Smith said '...2008 can't come quickly enough for us. The aircraft is pretty close to perfect. It gives us a lot more cubic space, a lot more payload, and a lot more range, but it also sits in almost the same parking dimension as our largest aircraft today and only utilizes one slot. That's a great advantage.'

Lights, camera, action! The grand reveal of the A380, with Presidents, Prime Ministers and children! (Airbus)

Akbar Al Baker, chief executive of Qatar Airways, stressed the interior flexibility offered by an aircraft with more floor space than any airliner in history. *'We are looking at having innovations that other airlines have not yet thought about yet.'*

Flamboyant Virgin Chairman Sir Richard Branson said the A380 would give operators the chance to provide a new level of service. *'The A380 can take up to 900 passengers, but at Virgin we plan to only have about 500 passengers.'* Branson added the Virgin aircraft would feature beauty parlours and *'...larger bars, so passengers are not stuck in their seats and can get out and meet each other.'* He also said that the aircraft would also have casinos for gambling as well as a few private double beds, jokingly suggesting *'...so there will be at least two ways to get lucky!'*

The reveal also generated tremendous interest

Politicians gather at Toulouse for the inauguration of the new Airbus A380 on January 18, 2005. (Front, from L to R) British Prime Minister Tony Blair, French President Jacques Chirac, German Chancellor Gerhard Schroeder and Spanish Prime Minister Jose Luis Rodriguez Zapatero.

The Grand Reveal - Part Two! The A380 is presented to Airbus employees. (Airbus)

around the world. Television networks such as Sky TV and CNN beamed live pictures to screens on every continent and an unprecedented 640,000 unique visitors logged on to the Airbus website.

More than one in three logging into the site came from the USA, despite the time difference, while the next largest visitor numbers came from the United Kingdom; Germany, Sweden, Spain, Netherlands, and France followed. Over 14 million 'hits' were recorded by the site through the day.

The following day the whole thing was repeated for the benifit of more than 50,000 Airbus employees worldwide, about 5,000 of whom packed the hall for a re-run of the sound and light show. The crowd was mostly made up of employees who had won a place at the event through a prize draw, and included a driver for Airbus China in Beijing who made his first journey abroad to attend the ceremony!

With the show over, the A380, now appropriately registered F-WWOW, was returned to the cold outside to continue the build-up to outfitting for fuel and pressurisation tests, followed by a final systems and equipment upgrade with the replacement of non-flight items with flight-cleared ones.

A boost to the programme occurred in late January when China Southern Airlines ordered five A380s, the first two of which were to be delivered in time to help the airline take passengers to Beijing for the 2008 Olympics. The latest sale took overall firm orders to 154 aircraft from 15 customers

Ground vibration tests of MSN002, which would be the third to fly, were completed after validating frequency and structural damping modes used in models for upcoming flutter clearance flights.

Ground tests continued through February and March, and it was not until F-WWOW was handed over to Flight Test on 6 April that the engines and APU were powered up, with the de-storage of oil from the engine oil system causing spectacular white exhaust clouds behind the aircraft.

MSN001 was then finally cleared to carry out taxi tests and low-speed acceleration and stop checks. After all these years, it was difficult for the gathered Airbus employees to believe that the A380 was finally moving under its own power. After several more days of brake and system checks, the superjumbo was cleared to be taxied to the end of Blagnac's 11,480-foot runway 32L for high-speed runs and a full stop.

The urge to take the aircraft on its first flight was almost irresistible, but it would have to wait.

Chapter 8

To Test, To Fly, To Certify!

The weather on the morning of 27 April 2005 was exactly as had been predicted by the meteorologists. A ridge of high pressure had moved into France from the Atlantic, bringing clear skies, warm weather, and a gentle northerly breeze that would allow the A380 to take off away from the city of Toulouse, a necessary requirement before the first flight attempt could be sanctioned.

Flight Division Senior Vice President Captain Claude Lelaie and Chief Test Pilot Captain Jacques Rosay led the six-man crew; between them, Lelaie and Rosay had already amassed more than 13,000 flight test hours, including the first flights of the A318, A340-500, and -600. Flight Test Division Vice President Fernando Alonso was picked as flight test engineer responsible for overseeing flight controls and aircraft structural monitoring,

while the others included flight test engineers Jacky Joye, Manfred Birnfeld, and Gerard Desbois.

Preparations had been in hand for some time, for plans were in place for a first flight on 18 April and again on 20 April, but the weather refused to cooperate and it was not until the last week of April that things looked better. The media had been notified and were on standby.

Word spread around the world that first flight was imminent, and by the early hours of the morning of the 27th, about 50,000 people - if police estimates were to be believed - packed the fields and roads around Toulouse's Blagnac Airport. Thousands more Airbus employees were shepherded in guest enclosures on the airport itself. Under a cloudless sky the crew boarded the giant

The test crew for the first flight. On the flightdeck was Claude Lelaie and Jacques Rosay, 5th left, sitting in the cabin four engineers, on the left is Gerard Desbois, 2nd Left Fernando Alonso, 4th left Jacky Joye, among them (right) Manfred . (Airbus)

blue-and-white aircraft and started MSN001's - by now carrying the registration F-WWOW - four Rolls Royce Trent 900 engines. Shortly after 10:00 am local time, the aircraft taxied slowly to the holding point of Runway 32L and then onto the runway itself. It was 10:18.

At 10:29:32 the throttles were opened until they reached maximum power, Lelaie and Rosay guided the A380 down the centreline as it quickly gathered speed. Rosay pulled back on the side stick controller and the aircraft launched effortlessly into the air. At liftoff the ballasted aircraft weighed 421 tonnes - or 928,300 pounds - instantly winning the A380 a place in the record books with the heaviest ever takeoff of a commercial airliner!

Accompanied by the Airbus flight test chase aircraft, an Aérospatiale SN 601 Corvette, the aircraft flew straight ahead until, to the on-lookers at Toulouse, it dwindled into a dot in the distance. At about 10,000 feet Rosay retracted the landing gear, slats, and flaps before climbing farther to almost 14,000 feet for initial handling qualities tests. The first part of the flight, including the take-off, had been conducted in direct law, in which the flight control system's (FCS) envelope protection features are disabled. Later on in the flight, the FCS normal law was activated for a while.

'The takeoff was absolutely perfect...' chief test pilot Jacques Rosay reported back to the Flight test Centre by radio from the A380 flight deck as he flew at 10,000 feet just north of the Pyrenees mountains, about an hour into the flight. *'The weather's wonderful.'*

The crew also reported that the aircraft was handling well, while flight test engineer Fernando Alonso reported that *'...in every configuration there was very little buffet.'* With several initial handling and flight control law tests completed, the crew headed back to Blagnac International Airport for a landing at 14.23 local time (12.23 GMT) after successfully completing a first flight that lasted three hours and 54 minutes.

Moments after emerging from the cockpit of the A380 after its successful first flight, chief test pilot Jacques Rosay told the gathered media that flying the world's biggest passenger jet had been *'...like handling a bicycle.'*

As captain for the take-off and the initial part of the test flight, he lavished praise on the aircraft for its performance: *'This aircraft is very, very easy to fly. Any Airbus pilot will feel immediately at ease with this aircraft, a pure member of the Airbus family.'*

Flight test engineer's station on the lower deck of Airbus A380 test aircraft F-WWOW (serial 001). (Photo: Airbus SAS)

The flight test crew board F-WWOW for the first flight on 27 April 2005 watched by the world press, (Airbus)

Amongst the many representatives in the media centre at Toulouse that morning was CNN's Business Traveller show presenter Richard Quest, their established airline and aviation correspondent. He is seen here in full flow doing a piece to camera. (Simon Peters Collection)

Thousands of Airbus employees await the taxi-out and first flight. (Simon Peters Collection)

The crew confirmed that the new aircraft and engines had handled as anticipated. Claude Lelaie commented: *'We had a very successful first flight and thoroughly enjoyed every minute of it. There are of course a lot of things to be done, but after this first experience, we now really sense the potential of this magnificent machine. And even on the ground, as already felt during the initial ground tests, the A380 handles as easily as any other aircraft. Also, the systems and the Rolls Royce engines performed satisfactorily.'*

Jacques Rosay added: *'Within the first minutes of the flight, we were impressed by the ease of handling of the aircraft which was in line with what we had felt in the simulator. We have no doubt any Airbus pilot would feel immediately at home in the A380; it is a true member of the Airbus aircraft family. We could also appreciate that the new features in the cockpit, including interactivity, vertical display, new interfaces that make the work*

It flies! F-WWOW takes to the skies for the first time from Toulouse - the chase Aerospatiale Corvette can be seen in the background. (Airbus)

Landing back at Toulouse at 14.23 local. (Simon Peters Collection)

of the crew very easy and efficient and I want to thank the customer airline pilots who have greatly contributed to this design.'

During the flight, which took the aircraft around South West France, the six crew members explored the aircraft's flight envelope as expected. They tested the A380's handling using both direct and normal flight control laws with the landing gear up and down, and with all flaps' and slats' settings during the part of the flight at cruise altitude. They made an initial evaluation of the comfort levels in both the main and upper decks, confirming that the cabin was very quiet and the ride smooth.

Noël Forgeard, Airbus president and CEO, said he and Charles Champion, executive vice president for the A380 programme, were *'extremely proud of everyone who made this happen'*.

This maiden voyage, during which all primary flight test objectives were met, marked the beginning of a rigorous test flight campaign involving five A380s, including one for the certification of the Engine Alliance GP7200 engine on the A380, and some 2,500 flight hours, expected to last around thirteen months. It was to

Even the construction workers pause as the aircraft taxies back in. (Simon Peters Collection)

The flight deck crew. 2nd left is Fernando Alonso, with Charles Champion on the right celebrate in front of the media after the first flight. (Simon Peters Collection)

culminate in the aircraft's certification followed by its entry into airline service in the second half of 2006 with first operator Singapore Airlines. The scope and rigour of the A380 ground and flight test programme should also prepare for a smooth entry into service.

On 1 December 2005, the A380 achieved its maximum design speed of Mach 0.96, over its design cruise speed of Mach 0.85, in a shallow dive, completing the opening of the flight envelope. In 2006, the A380 flew its first high-altitude test at Bole International Airport, Addis Ababa and conducted its second high-altitude test at the same airport in 2009.

On 10 January 2006, it flew to José María Córdova International Airport in Colombia, accomplishing the transatlantic testing, and then went to El Dorado International Airport to test the engine operation in high-altitude airports. The A380 first arrived in North America on 6 February 2006, landing in Iqaluit, Nunavut in Canada for cold-weather testing.

On 14 February 2006, during the destructive wing strength certification test on MSN5000, the test wing of the A380 failed at 145% of the limit load, short of the required 150% level. Airbus later briefed A380 customers on the wing modifications it was making as a result of the premature rupture

of the static test specimen.

There were plans to retrofit reinforcements to certain stringers in aircraft that had already been built and to produce modified components for subsequent wings, said Airbus chief operating officer and A380 programme head Charles Champion. *'Our conclusion is that we are going to add a few strips on some stringers in the wing in the area involved. The strips will be fitted on top of the stringers to increase the resistance of the stringers at the limit [load]'.* The proposed changes were submitted to the European Aviation Safety Agency for approval.

A380 product marketing director Richard Carcaillet told the media that the modifications to already-built wings would add 30kg of airframe weight, comprising 16kg for the reinforcement strips and 14kg for the attachment bolts.

On 26 March 2006, the A380 underwent evacuation certification in Hamburg. With eight of the sixteen exits arbitrarily blocked, 853 mixed passengers and 20 crew left the darkened aircraft in an incredible 78 seconds, less than the 90 seconds required for certification. Three days later, the A380 received European Aviation Safety Agency (EASA) and United States Federal Aviation Administration (FAA) approval to carry up to 853 passengers.

Making use of the FMS

The A380 employs an Integrated Modular Avionics (IMA) architecture, first used in advanced military aircraft. The main IMA systems on the A380 were designed and developed by Airbus, Thales and Diehl Aerospace, the IMA suite was first used on the A380. The suite is a technological innovation, with networked computing modules to support different applications and came into its own during flight testing.

The data communication networks use Avionics Full-Duplex Switched Ethernet, an implementation of ARINC 664. The data networks are switched, full-duplex, star-topology and based on 100baseTX fast-Ethernet, which reduces the amount of wiring required and minimises latency.

Airbus used similar cockpit layout, procedures and handling characteristics to other Airbus aircraft, reducing crew training costs. The A380 has an improved glass cockpit, using fly-by-wire flight controls linked to side-sticks. The cockpit has eight 15 by 20 cm (5.9 by 7.9 in) liquid crystal displays, all physically identical and interchangeable, comprising two Primary Flight Displays, two navigation displays, one engine parameter display, one system display and two Multi-Function Displays. The MFDs were introduced on the A380 to provide an easy-to-use interface to the flight management system—replacing three multifunction control and display units. They include QWERTY keyboards and trackballs, interfacing with a graphical 'point-and-click' display system.

The Network Systems Server (NSS) is the heart of A380's paperless cockpit; it eliminates bulky manuals and charts traditionally used. The NSS has enough inbuilt robustness to eliminate onboard backup paper documents. The A380's network and server system stores data and offers electronic documentation, providing a required equipment list, navigation charts, performance calculations, and an aircraft logbook. This is accessed through the MFDs and controlled via the keyboard interface.

Power-by-wire flight control actuators have been used for the first time in civil aviation to back up primary hydraulic actuators. Also, during certain manoeuvres they augment the primary actuators. They have self-contained hydraulic and electrical power supplies. Electro-hydrostatic actuators (EHA) are used in the aileron and elevator, electric and hydraulic motors to drive the slats as well as electrical backup hydrostatic

The flight deck of F-WWOW. Much of the operation here is completely 'paperless', even to the point where the airport landing plates are displayed on the computer screens. (Simon Peters Collection)

actuators (EBHA) for the rudder and some spoilers.

The A380's high pressure hydraulic system reduces the weight and size of pipelines, actuators and related components. The 350 bar pressure is generated by eight de-clutchable hydraulic pumps. The hydraulic lines are typically made from titanium; the system features both fuel- and air-cooled heat exchangers. Self-contained electrically powered hydraulic power packs serve as backups for the primary systems, instead of a secondary hydraulic system, saving weight and reducing maintenance.

The A380 uses four 150 kVA variable-frequency electrical generators, eliminating constant-speed drives and improving reliability. Aluminium power cables instead of copper are used for weight reduction. The electrical power system is fully computerised and many contactors and breakers have been replaced by solid-state devices for better performance and increased reliability.

Delays and Flight Test Problems
It had been acknowledged that the first flight took place at least a month later than Airbus originally planned, and Airbus had to face up to the fact that deliveries would not happen as first scheduled. First details of the slippage emerged in May 2005 when the company revealed that it was sending out teams to 'negotiate' revised delivery times with the initial aircraft customers. Singapore Airlines - the first airline to take the aircraft for commercial service - still hoped to have its initial deliveries by the end of 2006 but knew that the chances of making it by December that year would be tight.

Others airlines affected by the slippage included Emirates and QANTAS, the latter being advised that first deliveries would begin in April 2007 rather than October the previous year. It was not only the delays to the start of flight tests that had complicated the schedule but also the intense work of finalising cabin configurations. Air France also acknowledged it was talking to Airbus and revising its acceptance schedule, having originally planned to take first delivery in April 2007.

Initial production of the A380 was troubled by delays attributed to the 530 km (330 miles) of wiring in each aircraft. Airbus cited as underlying causes the complexity of the cabin wiring some 98,000 wires and 40,000 connectors - its concurrent design and production, the high degree of customisation for each airline, and failures of configuration management and change control. The German and Spanish Airbus facilities continued to use CATIA version 4, while British and French sites migrated to version 5. This caused overall configuration management problems, at least in part because wiring harnesses manufactured using aluminium rather than copper conductors necessitated special design rules including non-standard dimensions and bend radii; these were not easily transferred between versions of the software.

The problems could be traced back to the summer of 2004 when large sections of theaircraft's forward and rear fuselage had been arriving unfinished from Airbus's other main A380 production site in Hamburg. By late autumn, a team of around 200 German mechanics was in Toulouse along with several hundred kilometers of electrical cables to be installed in the first aircraft. But after weeks of painstakingly threading thousands of veins of copper and aluminum wire around the walls and floor panels of the airframes, the teams had run into a maddening snag: the cables were too short.

One German mechanic, who asked not to be

The International Civil Aviation Organisation wanted to increase the seperation distances between the A380 and other aircraft following it when on approach...

identified for fear of losing his job allegedly told the media *'The wiring wasn't following the expected routing through the fuselage, so when we got to the end they weren't long enough to meet up with the connectors on the next section. The calculations were wrong. Everything had to be ripped out and replaced from scratch.'*

Throughout the autumn of 2004, assembly line managers duly reported the problems at theaircraft's regular progress review meetings. But no one, at that stage, seemed to believe they were significant enough to merit a red flag to top management.

Airbus did not acknowledge the the problem until 1 June 2005, when company executives made their first public admission of manufacturing troubles and announced a six-month delay in the aircraft's delivery schedule. This reduced the total number of planned deliveries by the end of 2009 from about 120 to 90–100.

By late December 2005 Airbus were approaching the quarter-distance mark in the A380 flight-test programme, having cleared a number of key hurdles, but faced a daunting 10 months of trials to complete certification and prepare the aircraft for entry into service with Singapore Airlines.

The tests would stretch the A380 to the very limits. MSNO01 and 004 would perform the bulk of the tests with 600 flight test hours due to be chalked up by each of them by mid-2006. The second pair, MSN002 and 007, would between them be scheduled to contribute about 900 hours of testing to the programme, including work on the cabin systems and early long flights with full passenger loads of staff volunteers, and later route proving.

Tests ranged from takeoff and climb performance and stalls, to wake vortex effects, braking and rejected takeoff performance, cross wind landings, noise certification, cold and hot weather tests, emergency evacuation work, and 'hot and high' performance evaluation.

The flight envelope had been cleared, and the difficult negotiations with customers to reschedule deliveries following the programme slippage had been completed. At Toulouse executives were confident that the A380 programme would be able to keep to its revised timetable, but could barely disguise their anger and surprise over the recent interim recommendations by the International Civil Aviation Organisation (ICAO) to greatly increase separation distances for the aircraft.

Vice-president flight tests Fernando Alonso

John Leahy is the current chief operating officer - customers at Airbus after being appointed to the position in July 2005. Leahy continues as Airbus' chief commercial officer, a role he has held since August 1994.

said that Airbus was quite surprised by the ICAO interim policy letter issued on 10 November, which recommended a dramatic increase in the separation requirements for the A380 from the standard 'heavy aircraft' distances of 4nm, 5nm and 6nm during approach, depending on the size of aircraft following, to 10nm regardless of the category in trail. ICAO has also increased the 5nm cruise separation to 15nm for the A380. *'The ICAO policy is based on a type of computation that has not been validated by flight test measurements – we disagree with its recommendation,'* adding that *'...there has been no demonstration that the 747 is the limit for the 'heavy' category'.*

By the beginning of December the three flying A380s completed 586 of the expected 2,500 flight hours, and 161 flights, with the fleet averaging 65-70 flight hours a month. Airbus senior vice-president flight test Claude Lelaie said that a total of 43 pilots had flown the aircraft, including representatives from customers and from European and US aviation authorities. *'The first customer airline pilots flew the aircraft after the Dubai air show when we had eleven Emirates pilots – including three who had never flown an Airbus – fly two touch and goes each at Ras Al Khaimah,'* said Lelaie.

The successful demonstration of the A380's maximum design speed (Vmd/Mmd) of Mach 0.96 on 1 December marked the completion of the opening of the A380's flight envelope, flutter testing having been concluded in November. Lelaie said that a Vmd attempt earlier in the flight test programme had to be aborted at Mach 0.93

when they detected a shock wave, but it was rectified by calibration.

Lelaie says that the A380 was dived from around 39,000ft and reached Mach 0.96 quite easily with a lower rate of descent than previous Airbus aircraft – the pitch down attitude was only 7°– which shows that aircraft drag was low. Initial water ingestion trials at the Istres test centre had been carried out, with the A380 being accelerated to and decelerated from 70kt through a water trough, but these tests had to be completed once some modifications were incorporated, as the tests had to be aborted when some hydraulic pipes to the brakes were bent.

MSN004, which joined the flight test programme on 18 October, was dedicated to performance measurements and engine development. *'It completed the main evaluation of cruise performance on 9 November and there are complementary evaluations continuing until the end of December'* reported Fernando Alonso. Lelaie said there are indications that the A380 could end up cruising slightly faster than its nominal published speed of M0.85, but *'We'll have to wait for all the results before we know for sure'*. That aircraft spent a week at the Dubai air show in November wowing the crowds in its Emirates colour scheme, mid-way through an extensive two-month evaluation of low-speed performance test. Lelaie said the next major task for the flight test team was to fine-tune the fly-by-wire flight control rotation law.

Other ongoing flight test activities included:

Cold weather trials were nearly thwarted when unseasonably high temperatures brought concerns on Baffin Island, Canada. 'Earlier this week, temperatures were very unseasonably mild — down around the -15C (5F) mark,' said John Graham, manager of the Iqaluit Airport. 'Technicians are cold-weather testing the 555-passenger Airbus A380 this week at the small airport in the Nunavut capital. ' It all worked out. We got down to about -29C (-20F) when the airplane landed at Iqaluit airport on Monday' Graham said.

A dramatic image of the A380 ploughing through the water troughs at Istres. The tests were designed to check water ingestion into the engines and the effect of water hitting the aircraft and other components. (Photo: Airbus SAS)

structural identification; further autoland work and development of various systems – fuel, electrics (including testing of ram air turbine performance) and air conditioning (with complete ducting).

In October, MSN001 was used for four days of noise evaluation tests at Moron air base in Spain, where Airbus verified whether the target for the A380's external noise levels could be achieved with current configuration. The aircraft completed over 100 flyovers to measure approach and take-off noise.

'Cold soak trials are set for early in 2006, while the maximum-energy rejected take-off test will be undertaken at Istres, France, and is currently planned for March/April', said Lelaie. *'The braking system is not yet fully tuned,'* he added.

Since the beginning of the flight-test programme, Airbus had been monitoring wake vortex measurements at Toulouse and Istres, and while it acknowledged that the data collected so far indicates that A380 levels were slightly higher than the 747, it could not understand why ICAO had decided to create a special category for the A380 over and above any other aircraft. Airbus flew a back-to-back test during 2006 involving an A380, a 747-400 and a 777, as well as an A320, to generate some solid comparative data for analysis.

Meanwhile, Airbus chief operating officer and head of the A380 programme Charles Champion reported that A380 production was ramping up in Toulouse and at plants across Europe: *'A total of*

eleven A380s have been assembled, including the static and fatigue test specimens. Final assembly in Toulouse of the tenth flying airframe (MSN010 – the fifth SIA aircraft) began in early December,' he said. Champion added that at other Airbus plants production of sections for MSN025 were underway, as were parts manufacturing of components for MSN030.

Although testing had gone reasonably smoothly, Airbus carried out several unscheduled removals of Trent 900 engines. Champion said that MSN001 suffered two engine-related incidents: *'Engine 4 was changed at the end of September because of too high oil consumption, and then on 24 October engine 1 suffered an in-flight surge because a bolt was lost due to high-cycle fatigue. R-R asked for engines 2 and 3 to also be changed as a precautionary measure'* he said.

On MSN004, engine 1 was changed due to increasing oil consumption as a precautionary measure because the aircraft was going to Dubai for the air show.

Completion of the first of two test A380s with fully furnished cabins was under way at Hamburg and the aircraft (MSN002) was due to return to flight testing in April ahead of operating a series of early long flights in May from Toulouse with Airbus personnel on board. *'We will make a virtual first flight of the cabin of MSN002 in March on the ground with full passenger complement and ground infrastructure.'* said Champion. Prior to this, a similar exercise would be undertaken using the Cabin Zero test rig in Hamburg with a limited number of passengers.

MSN002, which was tasked with 500 hours of flight testing, was equipped with a 474-seat, three-class cabin. However, before being completed the cabin was modified into a high-density 853-seat arrangement for the evacuation trial in around March. Head of A380 industrial design Michael Lau: *'This will be achieved by removing bulkheads and galleys to incorporate the extra seats.'*

The fourth test A380, MSN007, was due to be ferried to Hamburg for its cabin installation in February, and was set to undertake the route-proving programme in around August. It would later be re-engined to conduct route proving of the

Engine Alliance GP7200-powered version.

Assembly of the main Engine Alliance flight test aircraft (MSN009) had been completed, and its first flight was scheduled for April. Champion said that certification of this version was expected in the first quarter of 2007 to enable deliveries to begin to launch customer Emirates in April 2007.

MSN009 registered F-WWEA - flew on 25 August 2006. On 4 September 2006, the first full passenger-carrying flight test took place. The aircraft flew from Toulouse with 474 Airbus employees on board, in the first of a series of flights to test passenger facilities and comfort. In November 2006, a further series of route-proving flights demonstrated the aircraft's performance for 150 flight hours under typical airline operating conditions.

One test required was the VMU-Test. For this, a tail bumper was installed on A380 F-WWOW so that the rear end could be dragged along the runway. This determined speeds which are called VMU (Velocity Minimum Unstick). Airbus needed to know the VMU as the computed take off speeds incorporate a margin above VMU, just as they also do for VS (Stall speed), VMCG (Minimum control speed ground) and VMCA (Minimum control speed air). These 'V' speeds form the basic building blocks of take-off performance. (Photos: Airbus SAS)

A380 Airbus Chief Operating Officer Charles Champion (centre) with British Chancellor Gordon Brown and test pilot Ed Strongman in the A380 cockpit at Heathrow. (Photo: Airbus SAS)

The team knew it faced a truly mammoth task for a mammoth aircraft. However, given its success to date and the gritty determination it had shown to overcome the odds and develop the A380 in the first place, Airbus was convinced it was up to the task. It accepted that the schedule had been tight to begin with but vowed to catch up as quickly as it could and ensure that the entry into service would be as smooth as possible. They knew the A380 was a world beater . . now they were out to prove it.

Airbus obtained type certificates for the A380-841 and A380-842 model from the EASA and FAA on 12 December 2006 in a joint ceremony at the company's French headquarters, receiving the ICAO code A388. The A380-861 model obtained its type certificate on 14 December 2007.

Changes at the top

By early 2006, there were still many A380 problems unresolved. The cost overruns and delays to the superjumbo project were raised at a 12 May meeting of the EADS board convened to certify the company's financial results for the first quarter, which were due to be published the following week.

Minutes from that meeting show that several board members questioned whether the delays were significant enough to merit a warning to investors. The board was unable to give a precise estimate of the delays, suggesting that they could be anywhere from one to five months.

One month later, on 13 June, Airbus announced a further six-month postponement to the A380 and said it would only deliver nine of twenty-five aircraft it originally promised customers by 2007. EADS warned the delays would reduce its earnings by €2 billion over four years, news which sent its shares tumbling 26%.

The announcement led to the departure of EADS CEO Noël Forgeard, Airbus CEO Gustav Humbert, and A380 programme manager Charles Champion. EADS managers once again sought to reassert their control over Airbus, appointing an outsider, Streiff, as chief executive, but keeping him on a short managerial leash.

On 3 October 2006 Airbus informed its customers about a further delay in the delivery schedule of the A380. According to this revised plan, the first A380 would be delivered in October 2007 - thirteen more would be delivered in 2008 and twenty-five in 2009. The industrial ramp-up would be completed in 2010, when forty five A380s were scheduled for delivery.

Fully aware of the impact this had on their development plans, Airbus was in close contact with its customers and stated that it *'is doing its utmost to find ways and means to alleviate the burden this represents for them'*.

In June, the amount of work to be done to finalise the installation of the electrical harnesses into the forward and rear section of the fuselage had been underestimated. Beyond the complexity of the cable installation, the root cause of the problem was that the 3D digital mock up, which facilitated the design of the electrical harnesses installation, was implemented late and that the people working on it were in their learning curve.

A press release from the company said that *'Under the leadership of the new Airbus President and CEO Christian Streiff, strong measures have been taken, which, in addition to management changes, include the implementation of the same proven tools on all sites, as well as the creation of multi-national teams to better use the best skills available. Simultaneously, training is being organised to swiftly bring the employees using those tools to the optimum level. With the right tools, the right people, the right training and the right oversight and management being put in place, the issue is now addressed at its root, although it will take time until these measures bear fruit'*.

As Airbus prioritised the work on the A380-800 over the A380F, freighter orders were cancelled. On 4 December 2006 US lessor ILFC deferred its order for ten Airbus A380s to 2013 and beyond, as part of a major renegotiation deal that included the switch of its freighters to passenger aircraft.

Airbus chief operating officer customers John Leahy spoke in Paris, saying that that the ILFC deal had been renegotiated the previous month. *'We've agreed to defer the A380s until 2013-14. ILFC always had the right to switch its five freighters to the passenger version and they've exercised that right.'*

It marked a further blow to the A380 freighter programme, leaving cargo carrier United Parcel Services – with its order for ten – as the only customer for the type after Emirates and FedEx cancelled their orders. UPS was to cancel their order for ten aircraft in late February 2007.

Airbus subsequently suspended work on the freighter version, but said it remained on offer, albeit without a service entry date.

For the passenger version Airbus negotiated a revised delivery schedule and compensation with the thirteen customers, all of which retained their orders, with some placing subsequent orders, including Emirates, Singapore Airlines, QANTAS, Air France, Qatar Airways, and Korean Air.

Route Proving and World Tours
For around two years the A380 toured the world, visiting every continent but Antarctica.

In November 2005, F-WWOO went to Dubai in the United Arab Emirates for the Dubai Air

The new Airbus A380 painted in full Emirates Airlines Colors, photographed at the 2005 Dubai Airshow. The aircraft, seen here with the French Patrouille de France aerobatic display team, is flying over the world-famous 'Palm' islands. (Photo; Airbus)

Show. Tim Clark, President of Emirates: *'When we ordered this aircraft in 2000* [Emirates had ordered 45] *we wanted it within a year or two, so we cannot wait to get our hands on it.'*

The A380 in full Emirates livery, dubbed 'the empress of the sky' by the flight display commentator, was the unrivalled star of the show, drawing crowds of people on its arrival and for each of its daily flight display as well as hundreds of visitors.

The show gave Middle East A380 customers the opportunity come on board and to see the aircraft first hand. In addition, on Friday, the French aerobatics team 'la Patrouille de France', which participated in the flying display every day during the air show, flew in formation with the A380 over Dubai.

F-WWOO visited the Asian Aerospace Airshow in Singapore and displayed before Singapore Airlines CEO Mr Chew Choon Seng. Airbus underscored its strong presence by highlighting the flagship A380 and the new A350. Held at the Changi Exhibition Centre in Singapore from 21st-26th February, the exhibition showcased the A380 in daily flying displays.

The it was off to the biennial ILA Berlin Airshow held over 16-21 May 2006 at Berlin's Schönefeld Airport, which allowed Airbus to highlight its full product line from the 100-seat A318 to the 555-seat A380, and to underscore its confidence in the future.

The Farnborough International Airshow, held on 17-23 July 2006, featured flying displays of the A380 and A340-600, with Airbus managers on hand at the biennial event to update airline customers, industry partners and the media on sales status and development goals. A strong growing feature here was that daily news was provided on a special section of the Airbus corporate Website.

On 13 November 2006 an A380 took off on the first of four trips that formed the crucial 'final step' in the certification process.

Known as technical route proving, these flights - using MSN002 - were designed to demonstrate the aircraft's capability of operating on a continuous schedule representative of commercial operating conditions. In the course of 18 days, the aircraft was expected to fly between 150 and 170 hours, with stops at 10 airports around the world.

Flight AIB 101 13 November - Toulouse to Singapore.

Time is 14:51; weather bright and sunny. 70 people on board as flight departs Toulouse-Blagnac. A

Mr Chew Choon Seng, the Chief Executive Officer of Singapore Airlines until the end of 2010. He is currently the Chairman of the Singapore Exchange and the Singapore Tourism Board.

three man crew flies the aircraft: Ed Strongman and Michel Gagneaux from Airbus and Didier Poisson from EASA.

The route was down across Europe, across Egypt, over the Red Sea into Saudi Arabia then to Bahrain, Oman and across the Indian Ocean into Singapore - a flight that lasted 12:30 hours.

The flight was used for a specific certification requirement, the crew workload assessment and human factor specialists closely monitoring what took place in the flight deck for the entire journey.

Over the Bay of Bengal some turbulence was experienced which brought the seatbelt signs ON, but overall it was a pleasant and uneventful flight. This was the third flight to Singapore and ground operations at Terminal 2 were almost routine for Singapore Airlines handling the aircraft.

In the A380 certification campaign the role of experimental test pilot Hugues van der Stichel was to act as the interface between the certification authorities, Airbus flight test and the design office. *'In practice, on major subjects, we have long-standing Airbus specialists but for some subjects that are new, and there are quite a few of those on the A38U - I am the interface.'*

In that role he covered subjects such as runways to demonstrate to the authorities that the A380 has been designed to take off and land on 45-metre wide runways. *'This is a is a very important subject on which both EASA and FAA have required complete substantiation. We monitored every flight of the A380 and compared the results with a data base of long range aircraft. We covered runways, obstacles, failures, compatibility, every possible occurrence to demonstrate the capability of the A380.'*

The flights to Singapore and back were the only ones that included a certification exercise in addition to the technical route proving. Hugues's

A380 TECHNICAL ROUTE PROVING FLIGHT 2007 DETAILS
(all times are local)

Flt No.	Route	Dep time	T/O Weight	Cruise Alt	Cruise Speed	Distance	Pax/crew	Arr time	Block
AIB 101	TLS-SIN	14:44	494 tonnes	41,000 ft	Mach 0.86	6,500 nm	70	09:04	12.40 hrs
AIB 102	SIN-ICN	06:04	406 tonnes	41.000 ft	Mach 0.85	2706 nm	67	12:51	06.00 hrs
AIB 103	ICN- SIN	05:00	404 tonnes	40,000 ft	Mach 0.85	2670 nm	63	11:10	06.05 hrs
AIB 104	SIN-TLS	14:26	524 tonnes	34/40,000 ft	Mach 0.86	6,242 nm	58	21:20	13.55 hrs
AIB 201	TLS-HKG	17:26	490 tonnes	43,000 feet	Mach 0.85	5.892 nm	60	11:24	11.58 hrs
AIB 202	HKG-NRT	05.48	383 tonnes	41,000 ft	Mach 0.80	1,832 nm	68	10.58	04.10 hrs
AIB 203	NRT-TLS	11:81	514 tonnes	40,000 ft	Mach 0.85	5,780 nm	70	17:26	12.50 hrs
AIB 301	TLS-CAN	17:22	510 tonnes	41.200 ft	Mach 0.85	5.679 nm	58	12:05	11.46 hrs
AIB 302	CAN-BJS	07:35	402 tonnes	37.000 ft	Mach 0.85	1.029 nm	67	10:29	03.00 hrs
AIB 303	BJS-PVG	18:24	370 tonnes	37.400 ft	Mach 0.85	680 nm	71	18:18	01.55 hrs
AIB 304	PVG-TLS	14.04	510,85 tonnes	various	Mach 0.85	5.670 nm	60	20:22	13.20 hrs
AIB 305	CAN-CAN	-	-	-	-	-	-	-	1.20 hrs
AIB 401	TLS-JNB	20:12	488 .3 tonnes	37/41,000 ft	Mach 0.85	4,370 nm	76	08:20	10.10 hrs
AIB 402	JNB-SYD	08:18	55 tonnes	35,000 ft	Mach 0.85	7,300 nm	69	08 :46	15.28 hrs
AIB 403	SYD-YVR	22:49	556 tonnes	39,000 ft	Mach 085	7.113 nm	79	07:33	14.55 hrs
AIB 404	YVR-TLS	16:19	505 tonnes	41,000 ft	Mach .85	5,523 nm	83	13:40	11.20 hrs
AIB 405	JNB-JNB	-	-	-	-	-	-	-	1.40 hrs

TLS -	Toulouse-Blagnac International Airport, France		BJS -	Beijing Capital International Airport, China
SIN -	Singapore Changi International Airport, Singapore		PVG -	Shanghai Pudong International Airport, China
ICN -	Incheon International Airport, Seoul		JNB -	OR Tambo International Airport, South Africa
HKG -	Hong Kong International Airport , China		SYD -	Sydney Kingsford Smith International Airport, Australia.
NRT -	Narita International Airport, Tokyo, Japan		YVR -	Vancouver International Airport, Canada
CAN -	Guangzhou Baiyun International. China			

task was to supervise the certification of minimum crew workload and to co-ordinate the exercise.

'We have chosen a typical long range flight with a crew who have been prepared and are monitored by human factors specialists. The aim is to compare the workload in this aircraft with its new interfaces to previous aircraft,'

We simulate events or failures related to the cockpit and specific to the A380. These failures, which are perfectly compatible with the people on board, are expected to increase slightly the crews workload. They do not represent a security risk as they are not major failures and totally reversible.

We keep permanently in contact with the crew and we also have video monitoring of the cockpit, then at specific times vie ask them to assess their workload on a previously agreed scale.'

This human factors study is only a complementary evaluation the visible part of the iceberg. There have been three global evaluations, in 2004, 2005 and 2006 conducted in the simulator with airline pilots in representative situations.

Hugues also participated in the fourth mission, round the world and over the poles. *'I feel really lucky. For me it is the crowning of the campaign. Normally I am not a great fan of very long flights but this gives me the opportunity to see the aircraft in very different locations. I also look forward very much to the last leg of the technical route proving*

which will be done with one of the FAA pilots with whom I have been in permanent contact for the past three years. It makes this flight very special.'

Pilot Michel Gagneaux's impressions…
The flight from Toulouse to Singapore was very long and overnight but not too tiring. We were three pilots and therefore I few for six or seven hours then I had a rest before coming back to the controls.

Usually on flights as long as fifteen hours, pilots try to work for about three or four hours stretches. I didn't feel too tired, which is surprising, but then I was able to sleep in the crew rest area where you have a real bed, located just behind the cockpit and where it is quiet.

I have already flown some 100 hours on the A380. It is a nice and easy aircraft to fly - all Airbus aircraft are - as easy as riding a bicycle, to quote our chief pilot!

Flight AIB 102. 15 November. Singapore to Seoul, Korea.

This was the A380s first visit to Seoul and the flight was met by a large crowd of media and visitors. First on board was Chairman Cho Yang Ho from Korean Air, who was shown around by Arman Jacobs.

Amongst the visitors was Soon Lee, Vice President Purchasing for Korean Air. *'The first visit*

F-WXXL lands at Seoul Airport on 15 November 2006 at 1400 hours local time. It departed at 0800 the next morning.
(Kim Pak Choi)

of the A380 has been quite an event with many journalists as people are interested in the airplane,' he said and added: *'People are also interested in the aftermath of the delay but we have confidence in the aircraft itself.'*

The main reason for the selection of the A380 by Korean Air was the requirement for extra capacity. *'The A380 is the perfect aircraft to fit our needs. We intend to use it to go to New York JFK, Los Angeles, Paris CDG, Frankfurt, the long flight routes,'* Soon Lee said.

Flight AIB 103/4 was backtracking to Singapore and finally Toulouse.

Flight AIB 201 - 17 November Toulouse to Hong Kong.

Dusk was just settling over Toulouse as the A380 gently took to the air. On most overnight flights, switching off the seatbelt fastened sign is generally followed by people settling down with a good book or curling up for a sleep, but on this flight it unleashed a hive of activity that would have most cabin crews tearing their hair out. Within seconds virtually everyone was out of their seat and launching tests or,

for people making their maiden voyage on the A380, simply exploring the aircraft -this may have been a aircraft full of aviation 'professionals' but they were just as keen as anyone else to play with buttons, flaps and gadgets!

With so much space on the two decks and 60 people moving freely around the aircraft, it felt more like a hotel lounge area than an aircraft. That feeling was perhaps even stronger because with total darkness outside and very little cabin noise inside, it's actually easy to forget that you are flying.

And so the A380 settled down for the next stage of route proving. Over the next eleven and a half hours the level of activity gradually decreased as people tried to grab some sleep. Every now and then the darkness was punctuated by city lights spread out below, while the aircraft slipped unnoticed across Switzerland, Austria, Germany, Czech Republic, Poland, Belarus, Kazakhstan and Russia.

As dawn breaks, the A380 glided smoothly alongside the Himalayas, revealing an unforgettable view, and passed over mainland China to complete its 6,000 nautical mile trip and

Above: F-WXXL lands at Hong Kong International for the first time.

Below: The huge tail of F-WXXL towers over the other airlines at Hong Kong International while on the route-proving flight

begin the descent into Hong Kong.

The A380 made a flawless landing when it touched down at Hong Kong International Airport on its first visit to China. As the aircraft taxied around to the terminal building, the number of airport staff on the ground trying to get a closer look steadily increased, until the A380 finally stopped on the apron in front of gate 62 in a sea of yellow vests and camera flashes.

The A380 was expected to slot into normal operations at Hong Kong with no problem

whatsoever as it was always designed to meet the Code F requirements for so called, very large aircraft

For experimental test pilot Peter Chandler, flying into Hong Kong was a familiar feeling as it was a route he flew often as a commercial pilot before joining Airbus. But the trip had a rather different ending this time and as soon as the aircraft doors were open, Peter was whisked away to meet the press waiting at a special welcome reception.

Airport Authority CEO Dr David Pang hosted the ceremony in a glass sided part of the terminal building, which offered the assembled guests and media an excellent yiew of the A380 parked alongside at the gate.

Thanking Dr Pang for his warm welcome, Peter explained why the A380 was such an ideal aircraft for the region in terms of efficiency, capacity and environmental performance before taking the first group of VIP guests from the airport and Hong Kong based airlines.

Flight AIB 202 - 19 November. Hong Kong to Narita, Tokyo.

A damp day outside could do nothing to dampen the warmth of the welcome laid on for the A380 when it arrived at Narita International Airport for the first time.

Dozens of journalists, photographers and television crews, who had participated in a special A380 briefing just before the aircraft's arrival, crowded round to watch the colourful welcome ceremony, which was held in front of large windows framing the A380 parked immediately behind.

Mr Kobori, Senior Vice President of Narita International Airport extended a warm welcome to the A380 crew and Henri Coupron, Airbus

Executive Vice President of Procurement.

'I am really excited to be able to witness what is a historic moment both for Narita and the aviation industry,' said Mr Kobori. 'Large aircraft like the A380 are very welcome at Narita, where our runway capacity is limited. What is really surprising is that despite its size, the A380 is ranked at level A, the lowest of our six noise categories, which is one of the measures used to estimate airport landing fees. As an inland airport we have a problem with aircraft noise and repeatedly ask airlines to introduce aircraft that will reduce this, so the A380 meets our needs exactly. I hope that it won't be long before we see many A380s in the airport every day,' concluded Mr Kobori.

Thanking Mr. Kobori for his kind welcome, Henri explained why everyone at Airbus was delighted to be able to bring the aircraft to Japan. Beyond carrying out typical airport operations, it will be a pleasure to show the aircraft to our friends and business partners here in Japan, including the 21 companies that had contributed to the manufacture of the A380.

He went on to explain why he thought the aircraft would be important to the region: 'Tokyo has, combined, the largest airport traffic, so many A380 customers will operate the aircraft here. Congestion in busy airports is a lasting problem, which we believe that the A380 will solve, while significantly reducing the cost of transporting each passenger and the environmental impact, too.

'This new flagship, in the colours of major world airlines, will be seen in Japanese skies very soon. It will change the may that people fly and I hope that people in Japan will experience it before long,' he added.

AIB 203 was direct from Tokyo to Toulouse, arriving back on 20 November.

Flight AIB 301 – 21 November. Toulouse to Guangzhou, China

The previous day MSN 002 returned from Tokyo and was being readied for a 12-hour flight to Guangzhou in China. Onboard the flight test and cabin engineers calibrate their instruments, it was the beginning of a long night for them too.

The trip report records the details. 'Engine start and push back was characteristically silent, all in the cabin have their in-flight entertainment systems set to the external tail camera view. Rolling down runway 32L shortly after 18:37, rows of twinkling runway lights glide past on every screen. Climb out from Toulouse is swift and despite a take-off weight of 510 tonnes, the initial cruise altitude of 34,000ft was reached in a remarkably short 25 minutes. With that kind of performance, its no wonder pilots love flying the A380!

Inside the aircraft, the cabin system engineers are ensuring the same will be the case for future passengers. Their task is a difficult one, how to make the best cabin in the sky even better. As we slip across cities that from our comfortable vantage point, hundreds of cabin wind velocity and temperature probes send data to test stations which show where the environmental control system should be tweaked. The mood lighting system is cycled through its preprogrammed settings, bathing the cabin in soothing shades of blue and pink. In the A380 gone are the days where the breakfast meal service was announced by the harsh flickering of white fluorescent tube lights. Temperature, lighting, airflow and countless other parameters can be controlled by the cabin crew in eight different cabin zones.

With noise levels confirmed to be the lowest of any aircraft flying today, there is at least one parameter that does not have to be perfected.

As the final cruise altitude of 42,000 ft is reached, we find ourselves zipping along at M 0.85 chasing an early sunrise skirting the northern side of the Himalayas.

Shortly after the first rays of sunlight illuminate the cabin, the excitement shifts from data gathering to window watching. Majestic peaks break through the clouds below as we continue our course ever eastward.

Crossing China, all looks good for an on time arrival for 13:00 local time, all the more important given that Chinese national television is devoting more than 1 hour of live broadcasting the A380's arrival. As we touch down, spot on the numbers and spot on time, at the brand new Baiyun airport, we see hundreds of people in front of a red podium set up next to the parking position. As soon as the doors open, the wave of enthusiasm outside floods the aircraft. Welcome to China!

This was the first experience of the Chinese red carpet treatment. Officials and guests were lined up as the pilots come down the steps to be greeted by China Southern hostesses with bouquets of flowers, watched by hundreds of spectators at the airport and broadcast by dozens of cameras. The arrival of the A380 was the final phase of the welcome ceremony, which started much earlier in the day with live TV broadcast and press briefings.

Successively Laurence Barron, president of

Landing at Guangzhou. Every attempt was made to arrive exactly on time, for the flight crew knew that their arrival was being carried live by Chinese TV in a one-hour special. (Shen Kang Rui)

Airbus China, Liu Shaoyong, president of China Southern, Liu Ziiing, president of Guangzhou Baiyun Airport and several senior officials deliver short speeches before Laurence Barron offered a souvenir of the ceremony to president Liu Shaoyong.

Flight AIB 305 - Local flying.

Guangzhou is the home base of China Southern Airlines, an Airbus customer operating nearly 90 Airbus aircraft, which became the first A380 customer in China with an order for five A380s in April 2005. So it was only fitting that Guangzhou should be the one stopover with a local flight, which took off at 1400 with more than 60 China Southern officials including the airline' president and its chief pilot. With much excitement the passengers boarded the flight while the president of China Southern, an A340 captain, took the left-hand seat in the cockpit to perform his first ever take-off with the A380. *'The president started the engines, taxied, did the take-off and later on he did the landing as well,'* explained Peter Chandler, Airbus test pilot, who acted as co-pilot. *'He did it with no training on the A380 at all. I told him to treat it the same as an A340 and he was fine. And the landing was the best I have ever seen for someone doing it without any training, very smooth, outstanding in fact.'*

After the take-off, the president let the chief pilot and a few other senior airline pilots take the controls. The experience was a good demonstration of how easy it would be for China Southern pilots to transition to the A380 in the future.

'I feel proud to fly the A380 today,' said Liu Shaoyong, as he came smiling out of the cockpit. *'My personal experience today confirms that the A380 is easy to control and very stable so I feel that it will provide our passengers with a comfortable in-flight experience. I am also confident in its safety.'*

Next day it was off to Beijing.

Flight AIB 302 – 23 November. Guangzhou to Beijing

The enthusiasm and curiosity of Airbus' guests had been sharpened by the intensive media campaign announcing the arrival of the A380 days before its actual landing. The pilots had barely time to walk down the red carpeted stairs to receive the traditional bouquets before the first visitors started to rush into the aircraft.

Among the official visitors coming on board were the vice-minister of the National Development and Reform Community, two vice-ministers of China Airworthiness Authorities (CAAC), the president of CASC, Airbus' partner in the training and support joint venture in Beijing, the president of Air China and members of the airline's management, airport officials and the vice-mayor of Tianiin, location of the future A320 Family final assembly line.

AIB 304 – 24 November. Beijing to Shanghai

It was dark and pouring with rain as the A380 came in to land for the first time in Shanghai Pudong International Airport. This is the home base of China Eastern Airlines, which became Airbus' first Chinese customer in 1985 and is

Airbus' largest customer in China with a fleet of 113 Airbus aircraft.

At 09.00 the following morning, when the first official visitors arrived at the aircraft, the sun had come out and shone on the A380 and the large red banner welcoming the aircraft to Shanghai. This was the last stop of the A380 in mainland China and the interest in the A380 did not flag. In groups of 20, some 150 VIPs, including airline presidents, airport and government officials, walked through the two decks of the aircraft, tried out the seats and wondered at the space in the cabins before stepping into the cockpit where Peter Chandler gave explanations to interested guests.

Outside, dozens of cameramen, photographers and visitors shot the scene from behind the safety ropes. Just another day's work for the A380 crew, who were becoming used to being in the limelight.

As the A380 left Shanghai and China on its may to its Toulouse home base, thousands of enthusiastic fans in China were bringing home souvenir photographs taken with Airbus ground crew in a shared moment of excitement.

Flight AIB 401 - 25 November. Toulouse to Jo'burg.

Crew - Pilots: Francois Barre, Philippe Perrin and Xavier Lescou. Engineers: Didier Ronceray, Bernard Masdoumier, Philippe Seve, Gerard Maisonneuve Andrew Daws. Cabin specialists: Thierry Gilard and Manual Martins Machado.

On Saturday 25 November at just after eight in the evening, F-WXXL took off from Toulouse-Blagnac airport. Within moments it was gently turning to set course for South Africa, Australia and Canada, via both the North and South Poles.

For nearly eight thousand kilometres the aircraft slid through the night skies over the African continent en route to Johannesburg, its first stop on this particular route proving mission. This was definitely route proving as it ought to be - a smooth, calm, uneventful ten-hour trip with breakfast served some 40,000 feet over Angola

Then as O R Tambo International Airport came into view, it was clear that once again the A380 was in for the kind of warm welcome that eclipses even the best African weather; this was quite handy as it wasn't really the best of weather - more sort of overcast and chilly! Nevertheless, thousands of people had sought out vantage points the length and breadth of the airport to watch the A380 glide in, while news crews circled overhead in helicopters.

Finally, as the A380 turned into the apron in front of the South African Airways technical facility at just after eight in the morning on Sunday 26 November, two of the airport's fire engines were on hand, shooting huge arcs of water across the aircraft from either side to form a most splendid guard of honour.

One and a half hours of media briefing was wrapped up in time for journalists, photographers and camera crews to take their places for the A380's landing, alongside thousands of other well-wishers, including many families. Most of the passengers and crew disembarked straight away, letting the aircraft get straight back onto the runway for series of autoland tests.

Most people are familiar with the autopilot system, which flies an aircraft automatically along the designated flight path. Less well known is the automatic instrument landing capability or 'autoland' system, which handles the aircraft's transition from the direct flight route, through a flare along the runway and eventually to a

F-WXXL departs Toulouse on the first leg of it's 'vertical' around the world proving flight. (Photo: Airbus SAS)

complete stop.

All Airbus aircraft have two identical autopilot systems, which are capable of autoland, and can be engaged in parallel for approach to provide back up should one of them experience a problem. That redundancy is called 'fail operational'. The A380 offers even more reassurance thanks to a third system on stand by, ready to take over at any time from either of the other two.

Pilots can choose to engage the system or land manually, depending on whether or not they expect to have a good enough reference point on the ground to land the aircraft manually. Manual landing is the usual practice, as aircraft separations at landing are increased when low visibility procedures are in force. Therefore, pilots will elect to land manually if visibility is good enough. Autoland is compulsory in so-called CAT3 conditions, i.e. when the decision to continue the landing could be taken as close as 50 feet to the ground, or even lower. Autoland is recommended when that decision height falls below 200 feet.

Such autoland systems face a challenge on the approach to Runway 03 Right at O R Tambo International Airport in Johannesburg, which has a very special profile. Not only is it situated at 5,800 feet with a runway incline which means the aircraft is traveling fast for landing, but there is a large step of nearly 100 feet just at the start, which is reflected in the radio altimeter and could affect the flare onto the runway surface.

The A380's visit to Johannesburg during route proving provided the ideal opportunity to confirm that the aircraft's autoland system worked as expected for the runway's unique profile.

The A380 tested the system four times. The aircraft initially took off from Runway 03 Left, before turning right and completing a circuit to arrive on the approach to Runway 03 Right. On the first three tests the aircraft performed a 'touch and go', which means that the aircraft took-off again after having travelled a few hundred metres along the runway. The first two circuits were right hand patterns. On the third pass, the aircraft turned in the opposite direction after take-off, so that it arrived from the left hand side for the final approach. The crew then let the autoland system bring the aircraft to a complete stop at the end of the runway As Experimental Test Pilot Hugues van der Stichel said afterwards: *'It was perfect. The landings were almost kisses!'*

For the last of the four tests, dozens of media teams poised alongside the runway were joined by Minister of Transport, Jeffrey Radebe, who was keen to get a close up view of the A380 in action before joining it back in the SAA technical facility to officially welcome the A380 crew and tour the aircraft's interior.

The minister was joined by Wrenelle Stander, CEO of Air Traffic Navigation Services (ATNS), who had been key in developing the route proving missions for the A380: 'It was absolutely exhilarating to see the A380 glide into the airport this morning and to be there for the autoland tests,' said Ms Stander *'The aircraft is bigger than I expected, but it is very, very quiet. Obviously we have a very big fleet here in South Africa, ranging from Chapter 1 to Chapter 3 and this is probably even better than that -the noise is very good .*

'ATNS provides air navigation services to 10% of the world's air space, including right down to the South Pole. So as well as having worked with the A380 team to prepare the trip to Johannesburg and this morning's autoland tests, we will be looking after the aircraft when it flies over the pole heading for Sydney,' she explained

The festivities continued with a press conference in the main airport terminal, where Claude Lelaie, Jacques Rosay and Fernando Alonso were on hand to present commemorative certificates to the Minister, Ms Stander, South Africa Civil Aviation Authority CEO, Zakes Myeza and Airports Company South Africa CEO, Ms Monhla Hlahla, on behalf of Airbus.

Flight AIB 402 - 27/28 November. Jo'burg to Sydney via 90° South, 153° West

Crew - Pilots: Jean-Michel Roy, Jacques Rosay. Hugues van der Stichel and Claude Lelaie. Engineers: Fernado Alonso, Jena Piatek, Jean-francois Bousquié, Gérard Maisonneuve, and Andrew Daws. Cabin Specialists: Thorsten Drewes and Olivier Abric.

At 14.18 hours on Monday 27 November the A380 was cruising at just less than 10,000 metres at Mach 0.85 en route from Johannesburg to Sydney, yet despite the fact that this is the world's largest civil aircraft, virtually all the passengers and crew were packed into just a few square metres.

Why? Because the floor space in question was in the cockpit and beside the test flight engineers station and the A380 was just moments away from becoming the first Airbus aircraft to cross the South Pole!

At the engineers station everyone had their cameras trained on the computer display, desperate not to miss the magic moment when the latitude counter ticked through 90 degrees. There was a spot of pre-pole excitement as the heading

Over the Antarctic!

Left: The view from F-WXXL high over the ice shelf.

Below: Alain de Zotti provides a briefing as to the route being flown using the latest high-tech device!
(Photos: Airbus)

Above: the view from the vertical fin camera, showing F-WXXL over the ice.

Right: the Captain's panel showing the approach to the South Pole. (Photos: Airbus)

Left: Everyone concentrates on getting the best pictures of the Ross Mountains in the polar region.
(Photo: Airbus SAS)

Although one of the most inhospitable places on earth, the flight from Johannesburg to Sydney over the South Pole was completely uneventful. (Phots: Airbus SAS)

indicator searched for the right direction and suddenly the moment had been and gone almost before the shots are taken: though perhaps the best photo would really have been the faces of the assembled group when Alain de Zotti from the flight test support team flicked the displays off for a just a second to test everyone's reflexes!

There was a similar flurry of excitement inside the cockpit as the controls started to register the magic moment. On the navigation display there was a green line that normally indicates where the aircraft is coming from and where it is heading. As the A380 drew nearer to the pole, the line fluctuated rapidly and one end turned pink to indicate that there was no information about the direction in which the aircraft was headed. As the pole was left behind, a quick flick of a switch to effectively flip round the map that it reads and suddenly the pink appeared at the opposite end, showing that the route ahead was clear and it was now the area that the aircraft had come from that was difficult to identify though for just a few moments.

Although the detour over the pole had been primarily scheduled to check that the autopilot continues to operate normally even though it reads north in every direction, that fact almost passed unnoticed in the excitement of this historic first.

Then it was most definitely Claude Lelaie and Jacques Rosay who had their hands back on the controls as the A380 banked tightly at 40 degrees to literally pivot the around the South Pole, before heading north to Sydney

Media briefings had been held at all the airport stopovers during the route proving and Sydney was no exception. As the A380 pulled into gate 57 and the iournalists, photographers and TV crews who had been out by the runway to match the landing, made their may back to the terminal's media centre, A380 crew members Claude Lalaie, Jacques Rosay and Fernando Alonso, and A380 marketing manager Corrin Higgs were whisked through the formalities of immigration, customs and security in time to freshen up.

With seconds to spare, they joined Airbus Vice President Australia Isabelle Floret and Julieanne Alroe, General Manager Asset Planning and Services for Sydney Airport to take centre stage in the packed auditorium.

Responding to questions about the departure from Johannesburg, the crew explained that the A380 had actually established a new airport record for take-off weight, taking off at 555 tonnes, five less than its maximum weight. Even at this weight, with 20-degree heat, the A380 took off using just 3,000 metres of runway. *'Despite the detour over the South Pole, we arrived in Sydney with 40 tonnes of fuel to spare,'* said Claude.

'This shows how easily the A380 could fly direct from Johannesburg to Sydney with a full payload,' added Fernando.

When an American journalist queried why the A380 had not yet been to the United States, Claude explained that it was simply a matter of formalities: *'Because we are not a transport* company, it is a bit more difficult to arrange visas. 'We hope to take the aircraft to the US next year, but the details are still being finalised so we can't announce any dates just yet.'

Mrs. Alroe, answering questions about the impact that operating the A380 would have on local communities who already complain about airport noise said: *'The local community will benefit in the sense that the A380 will be substituting almost every other aircraft of a similar size. This aircraft is going to be a lot quieter, so we certainly hope there is going to be a big benefit for the community around the airport. That's one of the most important things about this aircraft - we are seeing big advances in noise.'*

Rounding up the conference, Mrs. Alroe went on to explain that part of the complication in preparing to accept the A380 was that much of the information about configurations is commercially sensitive and confidential, but added: *'The co-operation that we have had with both the aircraft manufacturer and the airlines has been wonderful - this is one of the best projects I've worked on.'*

Flight AIB 403 - 29 November. Sydney Australia to Vancouver Canada.

Crew - pilots: Guy Magrin, Frank Chapman, Jean-Michel Roy, Francois Fabre (EASA). Engineers: Stéphanie Vaux, Patrick du Ché, Frédéric Gagneuz, Géeard Maisonneuve and Andrew Daws. Cabin Specialists: Michel Bonnet and Michael Diesing.

The functional route proving flights were being carried out to achieve certification, but at the same time, engineers were making the most of the opportunity to fine tune various elements of the aircraft, looking for ways to make further improvements and to ensure the maximum level of maturity when airlines put the aircraft into commercial service.

Among these were the engineers involved in the A380's satellite communication svstem. Christophe Cassiau-Haurie from Flight Test Support and Flight Operations Officer, Xavier Adhémard explains: *'The A380 MSN002 is equipped with SATCOM high speed data capacity, which allows connection to the internet from the aircraft, both in flight and on the ground,'* says Christophe. *'This feature provides crews working on the aircraft with a secure connection to the Airbus network, giving them remote access to professional applications such as the Airbus Flight Operations' flight planning system or the Test Flight Engineers' Technical logbook. They can*

also access their e-mail and other applications as though they were using a standard Airbus remote connection.'

The system had been used throughout the route 'proving campaign, but on fight AIB 403, the engineers carried out a few specific tests to monitor the system's performance.

Inmarsat is a system of four satellites used by the aeronautics and maritime industries for communication: primarily voice and data based.

As Xavier explained: *'The tests on this flight involve monitoring the quality of connections using SITA services within the Inmarsat spotbeam coverage during flights in the southern hemisphere and over the Pacific Ocean. It has been tested on all of the route proving flights and used operationally on this the southern hemisphere and over the Pacific Ocean. It has been tested on all of the route proving flights and used operationally on this one, with a stable reception throughout.'*

Although the system had only been used for working purposes on MSN002, it is designed to let airlines offer passengers internet and phone connections from their seats, should they wish to integrate such facilities into their cabin configurations. It had already been fully installed on MSN007 and would be available as an option in all future A380s.

Flight AIB 404 - 30 November. Vancouver Canada to Toulouse.

Crew - Pilots: Hugues van de Stichel, Gene Arnold (FAA) Jena-Michel Roy and Jacques Rosay. Engineers: Jean-Francois Bousquié, Jean Piatek, Géard Maisonneuve and Andrew Daws. Cabin Specialists: Thorsten Drewes and Olivier Abric.

To complete the vertical circumnavigation of the world and the flight proving trials.

Overall, these flight tests had been designed to assess the general handling qualities of the aircraft, operational performance, airfield noise as well as systems operation, in normal mode, failure cases and extreme conditions. For the extreme weather trials Airbus took the aircraft from the cold of Northern Canada, to the desert heat of the Gulf and hot and high altitudes of Ethiopia and Colombia, where it yielded excellent results and in many cases surpassed its design targets.

In addition to flight test success, further highlights included airport compatibility trials with a total of 38 airports visited around the globe during which the ability to operate the A380 in the same way as existing large aircraft were demonstrated.

The A380 cabin also underwent a series of tests

Airbus flew four A380s in formation early in September 2006, hard on the heels of the maiden flight of the Engine Alliance GP7200-powered version of the European manufacturer's ultra-large airliner. The formation flight comprised aircraft MSN001, MSN002 and MSN004 - which are all powered by Rolls-Royce Trent 900 turbofans - and the Alliance-powered MSN009. (Photo: Airbus SAS)

for certification, including the successful evacuation test, performed at Airbus' Hamburg site, Germany, on 26 March 2006. During this largest ever aircraft evacuation trial 853 passengers and 20 crew members left the aircraft within 78 seconds - 12 seconds less than required, validating 853 as the maximum passenger seating capacity for the A380-800.

Although not required for certification, but part of Airbus' commitment to smooth entry into service, Airbus undertook a series of four Early Long Flights in September 2006 where over 2000 Airbus employees took part to assess the cabin environment and systems in flight. These followed a 15 hour Virtual Long Flight, that took place in May 2006 in Hamburg, where 474 Airbus employees tested cabin systems in simulated long haul conditions.

Certification is achieved!

The world's largest commercial airliner, the 555-seat Airbus A380 received joint European Aviation Safety Agency (EASA) and Federal Aviation Administration (FAA) Type Certification on 12 December 2006. The certified aircraft was powered by Rolls-Royce Trent 900 engines.

The EASA A380 Type Certificate was signed by EASA's Executive Director, Patrick Goudou; and the FAA A380 Type Certificate by John Hickey, FAA's Head of Certification The documents were handed over to Airbus' Executive Vice President Engineering, Alain Garcia. The Ceremony, held at the Airbus facilities in Toulouse, France, was attended by the Honorable Marion Blakey, FAA Administrator, and by senior officials from Civil Aviation Authorities from several countries worldwide.

'This double seal of approval represents a key milestone for the A380 programme. It recognises the quality of the work performed by all those who have worked hard for many years on the development of this superb, new technology leading aircraft. My thanks go to all of them, including to the EASA and FAA teams, for this outstanding achievement,' said Louis Gallois, Airbus President and CEO. *'But more than anything, it provides clear evidence of the technical soundness of the A380, and confirms that the aircraft is meeting or exceeding the expectations in terms of performance, range, environmental friendliness, and cabin comfort. Both our customers and their passengers will love it.'*

The Certification by the two major international governing bodies comes after the A380 successfully completed a stringent programme of certification trials which took its airframe and systems well beyond their design limits to ensure the aircraft met - or even exceeded - all airworthiness criteria. The A380 was the first aircraft to which 21st century certification standards were applied.

The flight test campaign also revealed that the aircraft was meeting the guaranteed performance both in terms of fuel burn and range. Because of its very low fuel burn, contributing to the lowest operating costs, it produced very low emissions. An environmental champion, it is also quieter than any other airliner, meeting the stringent noise restrictions at London Heathrow. The A380 also has the quietest cabin in the skies and provides a very smooth ride.

A total of five aircraft were involved in the intensive flight test programme, four of which had Rolls Royce Trent 900 engines and one was powered by Engine Alliance GP7200 engines. To date, the aircraft had accumulated over 2,600 flight hours in 800 flights, with over 80 airline and certification pilots having flown the aircraft. During its test campaign, the A380 was also welcomed at 38 airports around the world, proving its easy airport acceptance and compatibility.

Airbus took a starring role at the 2007 Paris Air Show, announcing 425 firm orders from 19 customers, along with commitments for a total of 303 additional aircraft. This confirmed the worldwide market's strong endorsement of the A380 and A350 XWB, along with its continuing demand for the A330/A340, as well as the A320 Family. Two A380s participated in the Paris Air Show, one taking part in the daily flight presentations, while the other was on display in the static area.

Into the USA!
Then the news came out that Airbus was sending not one, but two A380s to the USA for simultaneous landings on both sides of the country. The flight to New York from Frankfurt was hosted by The Port Authority of New York and New Jersey and sponsored by Lufthansa and Airbus - it would also be the first passenger flight to the continent, for it carried a full load of invited guests. onto Runway 22 Left at JFK Airport.

Not to be outdone, the second A380 was sponsored by QANTAS, Airbus and the host airport of Los Angeles and flew in from Toulouse, France.

Aviation history was finally assured on 19 March 2007 when aircraft MSN007 from Frankfurt and MSN001 from Toulouse arrived in the USA. They were timed to arrive at the same time so that both Lufthansa and QANTAS could both claim bragging rights. The media was out in full force - it must have been of particular delight to New Yorker John J Leahy as spoke at the press conference inside the terminal: *'It's a great pleasure to be here on this very special day. I think you all know that not one but two Airbus A380s flying from Europe landed in the United States - almost simultaneously, but of course the first landed at JFK! All at Airbus are immensely proud of the A380 and we're very excited to bring it to New York in partnership with Lufthansa and the Port Authority of New York and New Jersey.*

For me personally, it's a special honour too,

MSN007 F-WWJB arrives at a snowy JFK from Franfurt on 19 March 2007. (Photo: Tom Brewer)

for as a native New Yorker who went to university here and drove a yellow taxi in 1970 and brought passengers to this airport when the 747 was first beginning to operate - that was the flagship of the 20th Century - today you have seen the arrival of the flagship of the 21st Century!

It's very fitting that the first A380 passenger demonstration flight was destined for New York, for the A380 and New York City have a great deal in common - both the city and the aircraft are big!

The city and the aircraft are truly unique - when Airbus began to build the A380, the best suppliers and aerospace companies in the world came together to help us make this aircraft a reality. More than any other country in the world suppliers in the United States were chosen to supply top technology components and materials. Airbus spent about 10 billion dollars with US suppliers last year alone - and that's really important. 10 billion dollars, every year is spent with US suppliers. This aircraft is a world aircraft - built in over 30 different countries, but 400 of those suppliers are here in the United States.

Today, with 500 plus passengers arriving on the A380 route proving, Airbus, Lufthansa and the Port Authority are testing actual facilities in a real airline operating environment - this shows that the A380 works. Clearly JFK is already off the mark - ready for the A380. We salute JFK and the Port Authority of New York and New Jersey for their great work.'

Meanwhile in Los Angeles, MSN001 arrived on Runway 24 Right and taxied to the Imperial Terminal of the airport's South side to be surrounded by a ring of traffic cones and police officials. The massive A380 descended out of a dank, gray sky and made a picture-perfect landing just before 09.30, about 15 minutes after the JFK flight landed as spectators cheered from both sides of the airport. The Los Angeles flight, operated by Australian airline QANTAS, was devoid of passengers.

Whilst at LAX, the A380 underwent ground-tests including airfield maneuvers, docking at the terminal gate and ground and gate handling exercises.

Los Angeles officials had fought hard to host the A380's inaugural landing, and wrote a letter to Airbus earlier that year urging executives to reconsider plans for an initial landing only in New York. Los Angeles officials contended Airbus was reneging on a promise to make the first US stop in Los Angeles, which kept its word to speed up construction of new $9 million gate for the aircraft. Los Angeles' airport agency ultimately planned to spend about $121 million to prepare for the A380, and had already spent around $50 million to improve runway and taxiway intersections. LAX, the fifth-busiest airport worldwide, was expected to be the first US destination for the A380 when it entered commercial service. The aircraft returned to Toulouse during the evening of 20 March.

Next day, on the other side of the continent, F-WWJB hopped from JFK to Chicago's O'Hare International Airport. As with new York, it was a time for speech-making and back-slapping.

MSN001/F-WWOO captured against a grey sky as it arrives at Los Angles International. (Photo: Ricky Moon)

MSN001/F-WWOO departs LAX for Toulouse on 20 March 2007. (Photo: Rickie Moon)

Everyone was welcomed by Nuria Fernandez, the Commissioner of the Department of Aviation for the City of Chicago, on behalf of Mayor Richard M Daley.

Rosemarie Andolino, Executive Director of the O'Hare Modernisation Program. then outlined the work that was going on to ensure the A380 could use the airport. *'Our construction crews have moved more than four million cubic feet of dirt and placed 41,000 square yards of concrete as we construct three new runway projects, including one Group Six capable runway that will feature a wider, reinforced runway and taxiway built to handle the increased weight and longer wingspan of the A380. Once this work has been implimented, O'Hare will have two new Group Six runways to handle the A380.*

Alan McArtor, the Chairman of Airbus North America Holdings then addressed the assembled media: *'This is a very exciting time for us, and I hope it is for you. As an aviator you have to get excited about the aircraft we are standing in front of. In our industry we're probably growing at a rate of about 5% a year - it's even higher off the Pacific Rim. When you look at the growth economies of the world - China, India, the Middle East - and how the trade routes of the world are strengthening, Chicago sits literally at the commercial crossroads of these major trade - routes linking the nodes of commerce around the world. The A380 with it's range of eight thousand nautical miles can connect Chicago non-stop with virually all of transportation and commercial centre of the world. It's not just about range, its about economics. The seat-belt costs on this*

airplane are about 20% less than the competing airplane against which it will fly. So as an airline, you simply cannot compete against this airplane. So anyone that is flying these long, over-the-pole routes is going to have to in one way or another fly an airliner like the A380.

He then introduced Captain Carl Sigel, Executive Vice President Operations, Lufthansa. *'We are very proud to be the only airline that has part of the A380 route-proving programme. The A380 is a beautiful aircraft - I had the chance myself to fly it a few months ago and I was very astonished how comfortable and how easy it was to fly. I fly normally the A340/A330 and and I was immediately able without any training to fly the aeroplane. I made several touch-and go landings without any problems.'*

Jens Bischof, Vice President, The Americas Lufthansa: *'At the moment we're in the processs of deciding which airports we're going to serve in the future, and Chicago O'Hare is very closely under consideration. Readiness is crucial in determining the desinations for the first porfolio of flights and I am sure Chicago is doing a great job in order to get everything ready for getting the first airplanes into the area'.*

In spite of all the grandstanding, clearly here was something worth taking notice of. One member of the media wrote a telling piece: *'Despite an edict from the City of Chicago's Department of Aviation warning people away from O'Hare Airport on Tuesday, the A380 crew plunked it down nicely on runway 4 Right to the cheers of the limited crowds who were able to find a place to watch.*

The city sent out a news release Tuesday telling the local riff raff they risked their vehicles being towed if they even appeared to clutter up the roads near the World's Busiest Airport. And for those of you non-Chicagoans, yes, this is the same Mayor Richard M. Daley who sent his bulldozers out in the middle of the night a few years back to transform Meigs Field into a new lakeside park.

In a continuing search for the truth, however, this reporter risked being ticketed and towed – I had my Visa card with me just in case though – and can only say that I watched a piece of history sail by for a few moments that day.

The A380 is a massive airplane with a length not much more than a 747-400, but a girth that looks like someone jammed a dozen elephants under the skin.

What amazed me was the comprehensive technological demonstration the aircraft put on as it passed overhead.

Surely the airplane was not at maximum landing weight, but even with all the drag it surely commanded a fair amount of power to cross the threshold. And from a noise perspective passing over head, as well as the noise it generated when it went into reverse after landing, the A380, will be a very quiet, yet formidable competitor.

There's certainly plenty that has gone right in the process that brought the A380 to Chicago this week, but thousands of detours have slowed the process as well, much as it might with anyone who assumes the risks of building airplanes today. One problem is a massive credibility gap at Airbus between what the company promises and what it can deliver.

I'd like to think I was watching the vanguard of a new segment in aviation and not merely an aircraft which might follow the Concorde into the history books as a technological marvel that failed on the ledger sheet.

It was then back to New York, and then to Frankfurt.

Now it was time to hand aircraft over to the airlines and to start earning revenue.

Chapter 9

Inaugural - Singapore Airlines

We are a small red dot in South East Asia. During my school days in America, my university friends thought that Singapore is a city in China. We are proud to be given the first new generation plane to operate, and to have Sydney as the first place of call reflects close bilateral relationship between Singapore and Australia. History was indeed set today in Singapore and though I wasn't there to witness the giant plane's departure, I feel proud to be a Singaporean.

Willy Teo, Singapore

Sydney Airport, Australia - The world's largest and most luxurious passenger aircraft completed its first commercial flight Thursday, travelling from Singapore to Sydney. With 455 passengers and 30 crew aboard, including four pilots, the Singapore Airlines Airbus A380 took off from Changi Airport and landed seven hours later in the Australian city.

So said one of the many press reports recording the first commercial A380 service.

A380 9V-SKA had been delivered on 15 October 2007 and entered service on the 25 October with flight number SQ380.

Most passengers arrived at Changi Airport at around 0600 that morning, but such was the excitement that a few arrived as early at 0415! Boarding was via gate F31 where breakfast was being served and all the ceremonies would be taking place. The holding area was slightly chaotic, with people mingling around and media crowding the area as well.

After the speeches by the assorted VIPs and the cheque presentation to the Singapore Community Chest, Suite and Business class passengers and Priority Passenger Service (PPS) Club members were invited to board first, all passengers making use of the three aerobridges.

Once boarding was completed, the usual Singapore Airlines standard of service was observed. Hot towels were distributed, Capt Robert Ting came on the PA system to welcome all onboard and gave some details of the flight. Push back happened more or less on time and made the short taxi to runway 20C for takeoff. There the flight was held for just a few seconds before the throttles were opened. Much to the

With thrust reversers deployed, A380 9V-SKB slows down at the end of its landing run (Singapore Airlines)

The dedicated check-in area at Changi Airport for the 'World's first A380 Flight' on 25 October 2007.

surpise to all the passengers on board, there was hardly any noise - there simply was no roar as with other airliners.

In the hands of Capt Ting and Capt Peacock, the A380 rapidly climbed up to cruising altitude of FL370. After the seatbelt sign was turned off, the crew began handing round glasses of champagne and presenting the certificates.

About an hour into the flight, brunch was served. Being a very special event, two members of SIA's International Culinary Panel, Sam Leong of Singapore and Matthew Moran, had specially created the menus. The two men themselves were on board the flight to '...*put the finishing touches to their gourmet creations.*'

The flight went quickly, and descent into SYD began at around 1650 local. An attempt was made at the flypast over Sydney Harbour Bridge, but the low cloud cover made it impossible to view anything. The aircraft made a few turns to get back on final approach to Kingsford Smith International's runway 34L.

The A380 broke through the cloud cover and right on schedule at 1725, the approach and landing were smoothly executed touching down gently to the thunderous applause of all the

passengers on board.

SQ380 arrived at Sydney seven and a half hours after departing Changi Airport in Singapore. Passengers looked tired but happy as they came out of the arrivals gate. The street-side area of the arrivals gate was a carnival atmosphere with a three-piece band playing music, media crews speaking to passengers everywhere and passengers showing off their framed certificates of flight.

The celebratory events were, in fact, over two flights and two days; most of the seats on the two legs of this flight - outbound and return - were sold on eBay, the global online marketplace, with all proceeds donated to charities.

The auction raised around S$1.9 million, all of which would be split three ways, between Singapore and Sydney charities, and a global humanitarian organisation: one third went to Singapore's Community Chest, one third between the Sydney Children's Hospital, Randwick, and The Children's Hospital at Westmead, both in Sydney and one third to Médecins Sans Frontières.

This was not just the launch of the world's first commercial A380 service - it was also the

The vast bulk of Singapore Airlines A380 9V-SKB looms overhead on final approach. (Singapore Airlines)

launch of Singapore Airlines new 'Suites' class. As the airline was proud to state in all their material; *'Our Singapore Airlines Suites, exclusively on board the A380 aircraft, provide the distinguished few with their very own haven of tranquility. You can luxuriate in your very own private space in our largest ever armchair hand-stitched by master Italian craftsmen Poltrona Frau.*

Each individual cabin features sliding doors and window blinds, offering you the freedom to decide on the level of privacy you prefer. While the leather and wood finishes, created in soothing natural hues, enhance the sense of serenity'.

Almost certainly since the days of the pull-down beds in the Boeing Stratoliners it was possible '...*to experience the pleasure of sleeping on a distinctively designed, standalone bed; not one converted from a seat. Our signature turndown service, with fine linen and plush, full-sized pillows, ensures a restful slumber. Whether in our largest seat or on our most comfortable bed, you have countless ways to enjoy this unique, personal space'.*

Clearly is was not just the Suites that much care and attention had been lavished on, but also what went with and in them. *'Lavish in our premium offerings in Singapore Airlines Suites where you may savour our special menus,* exclusively created by our celebrated International Culinary Panel. Elegantly, exclusively designed Givenchy tableware is the perfect setting for each gourmet masterpiece.

To complement your meal, we offer a selection of the finest wines to ever grace a cellar, each thoughtfully hand-picked by our distinguished panel of wine experts. Savour our unrivalled selection of Champagne, Grand Cru red Burgundy and Second Growth Bordeaux served in crystal ware.

Revel in KrisWorld, our state-of-the-art inflight entertainment system.

An exhaustive range of entertainment options, including audio and video-on-demand, leaves you spoilt for choice, all on your very own 23-inch wide LCD screen – the largest in the sky. For business, you will find an easy-access multi-port with power supply and USB ports'.

The flight was, as could be expected, made up of a mixture of passengers who had experienced the latest word in flight travel, with a ten month-old boy from Singapore joined by a 91 year-old man from the same country. Another of the passengers, Thomas Lee from California, had also been on the world's first Boeing 747 commercial flight between New York and London in 1970.

Those on board not only enjoyed the

Certainly this is 'a class beyond First', providing the ultimate in luxury and privacy. Setting a new standard in ultimate premium air travel, the Singapore Airlines Suites features a bold and unique cabin concept where each Suite is the customer's private cabin in the sky.

Behind its discrete sliding doors is a spacious and truly personal area, with lavish furnishing and finishes. The intelligent design of the full flat bed not only offers customers the choice to rest in their preferred sleeping positions, but also allows them to sit or lounge in bed as they might in the comfort and privacy of their own home.

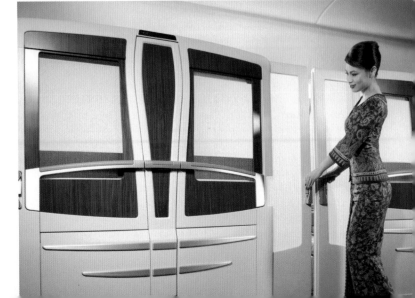

The Suites were designed for Singapore Airlines by leading French luxury yacht designer Jean-Jacques Coste, whose designs cleverly utilise space to make the flight experience even more luxurious. The Suites were manufactured by Jamco Corporationof Japan and Sicma Aero Seat of France. (all Singapore Airlines)

experience of the spaciousness and luxury setting of the vast machine, but were also treated to a champagne brunch, along with a selection of fine wines.

'I have never been in anything like this in the air before in my life,' said Australian Tony Elwood, who with his wife dined on marinated lobster and double boiled chicken soup before sipping on Dom Perignon Rosé. *'It is going to make everything else after this simply awful.'* Elwood had paid US$50,000 for two tickets.

David Henderson of Sydney watched the A380s arrival: *'I watched her approach from my office window at the end of the main runway. Traffic stopped as the plane appeared through the cloud and landed in front of us. We got a great view as she taxied to her stand. Wish I had been in seat 1A!'*

Michael Wilson, also of Sydney had a different perspective while listening to an airband radio: *'It was a little disappointing that the A380 was unable to do a low level flight down the harbour owing to low cloud and showers. It was interesting to hear the air traffic controllers calling the plane 'the big fella'.*

The media made much of the fact that the A380 'could' carry 853 passengers if configured purely for economy class. However Singapore Airlines decided instead to provide 471 seats in three classes - 12 private suites, 60 business class seats, and 399 economy-class seats.

Business class seats could be transformed into beds, while even the economy class spaces had more leg and knee room.

This 'first flight' was the culmulation of years of hard work from Singapore Airlines' Cabin Designer Mr Sim Kim Chui and Vice President, InFlight Services Ms Betty Wong in creating the ultimate A380 cabin. *'I think in the A380 for the first time we are developing all the product. Our first class, business class and new economy seat, new entertainment system, new lavatories, new cabin interiors - everything is new'*. For years, these ideas remained firmly under lock and key, for every other airline was seeking the tiniest clue as to what SIA were planning so as to outdo Sim's ideas and capture a competitive edge. *'It's not so intelligent to reveal to your competitors what you are going to do for it is easy for them to surpass you'*. All of Sim's ideas were not towards what many thought were the gimmicky ideas of casinos and jacuzzi's but in providing the passengers what he thought they really wanted - luxury and comfort.

Betty Wong: *'Being such a big aircraft and it's a clean sheet approach, everyone will be looking at what we do, and of course we intend to set the standard of premium air travel in the industry.*

Betty and her team were responsible for creating the world's first A380 travel experience. Toiletries, pillows, silverware, blankets, cutlery... every single item had to be carefully crafted to catch the passengers eyes while strictly conforming to all the regulatory standards applied to every airliner.

Betty Wong: *'We really like to give a total experience so that they can enjoy the food, wine, watch a great movie so that before they know it, it is the end of the flight - maybe they wont even want to get off!'*

Creating a hotel restaurant in the sky was not a simple task. To make sure that the A380 dining experience was the same as other inflight services SIA built a unique pressurised room to simulate high altitude air travel. In this room every meal presentation from their panel of world-class chefs was tasted to ensure that everything was perfect.

'It will feel like you're in a restaurant - you will get to pick and order things you would see on a restaurant menu and and you will eat it as if

Singapore Airlines Vice President, InFlight Services Ms Betty Wong

Singapore Airlines' Cabin Designer Mr Sim Kim Chui

you're in a restaurant' revealed Betty Wong.

The mock-ups of the new interiors - that had been three long years in the making - were finally revaled to the world's media at the SATS Inflight Catering Centre in Singapore on 17 October 2006.

The Return Flight

Next day it was time for the inaugural A380 flight from Sydney to Singapore.

Passengers were given some privileges, including a dedicated check-in, and cordoned-off drop off points. Check-in was earlier than usual to facilitate a welcome function that SIA had put together at Gate 57. Passengers from all classes mingled with champagne and finger food whilst SIA CEO Chew Choon Seng took New South Wales Premier, the Hon. Morris Iemma on a tour of the A380. SIA Chairman Stephen Lee was also present at the function.

Unfortunately, an electric storm blew up just as the aircraft's holds were being loaded, so all ground work was rapidly halted due to safety concerns for those working on the aircraft - an event which delayed the departure. Boarding was not finally called until 1700.

As in Changi the previous day, Singapore Airlines made use of the three aerobridges attached to the gate. Passengers were in effect 'pre-sorted' with Bridge 1 used for those with Suites, Bridge 2 for those in Main Deck Economy Class and Bridge 3 for those in Upper Deck –

Business Class and Economy Class.

Once passengers found their seats, they discovered a matte black laptop bag containing goodies that Singapore Airlines had provided that including a Singapore A380 model as well as a commemorative luggage tag marking the flight.

The In-Flight Entertainment System (IFE) in Singapore Airlines Economy (above) and Business (left) Class. Passengers can use USB and HDMI ports to connect their personal electronic devices to the KrisWorld IFE system, which allows them to view their own content on the high-definition screens. (Photos: Singapore Airlines)

As everybody settled down in their seats, the cabin crew started their rounds with hot towels. This crew was the same as that which operated the inaugural flight into Sydney, and they recognised a few of the passengers who came up on that flight. It seemed that the flight crew were very relaxed and enjoyed mingling and chatting with the passengers.

Captain Robert Ting came on the PA system to welcome everybody onboard, and introduce the other pilots. He also gave his thanks to ExxonMobil, who donated the jet fuel for the flight both directions.

Ground crew lined the apron watching the aircraft as it was pushed back and commenced to taxi through exits Yankee, Juliet and directly onto taxiway Alpha for 34L. The line up was smooth, and takeoff power was applied without holding.

Right: the departure gate at Kingsford Smith Airport Sydney welcomes media, business and first class passengers for the first flight back to Singapore.

Below: It seems that almost everyone wanted a picture of the Cabin Crew of SQ380 in Sydney - possibly because there seemed so many! (Photos: Annabel Chong)

Ready for take-off! A Singapore Airlines A380 departs Zurich. (Photo: Singapore Airlines)

Once again, everyone commented how quiet it was inside. At take off thrust, all that could be heard was the quiet sound of air rushing by, no noise or groans whatsoever from the engines and airframe.

A gentle, but positive rotation saw lift off after passing the Sydney Control Tower. Applause was heard all round. The A380 climbed through the cloudy Sydney evening en route to an initial cruising altitude of FL340. Step climbs were given en route and eventually a final cruising altitude of FL400 was reached.

Once the seat belt signs were turned off, the party really began. Passengers started getting up and walking around, exploring the aircraft - taking pictures and videos and generally having fun. Due to the delayed departure, a lot of passengers drank quite a bit, hence the toilets were all utilised soon after departure!

Since this was the inaugural flight, all the passengers received a certificate of flight. Premium passengers received theirs mounted, while Economy class passengers received theirs in a plastic clear folder. Each certificate was individually handed to passengers by a member of the cabin crew.

All too soon, it was time for the descent into Singapore. Captain Ting came back on the PA system to inform all of the planned approach into Singapore, as well as the fact that they would be the first passengers to experience an A380 autoland.

The flight was smooth up to this point and it got even smoother after that - the A380 hardly missed a beat. There was no fuss, no unruly wake up calls, no frightening sounds, nothing. Being on the upper deck, it was impossible to even hear the flaps or gears lowering. You are really disconnected from the flight.

Touchdown was a greaser - a total non-event, Everybody showed their appreciation for the smooth landing by applauding the computers.

A slow taxy on EP and the aircraft was soon docked at F31, the same gate from which SQ380 departed the day before. All the aerobridges were used to unload the passengers this time. A Malay percussion crew welcomed the passengers to Singapore and SIA management were on hand to greet the passengers.

The tagline used for the Singapore Airlines A380, 'Experience travel in a new light', is something nobody should ever doubt - it was time to get down to earning revenue.

Chapter 10

Into Service - British Airways

Introduction of any new airliner into passenger service can never be a quick thing. The public 'launch' event may be full of photo-opportunities and fanfare, but behind the scenes, much will have already been done over a considerable period of time. British Airways, for example, started months before taking delivery of their first machine – and that in itself was years after the interior design and layout was finalized.

Pilots require training and qualification, as do the Cabin Crew, and all the staff working at downroute locations and ground handlers need hands-on experience.

G-XLEB, British Airways' second A380, shows the size and bulk of the world's largest airliner in this head on view. (Photo: British Airways)

Flight Deck

The A380 takes superlatives to a whole new level. For British Airways variants the 747 had a maximum take-off weight of 397 tonnes - for the A380, it is 569 tonnes. The 747 has 14 cabin crew; the A380 has 22. Passenger totals for the 74 are 299/341 compared to 469 on the A380. The big gain though is in fuel savings; even with the size and weight increases the A380 has only a increase of 20% fuel burn.

British Airways became the first UK airline to operate the A380; with a total of twelve on order this was a relatively small fleet of aircraft which will only fly long-range, long haul services. The process of commissioning such a small fleet - termed the Entry Into Service (EIS) programme - was challenging, even with the use of an A380 simulator at Heathrow.

When in normal service the type each aircraft would only fly two sectors a day, yet required up to ten complete crews per aircraft to be fully trained and ready.

The first aircraft to arrive was G-XLEA, which spent most of August and September 2013 flying between European destinations from Manston in Kent and on the Heathrow to Frankfurt service. This was both to develop operational experience and to provide a high number of sectors for pilot training.

From late September sufficient experience had been gained on these short haul routes, coupled with the arrival of a second aircraft (G-XLEB) which allowed flights to be started to Los Angeles. Hong Kong was started in October, with Johannesburg online from February 2014.

Pilots everywhere found the A380 a delight to fly and benign from the handling perpective. There was no pitch power couple and the aircraft autotrims reduced workload on the flight deck. If an engine was lost, the aircraft handled most of the yaw automatically and used a much more sophisticated combination of flying controls than other types. Crews discovered that rudder input augmentation coupled with a combination of spoiler and aileron helped create a very benign and easily flyable machine.

The most noticable feature of the A380 was the huge wing, meaning that crosswind and cruise-ceiling limits are engine related. Fly-by-

Wire technology make crosswind landings straightforward by handling all the secondary roll effects from the de-crabbing yaw.

Where pilots found a considerable challenge was with aircraft momentum. The A380 weighed anything from 350 to 569 tonnes in service and, like the proverbial supertanker, once it was moving in a certain direction it took time and space to get it to go in another. This took experience and anticipation to handle.

Ground handling was another aspect that needed care, especially when responding to Air Traffic Control requests to expedite maneuvers and yet keep thrust to safe levels. As the aircraft is comparatively lightly nosewheel loaded, it can be difficult to corner at speeds greater than five knots in wet weather.

As with other current generation airliners, the amount of data available for presentation to the flight crew is enormous and could form a distraction trap for the unwary pilot, but a great deal of thought was put into the presentation and prioritisation of this information with the A380. Flight deck crew were trained in the adoption of 'Standard Operating Proceedures' (SOPs) so

that the aircraft does not distract them from their core task.

The A380 was designed from the outset to be a 'paperless' airliner with the aircraft library, charts, technical logbook and loadsheets being fully integrated into the aircraft systems. Given the world-wide radio and satellite communication network available nowadays, the flight deck crew can use the technical and load data recorded by the aircraft to cross check and approve it for performance calculations.

Cabin Crew
BAs In Flight Customer Experience Safety and Quality teams introduced a new 'Zero Harm' concept to coincide with the arrival of the A380. Their aim was to keep customers and crew safe by promoting the highest possible standards of best Standard Operating Proceedure practice. The A380 had been designed with safety in mind and all efforts were taken to ensure that key risks had been mitigated.

BAs 'safety champions' were asked how best to highlight the risks to the cabin crew community and these were identified in the

G-XLEB, British Airways' second A380 is tugged around Heathrow in the winter sunshine. (Photo: Author)

A380 as the crew rest area stairs and the front and rear staircases.

Simply by paying attention to detail, the problem with the rest-area stairs was solved by including a cut-out in the curtain so that the step was not concealed.

The wall-mounted staircase barrier on the aft stairs has two functions; to prevent the trolley from accidentally falling down the stairs when loading or unloading the after trolley lift and to stop customers using the stairs at certain times of the flight. but it must be open for taxi, take-off and landing to enable quick in case of an emergency.

British Airways A380s - as were many other A380s - were equipped with galley grab handles so that the crew had something specifically designed to hold on to in the event of unexpected turbulence.

Cabin crew training was intense; members had to adapt to the new electronic doors and the state of the art technology systems on board. Certain crew members were designated SMEs - Subject Matter Experts. This role was about

The British Airways A380 made its debut at the Royal International Air Tattoo on 19 July 2013 as it flew in formation with the famous Red Arrows above RAF Fairford in Gloucestershire. British Airways' senior first officer Peter Nye was at the controls with Captain Charles Everett in command of the aircraft. (Photo: Author)

delivering consistent customer service to ensure that every customer received a quality personal service and that the Cabin Staff product knowledge and delivery was excellent. Training ensured that the new service hallmarks were brought to everyone with reminders that the standards had to be delivered every time. Simple things like a warm welcome were so important as they set the standards for the rest of the flight.

With four standards of class on board, this gave a wider passenger profile from leisure to business and there were things on board that

could enhance the passenger travelling experience. Things like the mood lighting in every cabin, which could be changed - particularly in the evening and at night, to improve the customer's surroundings.

The hand run bar service in Club World was thought to be much more personal and meant that no trolleys or carts cluttered the aisles and the five course taster menu in First Class developed with the Langham Hotel, was expected to be another highlight of service.

British Airways' A380s are configured to

carry 469 passengers across four classes of cabin classes – with lucrative First and Business class passengers paying a hefty premium for the privilege. In First, there are 14 seats in a very spacious 1-2-1 layout across the lower deck. Club World has 44 seats ina 2-4-2 layout with a central pair of seats facing the same way. Also in the lower deck are 199 World Traveller seats in a 3-4-3 layout.

Upstairs are 53 Club World seats in a 2-3-2 layout, 55 World Traveller Plus seats in a 2 -3-2 layout and 104 World Traveller seats in a 2-4-2 layout.

The airline announced that the first long-haul return flight from London Heathrow to Los Angeles on 24 September would be priced from £621 in economy to £2,550 in business and £3,799 in First, while the first Hong Kong return on 22 October would be priced from £688 in economy to £2,499 in business and £5,800 in First.

Legroom is 31 inches in World Traveller class, 38 inches in World Traveller Plus, there's a 6ft-long bed in Club World and a luxurious 6ft 6 inch-long bed in First Class.

A BA spokesperson stressed that the new economy seats have been cleverly designed to be thinner-backed and hollowed out to increase seating space for passengers.

Base Staff and Route Planning
As with all other departments, preparations for introducing the A380 into service had been going on for months. Staff working at downroute locations selected as 'first service' routes were also working hard to ensure the highest possible level of service was provided to customers from the very first flight. A good example was BA's Hong Kong base, where International Cabin Crew (ICC) Base Manager Jolene Ho started preparing for the impact the new A380 service would have since the route was announced in March 2013.

Hong Kong was regarded by British Airways as almost the perfect A380 route, for with one of the world's major finance and business hubs. Hong Kong is the home of most of the world's leading banks and also the base for many manufacturing industries, including print,

The flightdeck of an A380, parked on Stand E15, Hong Kong International Airport, known locally as Chek Lap Kok Airport. With increasing demand from operators to use the A380, HKIA operates three parking stands that can accommodate it. In July 2010, the first stand with three aerobridges entered service. Located at Gate E15, the stand allows the passengers on a fully loaded A380 to disembark within twelve minutes, three minutes faster than a stand with two air bridges. (Photo: British Airways)

publishing and food. Many travellers use Hong Kong as a gateway to the wider southeast Asia region that includes China, the retail and clothing industry playing a major part in this demand and the fleshpots of Macau with its high rolling casinos also attracting many big spenders

The main competition for BA came from Cathay Pacific and Virgin Atlantic. Cathay offers much more in terms of onward connections with their long-established reach across the region.

British Airways saw the London Heathrow to Hong Kong service as a means to link the two financial capitals - the network planning teams analyse huge amounts of data and look for opportunities to match aircraft to routes - Given the importance of Los Angeles and Hong Kong as key cities, as well as their distance from London, BA felt that these two initial destinations would give the best returns and their customers would get exectly the kind of experience that they would expect from the BA brand.

British Airways knew that the A380 was more fuel efficient than its predecessors and also generated 50% less noise than its nearest rival. With 469 seats on board divided into four classes it offered much more capacity using fewer take-off and landing slots - perfect for the Hong Kong route.

Jolene Ho knew that because of the size of the aircraft, her team of 74 ICCs would have to increase, and that due to time constraints, recruitment would have to start immediately. This took a large amount of co-operation between area managers, Manpower and Scheduling departments to set up the New Entrance Courses. Ensuring the new and existing members of the team were fully trained on the aircraft and its systems was also a challenge.

New entrant training could take five to six weeks, and the logistics involved in getting new and existing staff trained without impacting on the current service was also problematic.

As Jolene said in BA Cabin Crew News: *'The training is crucial - not just the familiarisation with a brand new aircraft, but also with the service standards as there is a much larger premium area on the A380.*

I was very excited to hear that Hong Kong had been chosen as one of the key routes for the A380. I was very proud that my team was going to be one of the first to serve on this exciting new aircraft, though I knew it would mean a lot of hard work for us all'.

As with all the downroute locations, a focus on the commerical elements of the new service along with identifying local corporate accounts would help the teams. Servicing such a high profile aircraft could be seen as daunting, but Jolene Ho was confident that her team would rise to the occasion: *'...we will be working with the commerical and marketing teams to analyse the business reasons for choosing Hong Kong as one of the key routes for the A380 and looking at local Gold Card and Premium customers. We want to talk to our customer knowledgeably. The crew are looking forward to this exciting new challenge. I think they feel a bit of a responsibility to be experts on the route and the new plane, but I am confident that they have a lot of support and a fantastic attitude. We have a very established base here and this is an effective team'.*

'The Great Day' Arrives

For all the high-tech and glitz, it started with bacon butties, such a typically British thing. But then, there's nothing better on a cool and breezy morning at London Heathrow when staff, media and exhibitors gathered under leaden skies at the Maintenance Base. Bacon butties are exactly the sort of thing that only an engineer would understand!

Much was planned for the arrival of their first A380 at London Heathrow. Hundreds were on hand to greet G-XLEA in the hands of Captain James Basnett on it's arrival at Heathrow on Thursday 4 July, with 380 British Airways employees on the ground to walk alongside it.

Special live TV broadcasts of the A380's arrival were shown on screens at major locations, hosted by Sky Sports' Mark Durden-Smith and BA's own Nicola Pearson and a commemorative version of BA's 'Up to Speed' staff newspaper was printed to celebrate the occasion.

First to be interviewed was Nick Swift, BAs Chief Financial Officer. *'It's a fantastic day for BA. By happy co-incidence the new aircraft arrive at the start of the second half of our five year plan. The aircraft will give us capacity for growth because they carry more customer and they will save is loads of fuel'.*

Around 50 people were booked on board the flight from Toulouse, where an official hand-

BA's CEO Keith Williams and Airbus Chief Executive Fabrice Brégier, along with BA Chairman Martin Broughton are almost mobbed by cheering staff as they de-plane from 'LEA. (Photo: British Airways)

over ceremony took place between Airbus officials and CEO Keith Williams Other passengers included VIPs, journalists and competition winner Paul Cosgrove. Newcastle contact agent Phillip Ma won a BA 'Pimp my Plane' competion with his London Skyline design and Heathrow Turnaround Manager Cosgrove won the competion to name Phillip's design with 'One London One World'.

Twenty-two cabin crew members were also prepared to provide the first service on the A380 after weeks of training.

The crew for this first BA flight was as follows. On the flight deck were pilots Captain James Basnett, Captain Dave Thomas and Senior First Officer Peter Nye. In the cabins were Customer Service Manager (CSM) Robert Nichol and Louise Davidson: Future Talent CSM Joshua Raven and Douglas Moore. The main crew consisted of Janine Brooks, Jeffrey Callinan, David Warren, Matthew Henwood, Gary Goding, Sophie Jupp, Paul McGowan, Natalie Fraser, Jade Podmore, Alexandra Phipps, Claire Thorndale, Daniel Randall, Georgina Proddow, Cassie Patton, Colleen Gray, Chloe Pearson and Simone Egidi.

After touching down at Heathrow, the A380

was tugged to park up for a photo call next to another new arrival, the Boeing 787, which joined the fleet just a few days earlier.

'These arrivals mark a historic moment for our airline - our first new aircraft types in 17 years and a spectacular demonstration of our £5 billion customer investment programme,' said Keith Williams to those gathered. *'Planning started over six years ago but over the past six months we've moved into full throttle. Teams from across the airline have come together to ensure our people are trained and prepared. I want to say a massive thank you to everyone who has been involved in getting us to this point'.*

Following the arrival of the new aircraft, final preparations were made for the first customers to step on board. Ground trials took place over the next four weeks, with colleagues volunteering to take part in simulated flights.

Garry Goding is a SME on the BA A380 Fleet, and was on the first delivery flight. *'I felt incredibly proud and and privileged to be part of such an historic day that will have huge positive implications for our future.*

It was a once-in-a-lifetime occasion, so it was a real honour to be chosen to represent

BRITISH AIRWAYS

UP to speed special

JULY 5, 2013

They're here!

A publicity view of the interior of a British Airways A380 first class cabin. The 'ribbon' motif on the bulkhead is a stylised, much modified version of the old British Overseas Airways Corporation 'Speedbird' design. (Photo: British Airways)

British Airways on such a high profile flight to show our brand of customer service excellence to the rest of the world.

I only found out when my July roster was published. I knew the aircraft delivery was the July 4 from Toulouse and when I saw it on my roster, I had to look twice to be sure! It was an incredible feeling to know I would be a part of the beginning of a new era.'

BA Chief Executive Keith Williams wrote to the staff not long after the arrival of the first aircraft: *'I was fortunate to be on board our first A380 as it landed at Heathrow. Our first two 787s have also arrived. This is a landmark moment and a fundamental part of our business plan. Together, these new aircraft types take us a step closer to our vision to be the most admired airline.*

The A380 brings a new dimension to our long-haul flying. It is the largest commercial aircraft ever designed and will bring us new flexibility in operating from Heathrow and other slot-constrained airports. Customers will love the space and light on board, and the aircraft's excellent noise and emissions performance will help us make big strides towards our ambitious environmental targets.

These are our first new aircraft types for 17 years and, combined with the the expertise of our people and their commitment to delivering outstanding service, I am confident that this will result in a truly enhanced travel experience for our customers.

Since we first placed the orders for our 12 A380s and for the 42 787s in 2007, hundreds of colleagues have been involved in preparing for their arrival in to our Fleet - selecting routes, checking infrastructure, agreeing commercial deals, designing cabins, and training for maintaining, operating and providing outstanding customer service on these great aircraft. I am proud of the great team effort that has made these arrivals possible.

I'd like to extend my heartfelt thanks to everyone who has worked on these programmes, volunteered for the trials and who will welcome our customers on board in September when the Dreamliner heads to Toronto and when the A380 makes its inaugural flight to Los Angeles. We can all be very proud'.

Chapter 11

Turn Around - Emirates

EK1/UAE1 - DXB/LHR A388 A6-EEC STD: 03.45 ATD 03.49 STA: 1135 Landed 11.23. The slip from the Station Manager meant that Emirates flagship flight number EK1, also known as UAE1, flown this day by A380-861 A6-EEC was due to depart Dubai at 03.45am GMT (7.45am local), but actually departed four minutes late at 03.49. The flight was scheduled to arrive at London Heathrow at 11.35am

Emirates, the airline...
The airline itself is a subsidiary of The Emirates Group, which is wholly owned by the government of Dubai's Investment Corporation of Dubai. It is the largest airline in the Middle East, operating nearly 3,400 flights per week from its hub at Dubai International Airport, to more than 150 cities in 74 countries across six continents. Cargo activities are undertaken by the Emirates Group's Emirates SkyCargo division.

At the time of writing, the airline ranks among the top ten carriers worldwide in terms of passenger kilometres, and has become the largest airline in the Middle East in terms of revenue, fleet size, and passengers carried. In 2012 the airline was the fourth-largest airline in the world in terms of international passengers carried, and the fourth-largest in the world in terms of scheduled passenger-kilometres flown. The airline was also the third-largest in terms of scheduled freight tonne-kilometres flown. The company also operates four of the world's longest non-stop commercial flights, from Dubai to Los Angeles, San Francisco, Dallas/Fort Worth, and Houston.

During the mid-1980s, Gulf Air began to cut

Emirates A380-861 A6-EEC comes 'over the hedge' into London's Heathrow Airport. The landing speed of this gentle giant can be as little as 130 knots. Visible is the huge 'Emirates' name painted against a red background on the aircraft's belly that is visible even when the aircraft is overflying at 36,000 feet on a clear day! (author)

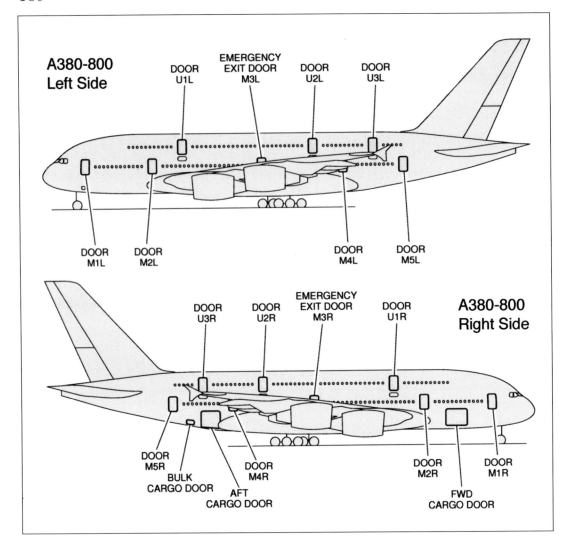

In order to understand an aircraft turn-around - more formally called 'Aircraft Servicing Arrangements' - is is necessary to understand 'what goes where'. The illustration above shows both the location and designation of all passenger and cargo doors on an A380-800 - the 'M' stands for Main, as in Main Deck, the 'U' for Upper Deck.

The forward and aft cargo bays are for either palletised or containerised cargo, the small (in relative terms) Bulk Cargo bay is for 'loose' cargo, such as the luggage of passengers who arrived too late at the check-in for their luggage to go into the containers, or for 'live' freight, such as domestic pets or animals for zoos or breeding programmes.

The diagram opposite shows a typical ramp layout, and the various Ground Servicing Equipment items in position during a typical turnround scenario. Each operator will have its own specific requirements and regulations for the positioning and operation on the ramp. Indeed, when the diagram is compared to the photographs, it is clear that Emirates operate a number of differences, not least that they use three passenger air bridges.

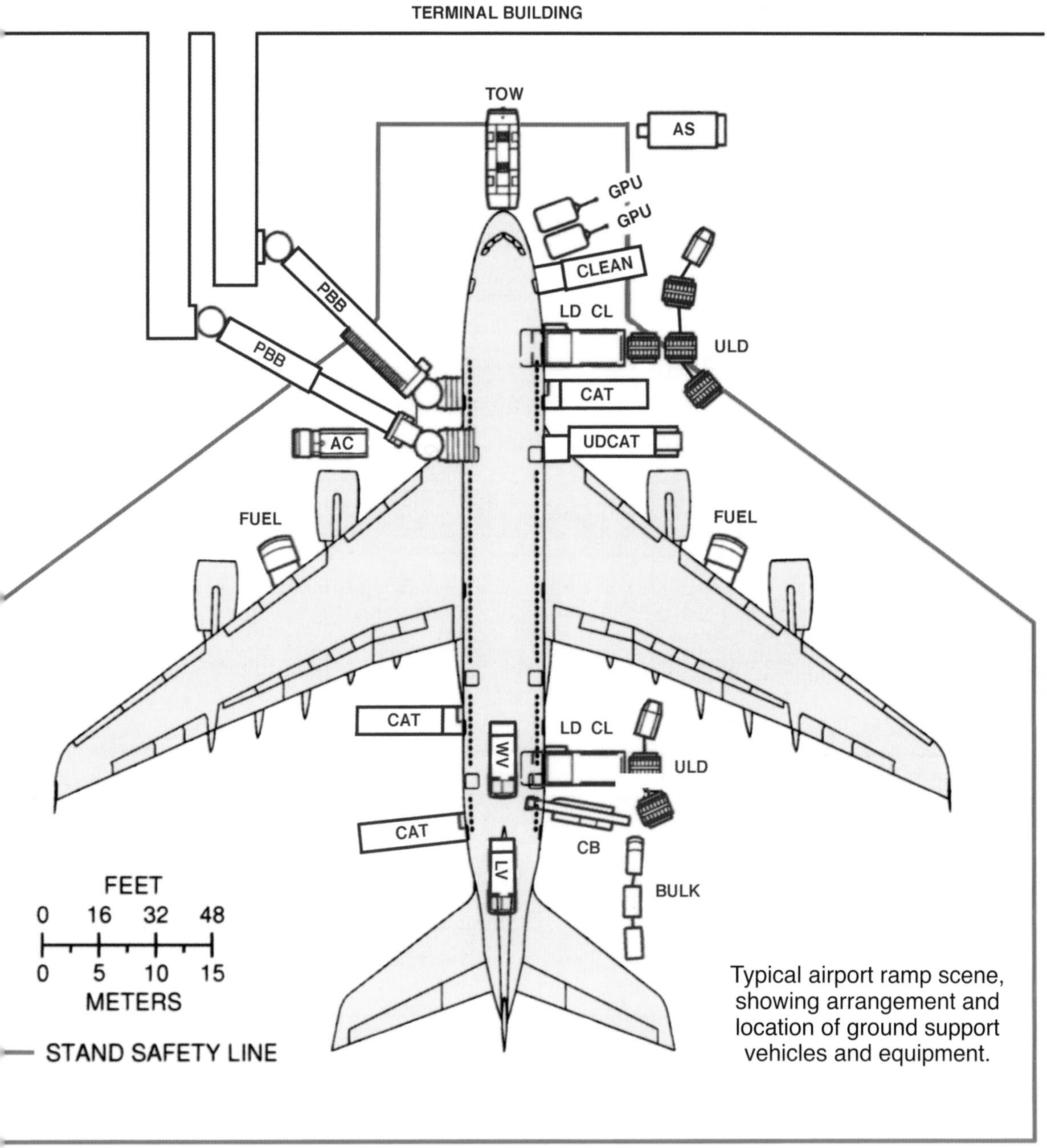

TERMINAL BUILDING
TOW
AS
GPU
GPU
CLEAN
PBB
PBB
LD CL
ULD
CAT
UDCAT
AC
FUEL
FUEL
CAT
WV
LD CL
ULD
CAT
CB
LV
BULK
FEET
0 16 32 48
0 5 10 15
METERS
STAND SAFETY LINE

Typical airport ramp scene, showing arrangement and location of ground support vehicles and equipment.

Key to equipment and devices

AC	Air Conditioning Unit
AS	Air Start Unit
BULK	Bulk Train of cargo containers
CAT	Catering Truck
CB	Conveyor Belt
CLEAN	Cleaning Truck
FUEL	Fuel Hydrant Dispenser or Tanker
GPU	Ground Power Unit
LDCL	Lower Deck Cargo Loader
LV	Lavatory Vehicle
PBB	Passenger Boarding Bridge
TOW	Tow Tractor
UDCAT	Upper Deck Catering Truck
ULD	Unit Load Device Train
WV	Potable Water Vehicle

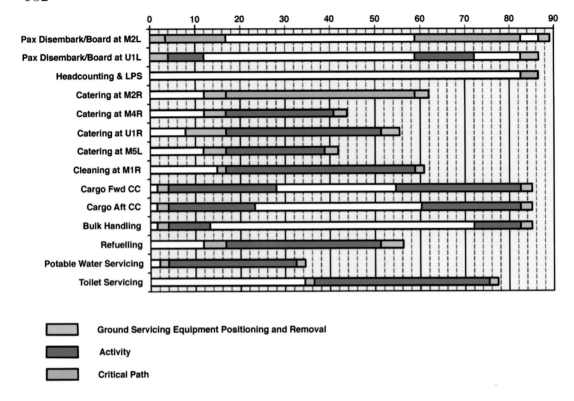

Airlines make great use of charts so that everyone is aware of what has to be done and when it has to be done and where it has to be done, given a particular set of circumstances. Although Emirates currently operate a 120 minute turn-around at London Heathrow, the chart above demonstrates a typical turn-around for a 90 minute aircraft servicing operation using a pair of air bridges. The white zones are for when 'nothing is happening' on that particular task. The Critical Path' denotes something that has to be done in the allocated time.

back its services to Dubai. As a result Emirates was conceived in March 1985 with backing from Dubai's royal family, with Pakistan International Airlines providing two of the airline's first aircraft on wet-lease. It was required to operate independent of government subsidies, apart from $10 million in start-up capital. The airline became headed by Ahmed bin Saeed Al Maktoum, the airline's present chairman. In the years following its founding, the airline expanded both its fleet and its destinations. In October 2008, Emirates moved all operations at Dubai International Airport to Terminal 3 to sustain its rapid expansion and growth plans.

Emirates operates a mixed fleet of Airbus and Boeing wide-body aircraft and is one of the few airlines to operate an all-wide-body aircraft fleet, at the centre of which is the Boeing 777. Emirates also has orders for 140 Airbus A380s and became the second operator of the type after Singapore Airlines.

Emirates has built up a strong brand name as a leader in the aviation industry, particularly in terms of service excellence, and its very rapid growth, coupled with consistent profitability. Emirates has won numerous awards – it was ranked eighth by Air Transport World for 'Airline of the Year' in 2012. The award has been given based on recognition of its commitment to safety and operational excellence, customer service trendsetters, financial condition including a 25-year consecutive annual profit. The airline was voted Airline of the Year in 2013. The same week this chapter was photographed, the airline announced at the Dubai Air Show that it had just ordered a further fifty A380s from Airbus, such was its confidence in the type.

The flight to London
A6-EEC took off from Dubai International Airport on Runway 30L - climbing out to the northwest before heading up Persian Gulf. It flew over Kuwait City, through Iraq, over Bagdad, into Turkey, then over the Black Sea,

crossing the coast into Romania over Constantia. By now the A380 was cruising at 40,000 feet, speed 460 knots. This morning Romanian airspace was relatively quiet as usual. Over Hungary, into Austria passing just below Vienna, then into Germany and the crowded skies of Western Europe. One hour out of Heathrow and the A380 was abeam Würzburg. It was then into Belgium, overhead Liege, briefly entering Dutch airspace before heading to cross the coast of the European mainland at Knokke-Heist. By now the airliner was at the top of the cruise, still at 40,000 feet, flying at 525 knots.

The descent from altitude started immediately the coast was crossed, some 260 km out of London. Approach into the capital followed what is almost standard procedure, descending over the North Sea heading towards Clacton, then a series of heading changes over Essex that amounted to almost 180 degrees before overflying North London and the Olympic Park at 4,000 feet then turning almost 180 degrees again to give the passengers great views of central London before joining the train

of aircraft on approach to Runway 27L. The A380 'crossed the fence on finals' at 132 knots, landing a few minutes early at 11.23am.

When taxiing around Heathrow, standard procedure as recommended by Airbus is to use the well-positioned taxi-cameras, located in the aircraft's centreline behind the nosewheel, which display on the pilot's primary flight display. Pilots claim that this allows the nose gear to be placed accurately on the centre line, and that it is extremely easy to taxi on congested ramps and narrow runways. At night, specific lights are located under the wing to provide illumination for these cameras.

A6-EEC came to a halt at Stand 307. Wheel chocks were put in place, the engines shut down and aircraft electrical power transferred to 'ground'.

A sophisticatedly choreographed ballet can only succeed on the stage if every movement has been intensively rehearsed in advance and all concerned are in harmony. The situation is similar with the A380. The airline has developed a meticulous schedule which coordinates all the

Emirates A380-861 A6-EEC at Stand 307, London Heathrow. Three jet bridges are in place, allowing the passengers to deplane. The furthest jet bridge from the camera is to the upper deck, the lower two to Doors ML1 and ML2. (author)

Ground power for A380 'EC, snaked out along the yellow trunking, then up into the aircraft via the red-coloured cables into the Electrical Connection Panel by the nosewheel. (both author)

NOSE LANDING GEAR

GROUND OPENING HANDLE
ACCESS DOOR
133AL

GROUND
ELECTRIC
CONNECTION

necessary services. Only when everyone plays their part according to the plan, is it guaranteed that an aircraft that has just landed can be processed speedily and take off again with a new load of passengers.

For this 'pit-stop' around 70 people work on the aircraft between flights. The turn-around of any aircraft within a two hour deadline has to be an enormous orchestrated symphony of different teams working together in perfect harmony - and with an aircraft the size of an A380, it is doubly so. It is probably best to think of the area around the aircraft in terms of specific zones: Front Left, Front Right, Rear Right, Rear left and Belly.

The extensive pit stop for the new queen of the skies has a previously unknown dimension: when an A380 has reached its parking position, 20 service vehicles simultaneously dock alongside it—more than ever before. Refuelling, fresh catering supplies, loading and unloading baggage, cleaning wash-rooms, supplying fresh water and electricity, engineering check—the list of activities is long and each one must be perfect. Up to 70 people are involved in quickly making the Airbus ready for take-off once again.

The first items in place after the aircraft arrived 'on chocks', earthed and then connected to ground power, are the three air bridges connecting aircraft to the passenger terminal, driven into place in the Front Left area - two for the main, and one for the upper deck. Three air bridges were needed by Emirates to minimise the chaos of deplaning. When fully loaded there could be 530 passengers aboard: 14 in First Class, 90 in Business Class and 426 in Economy. Given the propensity for every passenger to head for the exit the moment the aircraft stops, Emirates has a tried and tested formula in place for getting everyone smoothly off as quickly as possible.

Even before the last passengers have walked away up the air bridge, an army of cleaners have boarded. Obviously the upper deck has far fewer passengers to deplane than the main deck, and as that level is usually empty first, some of the team of 32 cleaners start work up there.

Whether catering or cleaning, each service provider must stick to the plan and precisely observe the time schedule for approaching and leaving the aircraft. The various service providers must not hinder each other and each one must

With three air bridges in place the Front Left quadrant of the area around the aircraft becomes quite difficult to access, for despite the size of the A380 it is remarkably low to the ground. (author)

Under the belly of the beast! Ground vehicles are everywhere - the cab of the truck of the left belongs to a scissor-lift wagon supporting a catering supply container to the main deck. The flatbed truck is the 'Potable Water' supply wagon pumping fresh drinking water up into the holding tank. The two vehicles on the right are a conveyor belt angled into the extreme rear cargo area, behind which is the Scissor lift cargo container handler for the rear main cargo hold. (author)

know exactly what the other is doing. This applies particularly to the work on board—because up to 50 persons have jobs to do aboard the aircraft. Here again, there are fixed scenarios. Every process is organized, every move clearly defined. To prevent even the smallest jam on board and save further time, a 'Highway Code' was introduced for all on board. Always move to the left, in other words, anti-clockwise, is the traffic rule in the cabin of the new Airbus.

With the incoming passengers and crew de-planed, the turn around crew can properly start work. Outside, the aircraft is re-fuelled direct 'from the mains' - gone are the days of fuel bowsers parked alongside. Fresh water - 1362 litres worth - is loaded from a potable water bowser and waste water is collected by the delightfully named 'honey cart' from the four waste water tanks on board, two 375 litres tanks for the upper deck, and two 675 litre tanks for the main deck.

Used linen is gathered in sacks by door ML5 - 'Main Left Five' - ready for collection. It is then either laundered or disposed of.

While working under the aircraft, staff have to be constantly aware of ice-cold water dripping down their necks, for as the aircraft descends from 40,000 feet into warmer, moist air ice forms on the airframe. This can remain on the underside of the surfaces for some considerable time, as can be clearly seen here from the different colours. It is not unknown for the aircraft to require the undersides to be de-iced before take off .

Airbus also maintain a fleet of engineers at Heathrow in case they are needed to supply specialist advice. (author)

Above: On the left hand side of the rear of the aircraft, a pair of Do & Co catering trucks are in position. The third truck is for aircraft cleaning.

Below: A City of London Animal Reception Centre truck collects a number of pets unloaded down the conveyor from the rear bulk cargo hold, aft of the main rear cargo bay door. (both author)

Freight - either palletised or in containers - is removed from the aft cargo hold.

The temporarily empty rear cargo hold, showing the roller-track flooring.
(both author)

Above: In the Front Right quadrant is the forward cargo hold

Below: The forward cargo hold. (both author)

Above and right: positioning the catering truck for the upper deck forward galley is critical - the location of the door can be seen above the wing on the opposite page..

...clearance between the leading edge of the wing is about eighteen inches, more or less the same amount as between the truck and the inboard engine cowl. The catering truck in this position has not only the extending walkway, but also the entire front end of the truck body extends out. (all author)

All the pictures on the next four pages relate to the numbers on the seating plan.

Left: Picture 1. On the main deck looking aft with a dedicated cleaning crew member replacing disposable headrest covers.

Right: Picture 2. Looking forward with cleaning crew working after, cleaning seatbacks and floor. (Photos: all author)

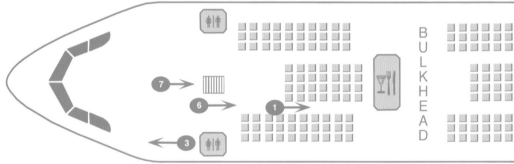

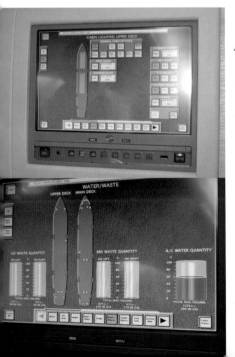

Left: Picture 3. A montage of two of the Cabin Services Display Screens showing the door status and the amount of water on board available for passenger use.

Right: Picture 4. Looking forward with cleaning crew working after cleaning the seatbacks and floor.

Left: Picture 8.
Inside one of the
main deck galleys.

Right: Picture 7.
The forward, or
'Grand' staircase to
the upper deck,
situated in the
forward vestibule.

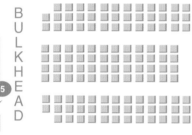

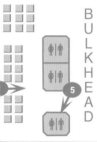

Left: Picture 5.
One of the standard
economy class
toilets.

Right: Picture 6.
Just inside the
forward vestibule,
looking back
alongside the
staircase into the
main economy cabin.

Moving up to the Upper Deck.

Left: Picture 9. Inside one of the two famous showers aboard the Emirates A380. The floor is heated. A traffic light system of warning lights inside the shower tells the occupant how much time they have left.

Right: Picture 10. At the top of the Grand Staircase is a small 'welcome on board' drinks area.

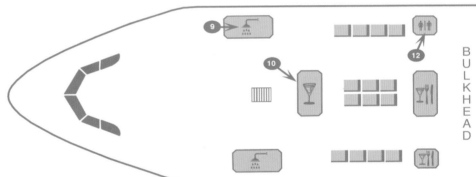

Left: Picture 11. A typical business class flat-bed seat with in-seat power supply for laptops along with extra-large table, a large-screen personal entertainment system and a built-in mini-bar.

Right: Picture 12 shows one of the Business Class toilets.

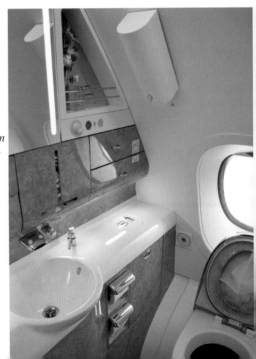

Pictures 13, 14 and 15 show the 'mood lighting' that changes from white for mid-day through to deep, dark purple for night above the desert.

The colours change between about six different shades depending on the time of day outside. Oh, and the ceiling lights up with a starry night sky when it gets dark outside!

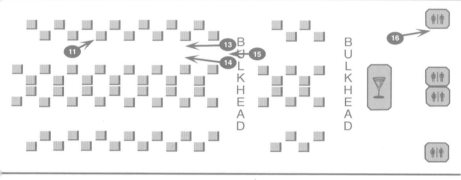

Left: Picture 16 is to the rear of the Emirates A380 Upper Deck, where there are more galleys, toilets and a further staircase, mainly used by the flight attendants to get between the upper and main decks.

(Photos: all author)

The rear public areas of the upper deck - the bar is not onlyclosed and custom-sealed as the aircraft is on the ground, but also covered with its grey goatskin protector to save the onyx top against the cleaners!

The lounge area either side of the bar, again with goatskin protectors over the highly polished wooden dividers. The curved seating areas on both sides of the bar have seat-belts for use in times of turbulence! (Photos: author)

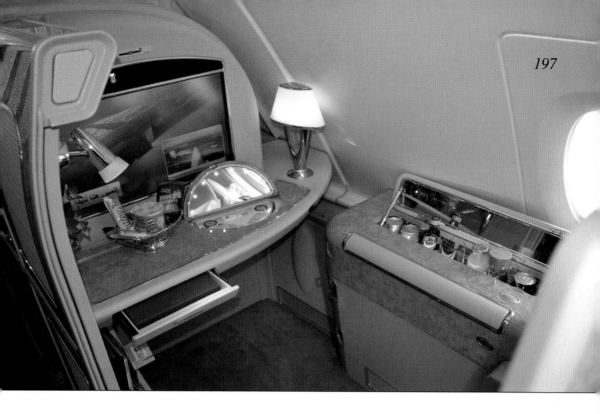

One of the First Class Private Suites that contain everything that a discerning passenger could possibly want. Each suite comes fully equipped with a sliding door, a personal mini-bar, adjustable ambient lighting, and its own vanity table, mirror, wardrobe, and privacy divider for central suites. As Emirates say in their passenger material 'And if you want to stretch out and sleep, our crew will convert your seat to a fully flat bed with a mattress, so you can arrive at your destination totally refreshed.'

A6-EEC loads the last of the underfloor cargo and prepares to depart as EL02 just as A6-EDU operating as EK29 arrives from Dubai. (Photo: Author)

Passenger's baggage - no longer carried 'loose' in the holds, but pre-loaded into shipping containers - is removed on scissor lifts, along with any cargo and courier items. On this particular flight some 'live cargo' had been carried, and this was unloaded down a conveyor belt from the extreme rear 'bulk cargo' hold - that also carried a aircraft towbar in case the aircraft was diverted to an airport that was not equipped for handling an A380. On this particular flight there were a number of pet dogs on board that were collected and taken to the City of London Animal Reception Centre for their own passport and immegration checks.

On board in the cabins all the 'used' linen was gathered up and put into bags, ready to be replaced. 'Linen' does not just mean towels - it's blankets from throughout the aircraft, duvets from First Class, disposable headrest covers, napkins... everything has to be replaced after every flight. Likewise, all used in-flight entertainment headsets are gathered up and replaced. Such is the quantity on an Emirates A380 that they designate a specific door - ML5 - for that purpose.

The detritus of the incoming flights catering is removed from the galleys and fresh, pre-prepared food - at the time of writing supplied in London by Do & Co airline caterers - is loaded in three positions, two at the rear of the aircraft, and one at the front, at a near over-wing position. Extra-

special care has to be taken when driving the loader into position for this task, as the truck is very close to one of the engines, and even closer to the leading edge of the wing before the truck body is raised elevated.

The food is placed in storage in the aircraft galleys and once the cleaning crews have removed all the rubbish, replaced the linen and checked the seat-back stowage the floors of the cabins are cleaned.

The arrival of the incoming crew marks almost the end of the turnaround and the start of the new flight. Once their personal bags are stowed, the first thing is the security check, through all the cabins and areas, followed by a double check that the aircraft is ready for the incoming passengers.

Boarding is on two levels, via three jetways, so even through there is is almost certainly more passengers boarding than on a 747 the process tends to be much more smoother. First and Business class board from an second floor lounge and an upper level jetway, while Ecomony passengers use two jetways from a lower level gate.

Once all the passengers are settled, the numbers check with the manifest, then the aircraft can be buttoned up.

Ground power is disconnected, checks are made that all ground vehicles have been moved away and the aircraft tug is connected to the nosewheel, ready to start pushback from the stand.

A6-EEC, now operating as Emirates EK02 from London Heathrow to Dubai is pushed back. (Photo: author)

Chapter 12

En Route - QANTAS

Aviation in Australia stretches back to the early pioneering days of manned and powered flight. In Australia, its development has been significant because of the vast interior of the country where long distances were a hindrance to many services. Until the Second World War, Australia was one of the world's leaders in aviation in terms of both air mileage and prominent aviation pioneers.

After the early development of powered flight in Australia in 1910, various air services were established: passenger and cargo transport, airmail, medical, and search and rescue services. The development of military aviation from 1912 and the engagement of the Australian Flying Corps in the First World War contributed greatly to pilot training and investment in infrastructure. Since the first air trial between England and Australia in 1919, international aviation has also played an important part in Australian aviation history.

Air trials between England and Australia were a high priority for civil aviation in the second decade of

the 20th Century. A prize was offered by the Australian Government for the first flight from England to Australia to be completed in 30 days. Ross Smith and Keith Smith won that prize in December 1919 when they touched down in Darwin in their Vickers Vimy.

In 1928, Bert Hinkler left England for Australia, following the same route that the Smiths had flown in 1919. After just 15 days he landed in Darwin, a little more than half the time of the Smiths' flight. An instant national hero, Hinkler received a special prize from the Government.

Charles Kingsford Smith was a pioneering aviator who flew across the Pacific from America to Australia in 1928 with Charles Ulm. In 1930, he soloed from London to Australia in 9 days 22 hours. Then in 1934, he and P G Taylor flew the transpacific route from Australia to America. On 10 November 1935, Kingsford Smith and his co-pilot died trying to set another England-to-Australia flight record when their aircraft went down off the coast of Burma.

Back in 1935 when this poster for a joint QANTAS/Imperial Airways' service to from England to Australia and return was produced, ten and a half days represented tremendous speed over the shipping lines six weeks or more.

In August 1920, former AFC officers Hudson Fysh and Paul McGinness bought an Avro aircraft and established what later became known as the Queensland and Northern Territory Aerial Service (then termed and written as Q.A.N.T.A.S). By 1922, a scheduled mail service operated between Charleville and Cloncurry, and operations had moved from Winton to Longreach. By 1927, the service had extended first to Camooweal, then Normanton. In 1929, the route extended to Brisbane with the company moving its headquarters there.

In October 1934 The MacRobertson Trophy Air Race - known as the London to Melbourne Air Race - took place as part of the Melbourne Centenary celebrations. The race was devised by the Lord Mayor of Melbourne, and a prize fund of A$75,000 was put up by Sir Macpherson Robertson, a wealthy Australian confectionery manufacturer, on the condition that the race be named after his MacRobertson confectionery company.

The race was organised by the British Royal Aero Club, and would run from RAF Mildenhall in East Anglia to Flemington Racecourse, Melbourne, a distance of approximately 11,300 miles. There were five compulsory stops: Baghdad, Allahabad, Singapore, Darwin and Charleville, Queensland; otherwise the competitors could choose their own routes. A further 22 optional stops were provided with stocks of fuel and oil by Shell and Stanavo.

Take off date was set at dawn - which happened to be 06.20 on 20 October 1934. By then, the initial field of over 60 machines had been whittled down to 20, including the three purpose-built de Havilland DH.88 Comet racers, two of the new generation of American all-metal monoplane passenger transports, and a mixture of earlier racers, light transports and old bombers.

First off the line, watched by a crowd of 60,000, were Jim and Amy Mollison in the Comet *Black Magic,* and they were early leaders in the race until forced to retire at Allahabad with engine trouble. This left the scarlet Comet *Grosvenor House,* flown by Flight Lt. C. W. A. Scott and Captain Tom Campbell Black, well ahead of the field. This racer went on to win in a time of less than three days, with an elapsed time 71 hours, despite flying the last stage with one engine throttled back because of an oil-pressure indicator giving a faulty low reading. It would have won the handicap prize as well, were it not for a race rule that no aircraft could win more than one prize.

In 1935, QANTAS took over the Darwin-Singapore sector of the Royal Mail route. By 1938, to meet the growing demand, the airline introduced Short C Class Empire flying boats. As flying boats needed only a mooring buoy, terminal building and fuelling facilities, Qantas established a base at Rose Bay in Sydney. The aircraft flew the entire Australia-England route, with the Qantas and Imperial Airways crews changing in Singapore.

Into Service with the A380

Since those pre-war flights QANTAS have evolved somewhat, grown in size and the journey times have reduced. Today, flights are promoted as 'a journey like no other' and styled *'We've drawn on 92 years of flying to design an extraordinary travel experience. Experience the comfort and exceptional service of your next journey on the Qantas A380'.*

QANTAS operate the A380 on five main routes: QF1/QF2 Sydney - Dubai - London; QF9/QF10 Melbourne - Dubai - London;

Qantas A380-842 VH-OQA 'Nancy-Bird Walton' completes its delivery flight from Toulouse via Singapore. Nancy-Bird Walton arrived on Australian soil as QF6008, landing on Runway 16R.

QF11/QF12 Sydney - Los Angeles; QF93/QF94 Melbourne - Los Angeles and QF127/QF128 Sydney - Hong Kong.

QANTAS put their A380s into service on 19 September 2008, starting flights between Melbourne and Los Angeles in October 2008. By the end of 2008, 890,000 passengers had flown on 2,200 flights totalling 21,000 hours.

Early Problems

On 4 November 2010, while climbing through 7,000 ft after departing from Changi Airport, Singapore, A380 registered VH-OQA, operating as Qantas Flight 32, en route from Singapore's Changi Airport to Sydney Airport, sustained an uncontained engine rotor failure (UERF) of the No. 2 engine, a Rolls-Royce Trent 900. Debris from the UERF impacted the aircraft, resulting in significant structural and systems damage.

The flight crew managed the situation and, after completing the required actions for the multitude of system failures, safely returned to and landed at Changi Airport.

The Australian Transport Safety Bureau (ATSB) found that a number of oil feed stub pipes within the High Pressure / Intermediate pressure (HP/IP) hub assembly were manufactured with thin wall sections that did not conform to the design specifications. These non-conforming pipes were fitted to Trent 900 engines, including the No. 2 engine on VH-OQA. The thin wall section significantly reduced the life of the oil feed stub pipe on the No. 2 engine so that a fatigue crack developed, ultimately releasing oil during the flight that resulted in an internal oil fire. That fire led to the separation of the intermediate pressure turbine disc from the drive shaft. The disc accelerated and burst with sufficient force that the engine structure could not contain it, releasing high-energy debris.

Following the UERF, the ATSB, Rolls-Royce plc, regulatory authorities and operators of A380 aircraft with Trent 900 engines took a range of steps to ensure that HP/IP hub assemblies with non-conforming oil feed stub pipes were identified and either removed from service, or managed to ensure their safe continued operation. Rolls-Royce also released an engine control software update that included an IP turbine overspeed protection system (IPTOS) that is designed to shut the engine down before the turbine disc can overspeed, in the unlikely event that a similar failure occurs.

Rolls-Royce has also made a range of changes to their quality management system to improve the way in which they manage non-conforming parts, both during the manufacturing process and when it has been identified that parts had unknowingly been released into service with non-conformances.

As a result of the discovery, EASA issued an Airworthiness Directive in January 2012 affecting 20 A380 aircraft that had accumulated over 1,300 flights. A380s with under 1,800 flight hours were to be inspected within six weeks or 84 flights; aircraft with over 1,800 flight hours were to be examined within four days or fourteen flights. Fittings found to be

Initial on-site inspection of the Rolls Royce Trent on VH-OQA identified that the fire was most intense in the lower left thrust reverser section and in the lower bifurcation. Sooting, glazing and the effects of heat were observed on a number of electrical, air, oil and hydraulic supply lines and the nacelle anti-ice bleed air ducts within the core section, lower bifurcation and accessories section on the fan casing. A significant amount of oil was smeared on the lower panel of the thrust reverser cowl. (Australian Transport Safety Bureau)

Qantas A380-842 VH-OQH viewed from the lounge at Kingsford Smith Airport, Sydney.

cracked were being replaced following the inspections to maintain structural integrity. On 8 February 2012, the checks were extended to cover all 68 A380 aircraft in operation. Despite hysteria whipped up by some sections of the media, the problem was considered to be minor and did not greatly affect operations. EADS acknowledged that the cost of repairs would be over $130 million, to be borne by Airbus. The company said the problem was traced to stress and material used for the fittings. Additionally, major airlines are seeking compensation from Airbus for revenue lost as a result of the cracks and subsequent grounding of fleets. Airbus has switched to a different type of aluminium alloy so aircraft delivered from 2014 onwards would not have this issue.

A typical flight with the Flying Kangaroo

The 4,595 mile journey between Sydney to Hong Kong can be covered in one 'hop' taking around nine hours aboard A380 QF127 of QANTAS Airways and is typical of their A380 operation. Eve Flostom divides her time between her family in Australia and her career in China, so is a well seasoned 'commuter'...

'QF127 leaves Sydney's Kingsford Smith Airport at 11.40 giving me something of a leisurely start on the morning of the flight. I usually fly Business, but for this trip and for assorted work-related reasons I upgraded to First. QANTAS offers Business and First class passengers very generous baggage allowances, but I didn't have that much to take but it meant that I was able to take a small trolley case on board with essentials for the six hour layover that I had in Hong Kong.

I'd arranged for a taxi to pick me up at 8am, thinking that I'd be at the airport at about 8.30am giving me almost three hours in the famed Qantas First Class lounge.

The journey to the airport was fine and I was dropped off by zone D, where the QANTAS Business class and First class check in desks are located. The check in area was quite busy but I didn't have to wait long. The check in agent was lovely, very friendly but professional. My bag was tagged and with both boarding passes and an Express Path card in hand I sat down to fill out my immigration card before proceeding through immigration and security. The Express Path card didn't really seem to make much difference as security was packed with all the usual suspects; people who don't know or care about the liquids rule, people who spend five minutes emptying out all of the coins from various pockets, people that walk through the scanner with all of their jewellery

QANTAS offer 14 individual suites or 'pods' on their A380s that are some of the best conventional seats in any aircraft. They have a seat pitch of 84 inches, extending into a full 29 inch wide by 80 inch fully flat bed when required. The low 'wall' shown in the picture on the right is the privacy screens in the stowed position - they can only be used in flight.

The suites are in Rows One through Five with three seats across the cabin and are certainly a step up from Business class and are a definite improvement on what some airlines offer. The QANTAS A380 seat is unusual in that it offers a motor to swivel - you face forward to take-off, land and dine but then rotate 45 degres to sleep!

Left and below is the passengers view from one of the QANTAS pods. The footrest also includes a subsidiary, occasional seat.

Each suite has a 17 inch High Definition TV monitor showing the usual Audio and Video On Demand (AVOD) programs which is motorised to rotate our from its wall stowage. The window shades are also motorised.

There is a seperate TV screen for the seat controls - or it can show a moving map - a great innovation so you can see where you are while watching a movie. All seats have 110 volts power outlets, plus a USP power outlet. (Photos: Eve Flostom)

QANTAS First Class is certainly luxurious, although the view outside is severely restricted, if not impossible, as these pictures show. The airline plans to reduce its First and Business Class, and increase Super and Super Economy seating.(Photo: QANTAS)

Sometimes you never know what you might see when you look up!

still on, I'm sure you've experienced it all before!

I made it to the lounge at 8.50 am and was welcomed in by name. The lounge didn't seem too busy, which was excellent news. I've never visited the First Class lounge in the morning, but I've heard stories of not being able to find a seat on some occasions.

I made my way over to the restaurant area and have a quick look at the menu although I already knew what I was going to order - the eggs benedict! I decided to wash this down with a glass of Tattinger. Yes, OK, I know it was barely even 9am, in those circumstances who cares?

I was able to sit and wait directly overlooking the A380 that would be taking me and several hundred other people to Hong Kong, VH-OQH, one that I had not travelled on before.

QANTAS use three air bridges for the A380 at Sydney: A for First, B for Economy and C for Business and Premium Economy. I made my way down towards the A bridge and was greeted warmly at the door and directed to my seat, I was actually the second person on board so I was able to get a few snaps of the cabin before others arrived and sort out all of my stuff.

With the suites upwards of approximately

The Business Class self-serve, non alchoholic snack bar area on the QANTAS A380.

QANTAS upgraded their Business Class Skybeds for the A380, now being fully lay-flat.

There were 72 Skybed seats on the QANTAS A380, having an 80 inch seat pitch (converting to a 78 inch long bed) with a 21 inch width.

These seats are located on the upper deck in a 2-2-2 configuration.

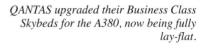

There are two Business Class cabins. The forward cabin is much more private, but has a private lounge on one side of the stairs, and a self serve bar on the other, creating noise and through traffic.

Above left: Each seat has it's own 12 inch AVOD monitor.

Above: A Business class seat, with storage space below the windows and privacy screen in the upright position.

Left: the passengers view of the other Business Class Skybed seats.
(Photos: Eve Flostom)

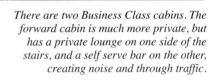

menu and waited for everyone else to board around me.

You can spot the frequent flyers from a mile away. As soon as the flight attendants hand them the coveted pyjamas (charcoal dark grey pjs for first, light grey for business) they're out of there like a flash, changed, and back in their seats before the aircraft has even taxied away from the gate.

The pjs are very comfortable, so I can see why they are popular. Oh, and you get your own socks and slippers too. The slippers even say 'first' on them.

Boarding was completed on time but had to wait a while before pushing back as apparently the wind had changed which affected the runway use. We eventually took off at 12.20, about 40 minutes past our scheduled push back time. The take-off was, as always with the A380, ridiculously quiet to the point where you actually wonder if you are going fast enough to leave the ground safely. I love the A380.

As the seat belt sign went off I reclined the seat and got comfortable. The IFE screen is both touch screen and controlled by a remote control which is embedded in the side of the seat. The screen is rather large and adjustable, making it easy to find a comfortable viewing position. I have to say that I'm a fan of the IFE on Qantas, they always seem to have a good selection of the latest films and TV programmes to my taste.

You can watch movies from the moment you get on board, to the minute you're ready to grab your luggage and disembark the flight. No more missing the end of a film you're engrossed in by just a few minutes. The screen is also quite large, at seventeen inches.

There's also a mobile phone charger in your suite, so you won't have to worry about getting a flat battery'.

QANTAS has several in-flight entertainment systems installed on its aircraft. Across the fleet, the in-flight experience is referred to as 'On:Q'. 'iQ' is featured in all classes of the Airbus A380. This audio video on demand (AVOD) experience is based on the Panasonic Avionics system and features expanded entertainment options, touch screens, new communications related features such as Wi-Fi and mobile phone functionality, as well as increased support for electronics (such as USB and iPod connectivity).

Eve continues: Talking of the seats, they swivel around, lie flat and offer massages It's pretty nifty. One moment you're facing the front of the aircraft, with limited legroom. The next moment you're

Another view of VH-OQH 'Reginald Ansett' at the gate in Sydney. (Photo: Eve Flostom)

$13500 return on the A380 jets, I knew I was in for a treat.

My first class 'pod' takes up the entire middle section of the jumbo A380 aircraft. That's the equivalent of four economy seats wide, and at least two in front. There's just a massive amount of room. Oh, and there are no overhead lockers above me. This makes the cabin feel more spacious.

Don't worry, with a maximum of just fifteen people in first class, you won't be short of room for your belongings. You can even keep them next to your seat.

I decanted my laptop, camera and various other bits into the bins and then settled down before being offered a pre-departure drink of Champagne, water or orange juice. I went for the Champagne, browsed the extensive lunch being turned to the side and reclined into a lie-flat bed. They are ridiculously comfortable and spacious. There are also several massage settings.

If you're on a night flight, when it's time to sleep the flight attendants will make up your bed for you including a large cotton pillow, bolster pillow, duvet and woollen blanket, and a fitted cotton sheet over the top of a sheepskin-covered foam mattress.

The only downside I found was that when people walked down the aisle it really thumped around, shaking me from my sleep. Perhaps it's because the pods are much lighter than the setups are in economy.

Also, you won't find yourself twisting your neck around in search of the elusive flight attendants. In first, they will cater for your every whim. Well, almost. They're very attentive.

First has an a la carte menu designed by Neil Perry. I requested a special meal and dined on roasted eggplant, potato cakes, capsicum, mushrooms and beans; gluten free bread with clear vegetable soup, and fruit. And some champagne, of course.

Oh, and want to pretend you're not surrounded by strangers? Well just pop up the privacy screens and you'll be able to zone out! There's also an extra seat, just in case you're travelling with a companion and they'd like to come by to eat with you. If you're flying solo it also doubles as a foot rest.

When you're facing a long-haul flight, it's nice to zip open the amenity bag and find SK-II products such as facial treatments, ear plugs, a toothbrush and toothpaste, mirror, tissues and even deodorant waiting for you. With the current liquid restrictions, many of us can't carry most of these rather essential items with us on board.

At about 8pm Sydney time the crew started to pack everything up in preparation for landing. The sun was just setting as we made our descent into Hong Kong, casting beautiful rays across the cabin.

The Captain advised us that we'd be landing a little later than scheduled due to traffic at Hong Kong and should expect to land just after 6pm local time (9pm Sydney). The approach was rather bumpy but the actual touchdown was smooth. Again, it seemed as if we floated onto the tarmac, such is the A380.

First class passengers are the first to get off the aircraft. So you don't have to deal with the shoulder-barging as people throw off their seatbelts, grab their luggage and race towards the exits, only to end up packed in like sardines, which often happens in economy. It's all rather relaxed in first and you have plenty of space to get organised without risking holding up the impatient hordes behind you.

As well as the headstart, you also get to cut the queues using the 'express passes'.

I've flown the Flying Kangaroo A380s a

The first daylight arrival of a QANTAS A380 at Dubai International Airport on 1 April 2013 is greeted with a typically extravagant Arabian water salute. (Photo: Dubai International Airport)

A QANTAS A380 gets airborne for another long-haul service.

number of times now, both First and Business, on day and night flights, and they have been some of the best trips I've ever had!

In July 2013 Qantas completed a reconfiguration of its flagship Airbus A380 fleet, with all twelve aircraft now sporting an increased number of economy and premium economy seats. The rejigged superjumbos can carry 484 passengers, an increase of 34 from the previous headcount of 450.

The overall tally sees 371 economy berths compared to the old 332 (a rise of 39 seats), with three more premium economy seats on top of the former 32. The business class cabin has been reduced in size from 72 to 64 seats, with several of the self-service bars and snack areas axed to release revenue-earning space for more seats as QANTAS continues to face tough competition on international routes.

In early 2014 rumours started to circulate that QANTAS might become the first airline to lease out an overcapacity of it's A380 fleet the airline presently has 12 with options for another eight. Turkish Airlines is seen as a client for four.

The airline's vast order book for new widebody aircraft does not include A380s, but Chief Executive Temel Kotil has indicated that the carrier now has enough traffic to start operating the aircraft on several high-density routes from its hub at Istanbul Ataturk Airport.

'The leasing companies are making their offers to us and we are fixing our decisions considering those offers. There is no firm board decision of Turkish Airlines yet concerning the lease of A380 aircraft, despite receiving offers from the market,

a representative of the airline said. She declined to confirm whether the discussions concern the wet-lease of four QANTAS A380s or aircraft destined for Japan's Skymark Airlines.

'The facts are that QANTAS has flagged the need to make tough decisions as part of strengthening our business. For our customers, this won't change our focus on being one of the world's best airlines.' a QANTAS representative said.

QANTAS will take the axe to its domestic and international fleet, weeding out older aircraft and delaying orders for new aircraft as part of an aggressive $2 billion cost-saving campaign amid growing competition in both international and domestic operations. It also plans to cut 15% of its workforce

The older aircraft are less fuel-efficient than more modern jets and also carry a higher maintenance bill, and their early retirement will allow QANTAS to speed up its 'fleet simplification' drive to reduce number of different aircraft types it flies. It is also seen as a move to convince the Australian government and investors it is worthy of the state assistance it says it needs.

Battered by high fuel costs and a strong Australian dollar, its credit rating was relegated to junk status last year amid a price war with Virgin Australia.

The airline is in partnership with Emirates on routes from Australia to Dubai and into Europe. A bill before the Australian Parliament to lift foreign ownership restrictions has passed the Canberra lower house (Representatives) but its chances in the Senate are said to be limited.

D-AIMB, a Lufthansa A380, inside the company's superhangar at Frankfurt.
(Photo: Gregor Schläger, Lufthansa Technik AG)

The focal points of the Lufthansa Technik maintenance center at Frankfurt airport are the four gigantic hangars with a floor space of altogether 90,000 square meters. The largest of them, the A380 hangar in the South of Frankfurt airport, covers an area of 25,000 square metres in the current phase of construction. It is as big as four football fields and has room for three Airbus A380 at the same time. The second phase of construction, to be completed by 2015, will provide the capacity for simultaneous maintenance work on six A380s, thus becoming the largest aircraft hangar in Europe. (Photo: Lufthansa Technik)

A screwdriver is a screwdriver and a hydraulic lift is a hydraulic lift - under normal circumstances. With the Airbus A380 it is somewhat different. The world's largest commercial aircraft sets new dimensions. Without numerous special tools and equipment, the maintenance work could not be carried out - and this is also true about the specialists from Lufthansa Technik. For example, 100 so-called large operating units like cranes and hydraulic lifts are necessary, as well as more than 500 specially produced tools that range from screwdriver to hydraulic testers.

All airliners have to undergo a regular and rigourous maintenance schedule - these are periodic inspections that follow specific programmes which may be or not similar to different commercial operators around the world.

Airlines and airworthiness authorities casually refer to the detailed inspections as 'checks', and commonly are one, or a combination of the following: A check, B check, C check, or D check. A and B checks are regarded as the 'lighter' checks, while C and D are considered deeper or 'heavier' checks.

A Check - This is performed approximately every 500 - 800 flight hours or 200 - 400 cycles. It needs about 20 - 50 man-hours and is usually performed overnight at an airport gate or, if available, inside a hangar. The actual occurrence of this check varies by aircraft type and relates to either the cycle count (one takeoff and landing is considered an aircraft 'cycle'), or the number of hours flown since the last check. The occurrence can be delayed by the airline if certain predetermined conditions are met.

B Check - This is performed approximately every 4–6 months. It needs about 150 man-hours and is usually performed within one to three days at an airport hangar. A similar occurrence schedule applies to the B check as to the A check. B checks may be incorporated into successive A checks, i.e.: A-1 through A-10 complete all the B check items.

C Check - This is performed approximately every 20–24 months or a specific number of actual flight hours as defined by the manufacturer. This maintenance check is much more extensive than a B Check, requiring a large majority of the aircraft's components to be inspected. This check puts the aircraft out of service and until it is completed, the aircraft must not leave the maintenance site. It also requires more space than A and B Checks— usually a hangar at a maintenance base. The time needed to complete such a check is generally one to two weeks and the effort involved can require up to 6000 man-hours. The schedule of occurrence has many factors and components as has been described, and thus varies by aircraft category and type.

D Check - This is by far the most comprehensive and demanding check for an aircraft. It is also known as a Heavy Maintenance Visit. This check occurs approximately every five years. It is a check that, more or less, takes the entire aircraft apart for inspection and overhaul. Also, if required, the paint may need to be completely removed for further inspection on the fuselage metal skin. Such a check can usually demand up to 50,000 man-hours and it can

lufthansa.com

D-AIMA

Line maintenance can take many forms - everything from a full engine change, to detailed inspection of the smallest part.

Above: Doors open, with safety lines across the gaps to prevent technicians from accidentally falling through.

Right: The A380 may be the world's largest airliner, but the delicate touch of a small paintbrush is needed to ensure the structure is sealed against the elements in order to prevent damage.

D-AIMA 'Frankfurt am Main' undergoes an in-depth visual inspection during line-maintenance at Lufthansa Technik in Frankfurt.
(All photos: Sonja Brüggemann, Lufthansa Technik)

Above: A380 D-AIMG undergoing routine, low-level maintenance before going back into service the next day. The blue painted, multi-level tail dock structure for servicing the vertical fin is particularly noticable. (Simon Peters)

Below right: the view from the top of the tail dock, looking forward and down, with all the doors on the upper deck open. (Photo: Sonja Brüggemann/Lufthansa Technik AG)

generally take up to two months to complete, depending on the aircraft and the number of technicians involved. It also requires the most space of all maintenance checks, and as such must be performed at a suitable maintenance base. Given the elevated requirements of this check and the tremendous effort involved in it, it is also by far the most expensive maintenance check of all, with total costs for a single visit ending up well within the million-dollar range.

Because of the nature and the cost of such a check, most airlines — especially those with a large fleet — have to plan D Checks for their aircraft years in advance. Often, older aircraft being phased out of a particular airline's fleet are either stored or scrapped upon reaching their next D Check, due to the high costs involved in it in comparison to the aircraft's value. On average, a commercial aircraft undergoes two or three D Checks before it is retired.

Lufthansa Technik started preparations early for work on the A380. A decisive step was the construction of the new maintenance hangar at the A380's home airport of Frankfurt. The building, which covers an area of 25,000 square metres and started operations in 2008, is already being used for the Lufthansa long-distance fleet. With a size of 180 by 140 metres, and a total height of 45 metres, the hangar has a multifunctional design, can accommodate two Airbus A380s or three Boeing 747s simultaneously. With the second stage of construction, by 2015 there will be maintenance capacity for a total of six A380s, and it will then be the largest hangar in Europe. The investment was about €150 million.

The colossal hangar is one part of the preparations at Lufthansa Technik for the A380, the adaptation of the equipment is the other. Although 500 normal tools can also be used, at least the same number had to be ordered specifically for the new aircraft - from the torque spanner with a particularly high performance, via working platforms right through to the under-slung crane. The investment cost a further €14 million.

Probably the most striking equipment in the maintenance hangar of the superlatives is the so-called tail dock which makes the work on the 24-metre high tail unit possible. The work platform approaches the aircraft precisely to a millimetre. The design is tailor-made like a made-to- measure suit. And: the engineers can work safely at dizzying heights.

When the A 380 arrives for a check or a repair, the engineers, specially-trained for the aircraft at Lufthansa Technik, are ready for every job. Really ingenious methods are used. How do you manage a tyre change, for example, on this wide-bodied jet? Quite simple, answer the experts, by letting the aircraft help. Because the hydraulics of the hoist takes air from the tyres, which are inflated to 14 bar, for its compressed air. Thanks to this 'air number' the almost 300 ton aircraft is raised up and the tyres can be changed. The permanent equipment also includes the under-slung crane which makes clever use of its strengths when engines are being replaced.

And should extensive repairs be needed on the undercarriage, the entire aircraft will be lifted. About 90 minutes of preparation for the attachment of special lifting equipment is necessary, before the aircraft hovers in the hangar, jacked up at three points.

One of the most innovative new large tools was the idea of a Lufthansa Technik employee. He designed a revolutionary mobile cherry-picker which is equipped with a winch and can move

One of the inboard Rolls-Royce Trent engines with the covers opened for engine inspection.
(Photo: Sonja Brüggemann/Lufthansa Technik AG)

The nosewheel bay undergoes a check - the forward nosewheel bay doors are open so that the interior can be checked and inspected. The picture on the left is from inside the nosewheel bay, looking down and aft, showing the massive structure that supports the nosewheel assembly.
(Photos: Gregor Schläger/Lufthansa Technik AG)

independently of it. The clever method, for example, makes the regular replacement of the escape chutes possible. Normally the winch and the cherry-picker are separate and their use complicated and time-consuming.

In the high-tech workshop the engineers find everything they need for the work on the super aircraft. Once the wide-bodied Airbus is parked in the hangar, according to their needs, the engineers can make use of special supply units which are usually sunk into the ground.

These 'ground pits', for example, provide electric current and or water, and nitrogen for the tyres. At the latest after 750 flying hours (every six to eight weeks) an Airbus A380 rolls into the maintenance hangar at Frankfurt Airport.

The hangar and its personnel already passed the first practical test in April when an Airbus A 380 was pushed into the super maintenance hangar by the largest and latest aircraft tractor. And this is just the beginning, being this is only the first stage of construction of the hangar system, the second section due for completion by 2015.

Above: a Lufthansa technician uses the onboard computer system to both check the flight systems and to use their diagnostic capabilities. The A380 is designed to be a 'paperless' aircraft, with no physical log-books.

Below: such is the size of the Lufthansa facilities at Frankfurt, tricycles with luggage capacity are used to get around! (Photos: Gregor Schläger/Lufthansa Technik AG)

Brake to Vacate

The A380 is a high-technology aircraft, and the Lufthansa examples are no exception and are equipped with a feature that makes coming to a stop just that little bit easier. Many travellers are aware of what is termed 'auto-land' where the Flight Management System 'flies' the aircraft to the point of touchdown and beyond - the A380 takes it one step further.

Many drivers are familiar with it from their everyday driving: the 'Sat-Nav', a technology which makes finding your destination so much easier. Also when they need to brake there are additional aids like power brakes and antilock systems. On the Airbus A380 wide-bodied aircraft both of them exist all-in-one and that is new: a brake with a built-in Sat-Nav device. 'Brake to vacate' (BTV) is the name of the technology.

The concept is based on an automatic targeted braking with pre-selected taxiing speed. In other words, a braking technology that permits the aircraft to complete the landing precisely at the point where it should also leave the runway (Exit Point). As a result of the optimized landing process, the flow, particularly at larger airports, is relieved. Because of this innovation Lufthansa's new flagship reduces the respective time spent on the runway. Thanks to this, the following aircraft can land or take-off faster, an advantage in heavy

With plastic sheeting over the economy seats, and protectors on the carpets, this technician works on checking one of the main deck cabin doors. The surrounding trim has been removed, showing something of the internal structure, likewise the cover has been removed from the safety slide pack.
(Photos: Lufthansa Technik AG)

traffic at airports with many flights.

'Brake to vacate' is satellite-controlled via the locating system GPS (Global Positioning System) and works on the basis of a navigation instrument in a database specially created for this purpose, the runway coordinates of airports are stored precisely to a centimetre.

Via this onboard 'Onboard Air Navigation System' (OANS), the pilot indicates with a mouse click where on the runway the aircraft should have reached the desired taxiing speed which, as a rule is six to ten knots. The interesting thing is: it does not matter at what point on the runway, the aircraft touches down. 'Brake to vacate' does the thinking and calculates the braking distance so that the pre-defined Exit Point is actually reached – with more or less braking energy and, if necessary, more or less reverse thrust. The refined technology, thereby, not only takes into account the 'map' of the airport, but also the data of the aircraft like weight and speed. The pre-programmed weather conditions are also considered. If the runway is wet, although it had been expected to be dry,

'Brake to vacate' also recognizes this and correspondingly controls the braking energy. The method offers numerous advantages: The landing procedure is even safer and more economical, brakes wear longer and deceleration is smoother. Gentle and intelligent braking is also more pleasant for the passengers. Another side-effect is that the air traffic controllers at the airport know more precisely at which taxiway the aircraft will leave the runway.

Linked in with the 'Brake to Vacate' are two additional warning systems which make the A380 even safer. The so-called 'Runway Overrun Warning' becomes active at a height of 500 feet, when it calculates that, under the current configuration, the runway would not be long enough for a landing. The pilot receives a warning, for example, in the event that the runway should be wet. In the event of 'Runway Overrun Protection' a safety mechanism is triggered if the pilot has landed nevertheless and, if necessary, the system activates maximum braking power in order to come safely to a stop on the runway.

Chapter 14

Deliveries

Air Austral

Air Austral is a French airline with its headquarters and main operating base at Roland Garros Airport in Sainte-Marie, Réunion - an island in the Indian Ocean. It operates scheduled services from Réunion to metropolitan France, South Africa, Thailand, India and a number of destinations in the Indian Ocean. The company has 900 employees. In November 2009, it was announced at the Dubai Air Show that Air Austral had placed a firm order for two A380s which will be operated from the La Reunion to Paris in an 840-seat single-class configuration, but later reports said that all options were on the table, including a mixed-configuration A380. Service entry is planned for 2014.

Air France

Air France introduced the A380 on 20 November 2009 with a service to New York's JFK Airport from Paris' Charles de Gaulle Airport. The first order - for ten -800s was announced on 24 July 2000 with options for a further four. Air France became the first European carrier to offer flights on the A380, with three operating during winter

2009-2010 on the Paris-New-York and Paris-Johannesburg routes in a configuration that seated 538 passengers.

The heavy investment involved covered a long period of time, corresponding to Air France's strategy of continually renewing and upgrading its aircraft, whose average age of nine years makes it

Above: The Premier Class area on the Air France A380s.

Below: Air France's A380 F-HPJA. (Photos: Air France)

one of Europe's youngest fleets.

The size and performance of the A380, particularly well-suited to the Air France network, will save the Company from 12 to 15 million euros per aircraft per year. By early 2014 nine aircraft had been delivered.

Amedeo

Amedeo, the German aircraft leasing and asset management organization formally called the Doric Lease Corp, and Airbus signed the contract for 20 A380s at the 2014 Singapore Airshow, originally announced at the 50th Le Bourget Airshow on 17 June 2013, the first of which was scheduled to enter service in 2016. The final agreement was signed by Mark Lapidus, CEO of Amedeo and John Leahy, Airbus Chief Operating Officer, Customers.

Mark Lapidus said, *'Today's signature with Airbus is a great day for aviation as we offer airlines a new, more flexible way to access the* *unique benefits of the A380 through our tailored leasing solutions. As world air traffic continues to double every fifteen years and airport infrastructure and slots do not, the A380 is the best solution for airlines to capture that growth and build passenger loyalty thanks to the on-board space and comfort combination that no other airliner can compete with and do so at the lowest per seat unit cost.'*

'This firm order from Amedeo is a clear recognition of the A380's long-term market appeal. The A380's unbeatable economics and passenger comfort are now available to airlines through operating leases from Amedeo,' said John Leahy. It was intended that Amedeo's customers would benefit from unbeatable seat-mile costs for their cabin configurations with a baseline three class, 573 seat layout. The cabin layout offered an efficient and at the same time flexible cabin configuration that minimised reconfiguration costs and eased transition from operator to operator with the main deck seating

Asiana Airlines' first A380 arrives in Hamburg, Germany, on 13 December 2013, to undergo painting and cabin furnishing. (Photo: Airbus SAS)

427 passengers in 18.5 inch wide economy seats, while the upper deck offered twelve first class, 66 business class and 68 economy seats.

Amedeo's senior management built a 6.8 billion US$ aircraft portfolio under management, including eighteen A380s acquired through sale-leaseback arrangements and adding four more during 2013.

Asiana Airlines

Asiana Airlines Incorporated is one of South Korea's two major airlines, with its headquarters in Asiana Town building in Seoul. The airline has its domestic hub at Gimpo International Airport and its international hub at Incheon International Airport. As a member of Star Alliance, at the time of writing it operates fourteen domestic and ninety international passenger routes, and twenty-seven cargo routes throughout Asia, Europe, North America, and Oceania.

In January 2011 the airline announced an order for six A380s for delivery in 2014, and planned operating on routes to Europe and the USA.

'With the A380, Asiana will be able to take its award-winning service to a new level, offering the very highest standards of comfort in the sky,' says Asiana's president and CEO Yoon Young-Doo.

British Airways

British Airways announced an order for twelve Rolls-Royce Trent powered A380 aircraft on 27 September 2007, the last scheduled to arrive by 2016. The first three were delivered during 2013, with a further five arriving by the end of 2014. Along with the Boeing 787 Dreamliner, the A380 will form the centrepiece of British Airways' £5bn investment in products and services to benefit customers.

The aircraft launches into commercial service flying customers to Los Angeles, followed by Hong Kong. It offers a choice of British Airways' First, Club World, World Traveller Plus and World Traveller cabins.

China Southern Airlines

China Southern Airlines Company Limited is an airline headquartered in Baiyun District, Guangzhou, Guangdong Province, People's Republic of China. It is the world's sixth-largest airline measured by passengers carried and

Three hundred and eighty British Airways staff 'wave the flag' to welcome Airbus A380 G-XLEA to the Heathrow base on 4 July 2013. (Photo: British Airways)

China Southern Airlines A380 B-6137 comes in to land. (Photo: China Southern Airlines)

Asia's largest airline in fleet size and passengers carried. It is the fourth-largest airline in the world in domestic passenger traffic and the sixth-largest in scheduled domestic passenger-kilometres flown.

From its main hubs at Guangzhou Baiyun International Airport and Beijing Capital International Airport, the airline flies to 193 destinations using a fleet of more than 400 aircraft. China Southern Airlines was established on 1 July 1988 following the restructuring of the Civil Aviation Administration of China. Since then, it

acquired and merged with a number of domestic airlines, becoming one of China's 'Big Three' airlines (alongside Air China and China Eastern Airlines). China Southern Airlines is a member of the SkyTeam Alliance. The airlines's logo is a red kapok on a blue vertical tail fin.

China Southern Airlines is the first Chinese airline to order and to operate an Airbus A380 with an order for five of the type announced on 28 January 2005.. The airline initially operated these aircraft on Beijing–Hong Kong and Beijing–Guangzhou routes, but, these domestic services

Emirates A380 receives the traditional firemans welcome into San Fransico for the first time arrival on 3 August 2008. (Photo: George Banks)

struggled to be profitable. Due to the demand limitation of the airlines' international hub at Guangzhou Baiyun Airport, few routes from Guangzhou have the demand to support an A380. In an effort to make its A380s viable, China Southern started operating them on its Guangzhou–Los Angeles route and on the Guangzhou–Sydney route.

Emirates

Emirates is an airline based in Dubai, United Arab Emirates. The airline is a subsidiary of The Emirates Group, which is wholly owned by the government of Dubai's Investment Corporation of Dubai. It is the largest airline in the Middle East, operating nearly 3,400 flights per week from its hub at Dubai International Airport, to more than 133 cities in 74 countries across six continents. Cargo activities are undertaken by the Emirates Group's Emirates SkyCargo division.

The airline is the largest customer for the A380 by a very large margin. Emirates announced an order in April 2000 for the Airbus A3XX (later named Airbus A380). The deal consisted of five Airbus A380s and two Airbus A380Fs. The deal was confirmed on 4 November 2001, when Emirates announced orders for fifteen more A380-800s. An additional order twenty-one A380-800s was placed two years later. In April 2006, Emirates replaced its order for the two variants with an order for two A380-800s. In 2007, Emirates ordered 15

A380-800s, bringing the total number ordered to 58. According to Emirates, the aircraft would allow the airline to maximize its use of scarce takeoff and landing slots at crowded airports such as London Heathrow. In 2005, the first A380-800 in full Emirates livery was displayed at the Dubai Airshow.

At the 2010 Berlin Air Show, Emirates ordered an additional 32 A380s worth US$11.5 billion. Emirates expected all of its 90 A380s ordered to be delivered by 2017. None of the additional 32 jets are intended to replace existing A380s; although Emirates received its first A380 in 2008, it does not expect to retire these early airframes before 2020.

In 2010, Emirates said they planned to operate over 120 Airbus A380s when new airport space is available. The target implied a future Emirates order for 30 of the world's largest airliner, worth US$10 billion at list prices, at an unspecified date.

Then, on 17 November 2013, Emirates announced at a press conference at the Dubai Airshow that they were placing an order for an additional 50 Airbus A380-800s, bringing the overall order total to 140.

Emirates has stated that its versions of the A380-800 will offer fuel economy of 3.1 litres per 100 passenger km. Emirates A380-800s also feature the Engine Alliance GP7200 engines, which save 500,000 litres of fuel per aircraft per year. Unlike many other airlines, Emirates are

happy to reveal aspects of their operations - For example, the company uses a programme called 'Flextracks'. Computer software that allows pilots to diverge from fixed or direct routes, making use of high-altitude jetsreams to an aircraft's advantage and avoid strong headwinds. Operations Centres calculates and publishes Flextrack information to enable them to make the most of prevailing weather patterns and winds which allow aircraft to improve flight time and reduce fuel usage, delivering considerable environment benefits through a reduction in emissions and reducing operating costs.

Emirates have also invested in a programme called 'tailored arrivals'. This allows air traffic control to uplink to aircraft en route. It first determines the speed and flight profile from the air onto the runway, this allows the crew to accept and fly a continuous descent profile, thus saving fuel and reducing emissions.

Etihad Airways
Etihad Airways is the flag carrier airline of the United Arab Emirates. Established by royal decree in July 2003 and based in Abu Dhabi, Etihad commenced operations in November 2003. The name derives from the Arabic word for 'union'.

The airline operates more than 1,000 flights per week to 96 passenger and cargo destinations in the Middle East, Africa, Europe, Asia, Australia and the Americas, with a fleet of 85 Airbus and Boeing aircraft. In 2012, Etihad carried 10.3 million passengers, a 23% increase from the previous year, delivering revenues of US$ 4.8 billion and net profits of US$ 42 million. Etihad Airways is the fourth largest airline in the Middle East and the second largest airline in the United Arab Emirates, after the Dubai-based airline Emirates.

Etihad announced an order for four A380s on 20 July 2004, which was increased to ten, with options on a further five on 14 July 2008.

On 8 March 2011, Etihad Airways and Engine Alliance announced that they had signed agreements worth up to $1.5 billion for the purchase of GP7200 engines to power Etihad's fleet of ten Airbus A380 aircraft and a long-term fleet management agreement for the maintenance, repair and overhaul of the engines, the airline announced yesterday.

'The GP7200 engines, provided by the Engine Alliance in this agreement, will offer significant fuel efficiencies and cost optimisation for Etihad's first Airbus A380s when they enter our fleet from 2014,' said James Hogan, Etihad Airways chief

executive officer in a statement released by Etihad.

By April 2014, president and CEO James Hogan said the first Etihad Airways A380 flight was likely to take place in the first week of December 2014 , between Abu Dhabi and London. and that the interior would be revealed at the 2014 ATM show in Dubai : *'What we will show is something very special, very unique. We have been waiting a long time and developing something that we believe is quite spectacular and different from what you see inside all the other airlines currently flying the A380,'* Hogan said.

Hong Kong Airlines
Hong Kong Airlines Ltd is a Hong Kong-based airline, with its main hub and corporate head office at Hong Kong International Airport. The airline operates scheduled regional passenger and cargo services to ten destinations within the People's Republic of China and Vietnam, including codeshares with its sister airline, Hong Kong Express Airways.

At the Paris Air Show in June 2011, Hong Kong Airlines had announced a signed contract for ten Airbus A380's but due to China's anger with the European Union over plans to force all airlines to take part in its carbon-trading scheme, the Chinese government blocked progress on the sale. Normally, airlines in Hong Kong are not required to seek approval from the Chinese government to proceed with aircraft orders. The A380 cancellation became an issue as Hong Kong Airlines' parent, Hainan Airlines, is registered in mainland China, not Hong Kong SAR. In early January 2012, HKA's corporate governance head Kenneth Thong stated in a TV interview that the order was going ahead.

In December 2012, CEO Yang Jianhong told the media that *'We won't resume long haul routes in the short term. The carrier is discussing changing at least some of its ten on-order A380s for A330s, and delaying deliveries.'*

Kingdom Holding Company
Kingdom Holding Company (KHC) is an investment holding company based in Riyadh, Saudi Arabia and is a publicly listed company on the Tadawul (Saudi Stock Exchange). KHC consists of a select team of experienced investment specialists directed by Prince Alwaleed bin Talal. The company describes itself as a diversified investment company, whose main interests are banking / financial services, real estate, hotels, media, entertainment, and internet/technology.

F-WXXL seen in flight on 8 March 2012 over Toulouse in a colour scheme thought to represent the ACJ380, or Airbus Corporate Jet. (Photo: Simon Peters)

In early 2007, reports began circulating that an extremely rich person had commissioned a private variant of Airbus' then-newly introduced A380 airliner, at a starting cost of $300M. Eventually the buyer, who was later revealed as Saudi Arabian royal Prince Al-Waleed bin Talal, was said to have spent an additional $100M to $150M to outfit the aircraft to his high standards to transport no more than a hundred people. But now the prince has apparently sold the plane before it ever took flight, to an unnamed billionaire desperate to skip the waiting list for the world's largest private jet.

Allegedly - and everything about this aircraft has to be couched in those terms, because the Prince is notoriously secretaive, and Airbus refuses to discuss these sort of details about client discussions - the company committed to purchasing an Airbus A380 'Flying Palace' for $485 million later that year.

It seems that Prince Al-Waleed contracted interior designer Edése Doret - a private jet and megayacht specialist - to transform the interiors into an airborne palace. That process started simply, at least by these standards. Doret designed a 14-seat dining table for the Prince and his guests, complete with cushy chromed chairs and a glass chandelier, all rendered in soothing neutral tones.

Adjacent to the dining area is a lounge area boasting three sofas, a pair of chairs, a shiny coffee table, and four rather hideous light fixtures. As if guests weren't impressed enough already by a half-billion dollar private jet, there was an illuminated nook in the divider to hold a scale model of the owner's absurdly large motor yacht. A huge flatscreen television, mounted on the wall opposite the ship model, provides more pedestrian entertainment.

Other rumours were circulating - lots of big numbers and fanciful scenarios have been floated about Alwaleed's 'Flying Palace.' Among them: there would be an on-board parking space for his Rolls Royce; a Concert hall with grand piano, seating for ten and stage for private entertainment; Marble tiled steam room with spa treatments; a 'wellbeing' room complete with flat screen TVs on the walls and floors that shows passengers what they are flying over; Five master bedrooms with king sized beds, private bathrooms and showers; twenty smaller private rooms; a private elevator that connected the master bedroom to the tarmac for quick entrances and exits; a Boardroom with holographic TV monitors and a prayer room with computer monitored prayer mats that automatically adjusted to face Mecca. Alwaleed was supposed to take delivery of the plane in 2013. It seems that all of those stories were wishful thinking.

What really happened to the aircraft is a tale of what appears to be Alwaleed acting like a second-hand car dealer with outsized expectations for a speculative flip prior to the 2008-2009 global financial crisis.

In October 2007, Alwaleed negotiated to obtain F-WXXL (002) a test flight version of the A380 that was essentially second hand. Aircraft manufacturers are notoriously secretive about their prices and any financial arrangements with their clients: there were rumours however that Alwaleed did a fantastic job negotiating with Airbus, and got the price down to $130 million, roughly 50% of

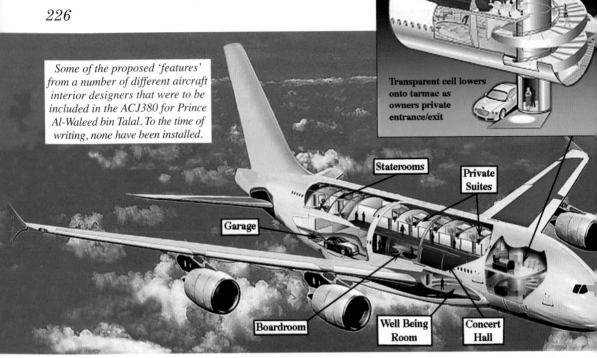

Grand star
and lift
three

Some of the proposed 'features' from a number of different aircraft interior designers that were to be included in the ACJ380 for Prince Al-Waleed bin Talal. To the time of writing, none have been installed.

Transparent cell lowers onto tarmac as owners private entrance/exit

Staterooms

Private Suites

Garage

Boardroom

Well Being Room

Concert Hall

which was to be paid in yearly instalments following a $19.5 million down payment; the remainder was to be paid upon delivery. Airbus agreed to deliver the plane 'as new', with new engines and new systems in July 2010. For comparison, the 'list price' for the A380-800 listed at $390 million.

Then the Prince's core asset – Citigroup shares — began to fall in value in late 2007. According to sources who do not wish to be named, Alwaleed's employees were instructed to find someone else to buy the aircraft. In March 2008, one employee supposedly found a UK aircraft leasing company willing to pay $268 million, but Alwaleed rejected the deal, saying he wanted nothing less than $300 million.

In 2008, when questioned by the media about why he had ordered the A380 when he already had a fully equipped 747, he reply was *'I want to sell it to someone else and make some money.'*

By the spring of 2010, the prince began negotiating to sell the aircraft to Saudi Arabia's King Abdullah, and eventually a contract was supposedly drawn up to sell it to the King for $150 million. By that time, Alwaleed had defaulted on several payments to Airbus, according to a number of sources, not so much because he didn't have the money, but because he didn't want the aircraft. At one point, sources said Alwaleed had to pay Airbus an additional $10 million to get a six month delay on the delivery of the A380.

On 26 June 2011, Airbus and 'Kingdom 5-KR-

199' - the corporate entity Alwaleed was using to buy the aircraft – entered into a 'novation agreement' that made the Saudi Ministry of Finance - essentially the King's bank account - the new buyer. The contract was signed by the Saudi Minister of Finance, Airbus executive John Leahy and what appears to be Prince Alwaleed on behalf of Kingdom 5-KR-199.

In February 2012, ahead of the 2012 Forbes Billionaires List, Kingdom Holding Chief Financial Officer Shadi Sanbar insisted to Forbes that the A380 had not been sold, and claimed it as an asset owned by Prince Alwaleed worth $330 million. Forbes had, it seemed, discounted the value of the A380 for the 2012 Billionaires List to $150 million. Sanbar's insistence that Alwaleed still owned the machine in February 2012 contradicted the facts as laid out in the June 2011 agreement signed by the Saudi Ministry of Finance.

In February 2013, Kingdom Holding's Sanbar told a US business magazine that the A380 had been sold, without disclosing a buyer, a sales price, the date of the sale or even an explanation for the sale. Asked again in early March about the A380 sale, Sanbar stated: *'The Prince has not disclosed nor wishes to disclose why he sold the plane. His Royal Highness asserts that it is none of anyone's business why he chose to sell the plane.'* Sanbar added that delivery of the A380 was completed at the end of 2012. As far as is known, the A380 is still sitting on Airbus property in Toulouse, void of any interior decoration.

Korean Air

Korean Air Lines Co Ltd, operating as Korean Air, is both the flag carrier and the largest airline of South Korea, with global headquarters located in Gonghang-dong, Gangseo-gu, Seoul, South Korea. Korean Air's international passenger division and related subsidiary cargo division together serve 130 cities in 45 countries, while its domestic division serves 20 destinations. It is among the top 20 airlines in the world in terms of passengers carried and is also the top-ranked international cargo airline. Incheon International Airport serves as Korean Air's international hub. Korean Air also maintains a satellite headquarters campus at Incheon.

Korean Air had ordered five A380s, plus three options on 18 June 2003 - that was later increased

to ten confirmed orders. Korean Air begin its inaugural services between Seoul/Incheon and both Tokyo and Hong Kong from 17 June 2011 onwards. The first aircraft arrived in Korea at 09:00 on 2 June (local time) after successfully completing final flight and ground tests in Toulouse.

The inaugural A380 commercial fight took off from Incheon International Airport at 09:10am on June 17, arriving in Narita International Airport in Tokyo, Japan at 11:30 am on the same day. The same flight returned to Seoul, departing at 20:00pm to Hong Kong International Airport, and arriving at 22:30pm (all local times) on the same date. The airline's premier A380 flight services was allocated the codename 'KE380' in order to mark this special and most historic occasion.

The first five of Korean Air's A380 aircraft were to be delivered by the end of 2011 and the remaining five by 2014. The airline gradually expanded its A380 service to popular short-haul routes in Asia, such as Bangkok in July, followed by long-haul routes to glitzy destinations in Europe and North America, such as New York in August, Paris in September and Los Angeles in October 2011.

Being the first A380 operator in Northeast Asia and the sixth operator worldwide, Korean Air took pride in the fact that it was to operate one of the most spacious A380s in the industry. Configured in a three-class layout with merely 407 seats in total, the lowest configuration of any A380 operator thus far, Korean Air's A380s featured unique, top-of-the-line amenities with 12 ultra luxurious First Class Kosmo Suites and 301 Economy Class seats on the main lower deck, and 94 fully flat-lying Prestige Sleeper seats in Prestige Class (business class) on the upper deck. Korean

Above: Korean Air's 'Duty Free Showcase' on their A380s.

Right: The first Korean Air A380 in service, along with the flight crew.
(Photos: Korean Air)

Air also took the bold step of being the first carrier globally to devote an entire deck of this giant aircraft to a single class. Moreover, in line with the airline's dedication to maintaining 'Excellence in Flight', all seats are installed with AVOD, Korean Air's much-praised inflight entertainment system.

In addition, Korean Air was the first airline in the industry to have a 'Duty Free Showcase' on its A380s. Featuring a great variety of duty-free products, such as cosmetics, perfumes, liquor and accessories, with a dedicated cabin crew member on hand to assist and advise passengers with all their shopping needs, the Duty Free Showcase is designed to offer a brand new and sure to be highly enjoyable in-flight shopping experience for Korean Air travelers.

Deutsche Lufthansa AG

Besides the actual airline named Lufthansa, Deutsche Lufthansa AG is also the parent company for several other airlines and further aviation-related branches, among the most well-known being Swiss International Air Lines and Lufthansa Technik. With over 620 aircraft, it has one of the largest passenger airline fleets in the world when combined with its subsidiaries.

Lufthansa's registered office and corporate headquarters are in Cologne. The main operations base, called Lufthansa Aviation Center (LAC), is located at Lufthansa's primary traffic hub at Frankfurt Airport. The majority of Lufthansa's pilots, ground staff, and flight attendants are based

there. Lufthansa's secondary hub is Munich Airport with a third, considerably smaller one maintained at Düsseldorf Airport.

Lufthansa is also a founding member of Star Alliance, the world's largest airline alliance, formed in 1997.

On 20 December 2001 Deutsche Lufthansa signed a contract with Airbus for the purchase of fourteen Rolls-Royce Trent powered A380s with options on a further two. At the time, this brought the total number of firm orders and commitments for the A380 to nearly 100.

Deliveries to the German airline were scheduled to begin in 2007 with Lufthansa planning to operate the aircraft on high density routes from its hubs in Germany to cities such as New York, New Delhi, Singapore and Bangkok.

'With this order, we are signalling a future-oriented investment, which will help strengthen Lufthansa's position long term in international competition,' said Lufthansa Chairman and Chief Executive Officer Jürgen Weber.

'We are very proud that Deutsche Lufthansa, one of Europe's most successful carriers, has selected the A380 for their future strategy. This contract signed today in the current environment underscores the demand for very large aircraft as the solution for strong long-term growth in air traffic,' said Airbus President and Chief Executive Officer Noël Forgeard.

Lufthansa's A380 celebrated its first long-haul flight in style with an array of special guests on board;

A typical scene on the ramp with Lufthansa's A380 'MB München (Photo:Lufthansa Technik AG)

The special flight operated by Lufthansa's new flagship on 6 June 2010, carried the German football team, a delegation from the German Football Assoication (DFB) and fans to the World Cup in South Africa. The A380, with flight number LH2010 on the Frankfurt-Johannesburg route, departed Frankfurt Airport at 20.30 hours arriving in Johannesburg at 8.15 hours local time. In addition to the team, DFB trainers and assistants, around 150 soccer fans made the journey on the A380. The fans attended the send-off for the team in the Business Lounge at the flight departure gate and took part in a talk session prior to the flight with Team Manager Oliver Bierhoff, Football Association General Secretary Wolfgang Niersbach and the players. They were also presented with an exclusive Lufthansa World Cup fan kit.

Captain Jürgen Raps, Member of the Lufthansa German Airlines Board and Chief Pilot, was in charge of the special flight on the flight deck. Supporting him in the cockpit were Captain Raimund Müller and Captain Werner Knorr. The cabin crew consisted of two pursers and nineteen flight attendants. *'The A380 is heralding a new dimension in aviation. I hope that the journey on this aircraft will inspire our national team to new dimensions at the World Cup,'* said Jürgen Raps.

'We are thrilled to be the first guests on board Lufthansa's biggest and most modern airliner and hope after a relaxed flight to realise our sporting ambitions at the World Cup in South Africa,' said Team Manager Oliver Bierhoff.

Malaysia Airlines

Malaysian Airline System (MAS) is the flag carrier airline of Malaysia and operates flights from its home base, Kuala Lumpur International Airport and with secondary hubs in Kota Kinabalu and Kuching. The airline has its headquarters on the grounds of Sultan Abdul Aziz Shah Airport in Subang, Selangor, in Greater Kuala Lumpur. It is a member of the Oneworld airline alliance.

Malaysia Airlines operates flights in Southeast Asia, East Asia, South Asia, Middle East and on the Kangaroo Route between Europe and Australasia. It operates transpacific flights from Kuala Lumpur to Los Angeles, via Tokyo.

In 2003, Malaysia Airlines' parent company, Penerbangan Malaysia Berhad, signed a contract with Airbus to purchase six Airbus A380-800 aircraft and on 7 June 2011, the first A380 for Malaysian entered into final assembly phase at the Airbus Final Assembly Line in Toulouse.

On 20 October, the first aircraft flew from

Malaysia Airlines takes delivery of it's first A380. (Photo: MAS)

Toulouse to Hamburg upon completion of the final assembly system tests for painting and fitting out, finally being delivered to Kuala Lumpur on 19 June 2012. The Malaysia Airlines A380 inaugural flight from Kuala Lumpur to London was on 1 July 2012.

Malaysia Airlines introduced double daily Airbus A380 flights on the London route on 24 November 2012, Paris route is effective daily from 1 March 2013 and Hong Kong route on 1 May 2013.

The aircraft have 494 seats in a three-class configuration - eight in first class, 66 in business and 420 in economy. The business class seats, together with 70 economy seats, will be on the aircraft's upper deck. First class seats on the aircraft have a seat pitch of 85 inches and a 87-inch lie-flat bed. The aircraft is also fitted with the Thales in-flight entertainment system and seats in all classes have a USB port and a satellite telephone facility.

'The investment in this latest aircraft, its technology, futuristic style and innovative design in cabin comfort are our initiatives to ensure that our passengers continue to experience an exciting new level of comfort, luxury and convenience. This is the identity that will move us from 'traditional classic' to 'premium contemporary' in our efforts to position Malaysia Airlines as a preferred premium carrier,' said the carrier's chief executive Ahmad Jauhari Yahya.

Queensland and Northern Territories Air Service (QANTAS)

QANTAS took delivery of the first of its 20 A380 aircraft in a moonlight ceremony at Airbus headquarters in Toulouse on 19 September 2008.

The Chief Executive Officer of QANTAS, Geoff Dixon, said the A380 symbolised a new era of travel for QANTAS, the world's most experienced airline.

'No other airline has flown as far as Qantas for as long as QANTAS, so we know very well the value of a well designed inflight product for long haul flights. The A380, with its extra space, new materials and advanced technology, has given us the ideal platform to reinvent the inflight experience.'

Mr Dixon said QANTAS had commissioned Europe-based Australian industrial designer Marc Newson to create stylish and comfortable interiors for its A380 fleet. 'We have been working with Marc on the A380 design for more than five years, and the

A QANTAS A380 (on the right) in formation with an Emirates Airbus A380 fly over Sydney Harbour Bridge and the Opera House on 31 March 2013. The two Airbus A380s display is believed to be the first of its kind between two seperate airlines to fly over Sydney's Harbour which will mark the alliance between the two airlines.
(Photo: Simon Peters Collection)

result, we believe, is the most innovative, functional and intelligent of any aircraft flying today.

'Marc has designed almost everything on board, from the seats and fabrics through to the coat hooks, achieving a look of understated luxury through the use of custom designed fabrics, innovative materials and premium finishes.'

Mr Dixon said QANTAS was the first airline to sign a contract with Airbus for the A380, after selecting the A380 as the cornerstone of its fleet renewal programme in the year 2000.

'We said at the time that in addition to giving us the opportunity to reinvent our product, this revolutionary new aircraft offered capacity and operating savings, as well as environmental improvements. Everything we have seen since our initial order has reinforced this view.'

QANTAS Chief Executive Officer Designate, Mr Alan Joyce, said the selection of the A380 was consistent with QANTAS' tradition as a leader in long-haul travel.

'I look forward to continuing that tradition as the next Chief Executive Officer,' he said. 'Taking delivery of the first of our A380s is an important occasion for us. It is both a culmination - following years of meticulous design development - and a beginning, with the A380 leading us into a new chapter in the story of QANTAS,' Mr Joyce said.

Qatar Airways

Qatar Airways Company Q.C.S.C. operating as Qatar Airways, is the state-owned flag carrier of Qatar. Headquartered in the Qatar Airways Tower in Doha, the airline operates a hub-and-spoke network, linking over 100 international destinations across Africa, Central Asia, Europe, Far East, South Asia, Middle East, North America, South America and Oceania from its base in Doha, using a fleet of more than 100 aircraft.

The airline has more than 30,000 staff, with 17,000 people employed directly and a further 13,000 in its subsidiaries. On 8 October 2012, CEO Akbar Al Baker announced that Qatar Airways would join the Oneworld alliance.

Right: a rendering of the interior of business class in a Qatar Airways' A380.

MSN137, first flew as F-WWST to become A7-APA. Although not yet fully in the Qatar Airways' colour scheme, the tail carried the pre-painted Onyx logo. (Photos: Qatar Airways)

Qatar Airways first ordered two A380s at the Dubai Air Show in January 2004, which was later raised incrementally to thirteen, with options on a further three, the first delivered in 2014. The aircraft are configured with three classes – First, Business and Economy with a fully customized interior, much of the work being carried out by the airline's own in-house design department. The 517-seat aircraft features 457 Recaro CL3620 economy seats, 52 B/E Aerospace Super Diamond business seats, and eight first-class seats. The first-class seats are of an all-new design, and are located at the front of the lower deck, together with an exclusive lounge area. Business passengers also benefit from a lounge area on the upper deck. To the rear of the business cabins, there is a small economy area.

As Qatar Airways CEO Akbar Al Baker stated in 2013 during the reveal of the interior: *'Seeing this image for the first time gives me great pride as Qatar Airways prepares to look forward to our newest aircraft type, the world's biggest, joining our fleet next year.*

'It is a striking example of how far our organisation has rapidly grown to its position of leadership as a truly global and world-class airline. The delivery of the first of our new A380s will mark a new chapter for the airline, while reinforcing our commitment to giving our customers the very best travel experience and service.'

The first Qatar Airways A380 was ferried from Toulouse to Hamburg during a test flight during September 2013 for fitting out and painting, with a delivery date set for the spring of 2014.

Qatar Airways' future home, the Hamad International Airport, scheduled to open in the beginning of 2014, has been specially designed to cater to the A380, with six contact gates designed with specifications required for the super jumbo.

In addition, the maintenance hangar at HIA is able to accommodate two of A380s simultaneously.

CEO Akbar Al Baker said that the airline is pleased to see the progress being made on their first A380. *'It is thrilling to see the A380 painted in Qatar Airways colours on display during its test flight from Toulouse to Hamburg. We have been awaiting the delivery of our first A380, and are delighted to soon operate passenger services with this fantastic aeroplane.*

Our mission is to provide our passengers the best – whether it is comfort, cuisine, the most expansive route network, or the best connectivity. By introducing the A380 to our ever expanding young and modern fleet, we are keeping to our commitment of ensuring that our passengers have the best possible experience when travelling with Qatar Airways,' he added.

Singapore Airlines
Singapore Airlines Limited (SIA) is the flag carrier of Singapore operates a hub at Changi Airport and has a strong presence in the Southeast Asia, East Asia, South Asia, and 'Kangaroo Route' markets. They were the launch customer of Airbus A380. SIA has diversified airline-related businesses, such as aircraft handling and engineering. Its wholly owned subsidiary, SilkAir, manages regional flights to secondary cities with smaller capacity requirements. Subsidiary Singapore Airlines Cargo operates SIA's dedicated freighter fleet, and manages the cargo-hold capacity in SIA's passenger aircraft.

On 29 September 2000, SIA announced an order for up to 25 Airbus A3XX (as the A380 was known at the time). The US$8.6 billion order comprised a firm order of ten aircraft, with options on another fifteen airframes. The order was confirmed by Singapore Airlines on 12 July 2001.

One of Singapore Airlines' A380s at Changi. (Photo: SIA)

'Like a diamond in the sky...' A Singapore Airlines A380 in flight. (Photo: SIA)

In January 2005, the airline unveiled the slogan 'First to Fly the A380 – Experience the Difference in 2006', to promote itself as the first airline to take delivery of the A380-800,

Skymark Airlines

Skymark Airlines Inc. is a low-cost airline headquartered at Tokyo International Airport (Haneda) in Ōta, Tokyo, Japan, operating scheduled passenger services within Japan. In addition to its base at Haneda, Skymark is the dominant carrier at Kobe Airport and is also the only domestic airline operating at Ibaraki Airport north of Tokyo.

Skymark Airlines was established in November 1996 as an independent domestic airline after deregulation of the Japanese airline industry, and started operations on 19 September 1998. It was originally established by a consortium of investors led by the travel agency HIS, and headed by HIS president Hideo Sawada. The airline incurred considerable losses in its first few years of operations, and briefly considered a recapitalization led by Commerzbank, but decided not to accept such an investment due to Air Do's issues with banks interfering in management. In August 2003, Sawada invited internet entrepreneur Shinichi Nishikubo to become Skymark's largest shareholder with a personal cash investment of 3.5 billion yen. On 11 December 2003, Skymark announced that it expected a profit of 470 million yen for the half-fiscal year ending on 31 October, the first profit made since the airline began operations.

On 17 February 2011 Skymark Airlines signed a firm contract with Airbus SAS for purchase of six

Rolls-Royce Trent powered Airbus A380s. As had been previously announced on 8 November 2010, six A380s including two options was ordered, the first aircraft scheduled for delivery in 2014 and will be deployed on international routes.

'Skymark appears set to offer the lowest-density seating arrangement yet on the Airbus A380, for it intends to configure the aircraft with just 394 seats,' said president Shinichi Nishikubo at the Paris air show.

The aircraft would fit 280 premium-economy seats on the lower deck and 114 business-class seats on the upper deck. Nishikubo said the long journeys from Japan on which the A380s would be deployed had sufficient business for premium economy and business, rather than economy services.

Airbus sales chief John Leahy - on the left - stands next to Skymark Airlines Chief Executive Officer Shinichi Nishikubo holding a model of the Airbus A380 aircraft during an announcement at the 49th Paris Air Show at the Le Bourget airport near Paris 23 June 2011. (Photo: Skymark)

Thai Airways

Thai Airways has its origins in 1960 as a joint venture between Scandinavian Airlines System (SAS), which held a 30% share of the new company valued at 2 million baht, and Thailand's domestic carrier, Thai Airways Company. The purpose of the joint venture was to create an international wing for the domestic carrier. SAS also provided operational, managerial, and marketing expertise, with training assistance aimed at building a fully independent national airline within the shortest possible time. The carrier's first revenue flight was on 1 May 1960.

The current Thai Airways is the national flag carrier of Thailand. Formed in 1988, the airline has its corporate headquarters in Vibhavadi Rangsit Road, Chatuchak District, Bangkok, and primarily operates out of Suvarnabhumi Airport. Thai is a founding member of the Star Alliance. The airline is the largest shareholder of the low-cost carrier Nok Air with a 49% stake, and it launched a regional carrier under the name Thai Smile in the middle of 2012 using new Airbus A320 aircraft.

From its hub at Suvarnabhumi Airport, Thai flies to 75 destinations in 35 countries, using a fleet of more than 80 aircraft. The airline was once the operator of two of the world's longest nonstop routes, between Thailand and Los Angeles and New York,

but due to high fuel prices, the withdrawal of aircraft, luggage weight limits, and rising airfares, the airline abandoned all non-stop US services in 2012 indefinitely. As of 2013, services between Bangkok and Los Angeles are served via Incheon Airport near Seoul. Thai's route network is dominated by flights to Europe, East Asia, and South/Southwest Asia, though the airline serves Johannesburg in South Africa and five cities in Oceania. Thai was the first Asia-Pacific airline to serve London Heathrow Airport. Among Asia-Pacific carriers, Thai has one of the largest passenger operations in Europe.

While celebrating its 50-year anniversary in 2010, Thai, spearheaded by Piyasavast Amranand, its president and a former energy minister, charted new plans for the airline's future, including a significant aircraft fleet renewal and an upgrade of existing services. Thai has since placed orders for a number of aircraft, including the six examples of the A380 configured in eight 'Royal' First Class, 80 Business or 'Silk' Class and 485 economy class.

Thai's A380 Royal First Class provides just 12 compartment-style seats, offering greater privacy in a separate cabin, combined with the highest degree of personal service. Seats have an 83 inch pitch, 26.5 inch width and 180° fully-flat bed configuration. The 23″ AVOD interactive touch screen entertainment and information system offers almost unlimited channels and there is full connectivity for Wi-Fi, mobile and SMS communications devices, with an in-seat PC power outlet. Other exclusive

Left: part of the Thai Airways delivery crew. (Photo: Airbus SAS)

Below: A Thai A380 at Frankfurt. (Photo: Thai Airways)

facilities include two larger than standard toilets, one of which features a spacious dressing area. An enlarged galley provides the flexibility to serve meals timed to suite individual passenger's preference.

Meanwhile Thai's A380 Royal Silk Class - with a 'Best in Class' strategy, is designed to provide the maximum in comfort and service for these premium passengers. The separate Royal Silk Class cabin contains 60 shell seats in a staggered layout for greater privacy and direct aisle access. Seats provide a 74 inch pitch, 20 inch width and 180° fully flat recline. The 15 inch personal AVOD interactive touch screen, Wi-Fi, SMS and mobile communications access, plus in-seat PC power point add to passenger convenience.

The airline took delivery of its first Airbus A380 aircraft in the last half of 2012, intending to eventually deploy the aircraft on its core European routes.

Transaero Airlines
OJSC Transaero Airlines, or simply Transaero, is an airline with its head office on the grounds of Domodedovo International Airport, Moscow . It operates scheduled and charter flights to more than 99 domestic and international destinations. Its main bases are Domodedovo and Pulkovo International Airport in Saint Petersburg.

Transaero Airlines, Russia's second largest airline, has completed a purchase agreement with Airbus for four A380 aircraft. The agreement was signed in June 2012 by Olga Pleshakova, Transaero Airlines CEO and Christopher Buckley, Airbus' Executive Vice President Europe, Asia and the Pacific on the first day of the Saint Petersburg International Economic Forum. This order follows a Memorandum of Understanding signed in October 2011. The deal will be financed with the support of VEB Leasing.

Transaero was the first customer for the A380 in Russia, the CIS and Eastern Europe. The Russian carrier planned to start operations with the Engine Alliance-powered A380 on its long-range network of high density routes from Moscow. The aircraft will feature a three class cabin layout, seating about 700 passengers. The world's largest aircraft - Airbus A380, will join the fleet of Transaero in autumn 2015. Speaking to the press, Olga Pleshakova, CEO of Transaero, said: *'The jet will be operating on international routes and possibly it will also be performing flights to Khabarovsk and Vladivostok. We will complete the development of cabin*

Above: Simon Peters' rendering of an A380 in Transaero Airlines colours and markings.

Right: Transaero Airlines, Russia's second-largest airline, CEO Olga Pleshakova (L) and Airbus Executive Vice-President Europe, Christopher Buckley, shake hands as they attend an agreement signing ceremony (Photo: Transaero Airlines)

236

layout by the end of February 2012. There will be
12 seats in Imperial class, 24 in business class
and 612 in economy class. The jet will be able to
seat 648 passengers.

The first class cabin (Imperial) will be located
at the lower deck. Business class will be located
on the second floor. Economy class will be located
behind the first class and the business class on
both decks. The new jet will be performing flights
to Bangkok, Phuket, Dominican Republic, Dubai
and Barcelona.

But taking into account the growth rates of
passenger traffic on routes to Far East, first of all
Khabarovsk and Vladivostok, we are discussing
technical procedures required for servicing A380
with the leadership teams of these airports.

'Our airline, with its strong innovation culture,
will be the first in Russia to fly the A380, the
world's largest passenger aircraft. I am sure that
the operation of the A380 will stimulate the
development of Russia's aviation sector, in
particular, its ground infrastructure. In addition,
our passengers will benefit from the completely
new air travel experience that the A380 offers with
its spacious, comfortable cabin, for their long-haul
flights.'

'We are delighted to welcome Transaero as our
new A380 customer,' said John Leahy, Airbus
Chief Operating Officer, Customers. 'We are
confident that this most efficient aircraft will
enable the airline to cope with the traffic growth
in Russia and offer its passengers unrivalled levels
of comfort on board.'

Virgin Atlantic
Virgin Atlantic, a trading name of Virgin Atlantic
Airways Limited, is a British airline majority-
owned by Sir Richard Branson's Virgin Group.
Virgin Atlantic's head office is in Crawley, West
Sussex, England, near Gatwick Airport. The airline
was established in 1984.

Virgin Atlantic uses a mixed fleet of Airbus and
Boeing wide-body jets and operates between the
United Kingdom, North America, the Caribbean,
Africa, the Middle East, Asia, and Australia from
its main base at Gatwick with secondary bases at
London Heathrow and Manchester.

As early as 26 April 2001, Virgin Atlantic
firmed up its commitment for six A380s plus
options by signing a firm contract for the 21st
century jetliner. The A380, the only all-new very

large aircraft on offer, had demonstrated its success
in the marketplace by - at the time - winning 62
firm commitments plus options from eight
customers.

Virgin Atlantic planned to introduce new
standards of passenger comfort such as casinos and
duty free shops on board the Superjumbo. It said
it would operate the A380, which offered 35%
more seats and 49% more floor space than the
largest aircraft flying, on routes to the US.

At the time, and on numerous instances since,
Sir Richard Branson, Chairman of Virgin Atlantic
Airways, commented: 'I am incredibly excited
about the opportunities these aircraft will bring -
our reputation has been built on innovation and
the A380 will give us the opportunity to create a
new flying experience for our passengers.'

'Virgin Atlantic's strategy is to maintain our
recent spectacular growth and these new aircraft
will play a large part in helping us to expand our
existing services and add new routes. As other
carriers are shrinking in size and cutting their
network, Virgin Atlantic will be offering
passengers more seats on more services to more
destinations.'

Virgin Atlantic continually delayed taking
delivery of six A380 superjumbos ordered from
Airbus more than a decade ago as the U.K. carrier
evaluates whether it still requires the world's
largest jetliner. While delivery dates slipped after
programme delays at Airbus that was originally
scehduled for 2006, Virgin itself put back service
entry as the global economy slumped and the
carrier mulled its own business model.

Virgin Atlantic, which placed a contract for the
double-deckers in 2000, deferred them yet again,
with the first delivery now due in 2018 rather than
2017, Chief Executive Officer Craig Kreeger said
in London.

'It's hard but not impossible to see a world
where we want to take the aircraft,' Kreeger said
in response to questions at the Royal Aeronautical
Society. 'It's not a clear choice.'

While airlines are looking to new planes such
as the A380 to reduce fuel consumption, the
superjumbo may be better suited to operators with
extensive hub systems - such as Dubai-based
Emirates, the biggest customer - than carriers such
as Virgin which generally rely on passengers
traveling point-to-point Kreeger explained.

Appendix 1

Boeing vs Airbus

EU/US Large Civil Aircraft WTO Disputes - Part One.

The US World Trade Organisation challenge to European Union support for Airbus.

Since 1992 direct and indirect government support to aircraft industry in the US and the EU has been regulated by the bilateral EU-US Agreement on Trade in Large Civil Aircraft. The EU in good faith has continuously met all commitments under this agreement, whereas US compliance had been less than adequate, in particular by covering up large hidden subsidies to Boeing including unprecedented prohibited production subsidies in Washington State for the 787 and other Boeing commercial aircraft.

The US and Europe filed counter-cases at the WTO in 2004 after the administration of President George W. Bush unilaterally walked out of a 1992 aircraft-aid accord with the EU. Toulouse, France-based Airbus, which had a record 1,419 orders in 2011 to extend its lead over Boeing, delivered 534 aircraft last year while its rival delivered 477. This came about after Harry Stonecipher, Boeing's chief executive officer held a meeting with US Trade Representative Robert Zoellick in March, 2004 during which he allegedly said *I think it's time we stop this launch aid stuff.'* Stonecipher was later forced to resign on 6 March 2005, following the scandal of an improper relationship with Boeing executive Debra Peabody.

On 6 October the US requested formal WTO consultations with the EU regarding alleged subsidisation of Airbus by the EU and certain of its Member States, and a WTO panel was set up thereafter.

The major bone of contention is that of EU Member State co-financing of Research and Development (R&D) for new Airbus aircraft – determined as 'Member State Financing' or 'reimbursable launch Investment'. This form of support was expressly agreed under the bilateral EU-US Agreement and had been used on three of the nine Airbus aircraft launched since 1990. It provided for government funding to Airbus repaid with interest under terms specified in the Bilateral Agreement (loan rates of return were cost to government plus 1%, and interest and principal is repaid on deliveries, even before the programs break-even). In some cases the terms were more onerous than those commercially available in that the lending governments are receiving royalty payments that will last through the life of a particular aircraft programme even though the original loan and interest are completely repaid. In fact, EU governments so far have made handsome returns on their initial 'investments', even though there are instances where Airbus has been able to obtain financing on more favourable terms from private lenders, compared with government offers. Airbus has repaid in excess of €7 billion. Since 1992, Airbus has repaid 40% more than it has received from EU governments. Airbus currently repays loans at the rate of €300 to €400 million year.

The US also claimed that a number of infrastructure projects were built or upgraded exclusively for Airbus, or that Airbus enjoyed preferential treatment. However, unlike infrastructure projects in the State of Washington - which were designed for Boeing and for which Boeing benefited from preferential treatment, - Airbus pays a market-based rent and clearly did not benefit from any preferential treatment for these projects, or they were for the use of the general public.

As regards research and technology support in the EU - be it at EU or EU Member State level, - such activities are co-financed by the industry and receive no more than a 50% maximum contribution from the EU or Member States, and the EU abides by the cap provided in the bilateral EU-US agreement for such support. The amounts budgeted by NASA and the Department of Defense for R&D support to Boeing's LCA business are estimated to be at least 10 times higher. Furthermore, not a cent of it is repaid.

The US also argued that Airbus benefited from preferential loans from the European Investment Bank (EIB). The EIB has indeed provided loans to Airbus but it has done so in full conformity with its lending rules and policy on conditions strictly similar to that of loans to other clients. For instance, the EIB has provided loans to European airlines for the purchase of Boeing aircraft, as well as to several other large US companies for investments in the EU.

The EU WTO challenge to US subsidies to Boeing. Following the United States' unjustified and unilateral withdrawal from the 1992 bilateral EU-US Agreement on Trade in Large Civil Aircraft and the initiation of WTO dispute settlement procedures against the EU, the EU for its part on 6 October 2004 decided to mirror the US steps by initiating WTO dispute settlement procedures regarding a number of US measures, including federal and state subsidies. A WTO panel was set up thereafter.

In its WTO case against the US, the EU challenged various US Federal, State and local subsidies benefiting Boeing, totalling US$ 23.7 billion in WTO inconsistent subsidies over the past two decades and up to 2024.

At federal level, Boeing benefits from numerous types of R&D support provided by NASA and the Department of Defense (DoD). This support includes contracts for R&D work to be carried out by Boeing - ultimately benefiting Boeing's LCA division and Boeing's aircraft models - reimbursement of Boeing's own R&D expenses, extensive cooperation with NASA and DoD engineers at no cost to Boeing, and use of testing facilities and equipment, also at no cost to Boeing. This support is coupled with the transfer of patents and other vital knowledge to Boeing, and reinforced by stringent restrictions on the application and use of such knowledge by foreign competitors. The EU estimates the benefits of US federal research programs to Boeing at around US$ 16.6 billion over the last two decades.

At federal level Boeing also enjoyed significant tax breaks under the Foreign Sales Corporation and successor legislation. That legislation has already been found to constitute prohibited export subsidies by multiple WTO panels and the WTO Appellate Body. The EU estimates these tax benefits at a value to Boeing's LCA division of US$ 2.2 billion over the period 1989-2006.

At the State and local level, illustrative examples of subsidies to Boeing included a US$4 billion package in the State of Washington (combining tax breaks, tax exemptions or tax credits and infrastructure projects for the exclusive benefit of Boeing) and a US$ 900 million package in the State of Kansas in the form of tax breaks and subsidised bonds, some of which are known as 'Boeing Bonds'. These will be enjoyed by Boeing until 2024.

The EU demonstrated before the WTO panel that the lavish subsidies benefiting Boeing had allowed Boeing to engage in aggressive pricing of its aircraft which has caused lost sales, lost market share and price suppression to Airbus on a number of select markets. It will also show that Boeing received illegal export subsidies: in addition to the Foreign Sales Corporation programme, the Washington State package was made contingent upon Boeing's export performance. Finally, the EU also demonstrated that the US has caused serious prejudice to the EU's interests by violating the EU-US 1992 Agreement.

Details of the US subsidies to Boeing challenged by the EU

1. State and Local Subsidies
    a. State of Washington: incentive package of measures benefiting the development, production and sales of US LCA. These incentives include but are not limited to tax and other advantages
    b. State of Kansas: incentives, including bond financing, tax benefits and other advantages, to the US LCA industry.
    c. State of Illinois: incentives, including tax incentives, relocation assistance and other advantages, to the US LCA industry.

2. NASA Subsidies
NASA transfers economic resources on terms more favourable than available on the market or not at arm's length to the US LCA industry, inter alia, by:
    a. allowing the US LCA industry to participate in research programmes, making payments to the US LCA industry under those programmes, or enabling the US LCA industry to exploit the results thereof by means including but not limited to the foregoing or waiving of valuable patent rights, the granting of limited exclusive rights data ('LERD') or otherwise exclusive or early access to data, trade secrets and other knowledge resulting from government funded research.
    b. providing the services of NASA employees, facilities, and equipment to support the R&D programmes listed above and paying salaries, personnel costs, and other institutional support, thereby providing valuable services to the US LCA industry on terms more favourable than available on the market or not at arm's length.
    c. providing NASA Independent Research & Development, and Bid & Proposal Reimbursements.

d. allowing the US LCA industry to use the research, test and evaluation facilities owned by the US Government, including NASA wind tunnels, in particular the Langley Research Center.

e. entering into procurement contracts with the US LCA industry for more than adequate remuneration.

f. granting the US LCA industry exclusive or early access to data, trade secrets, and other knowledge resulting from government funded research.

g. allowing the US LCA industry to exploit the results of government funded research, including, but not limited to, the foregoing or waiving of valuable patent rights or rights in data as such.

3. Department of Defense Subsidies

The Department of Defense ('DoD') transfers economic resources to the US LCA industry on terms more favourable than available on the market or not at arm's length, inter alia, by:

a. allowing the US LCA industry to participate in DoD-funded research, making payments to the US LCA industry for such research, or enabling the US LCA industry to exploit the results of such research, by means including but not limited to the foregoing or waiving of valuable patent rights, and the granting of exclusive or early access to data, trade secrets and other knowledge resulting from government funded research.

b. allowing the US LCA industry to use research, test and evaluation facilities owned by the US Government, including the Major Range Test Facility Bases.

c. entering into procurement contracts, including those for the purchase of goods, from the US LCA industry for more than adequate remuneration, including in particular but not limited to the US Air Force contract with Boeing for the purchase of certain spare parts for its Airborne Warning and Control System (AWACS) aircraft, the National Polar-orbiting Operational Environmental Satellite System-Conical Microwave Imager Sensor, the C-22 Replacement Program (C-40), the KC-135 Programmed Depot Maintenance, the C-40 Lease and Purchase Program, the C-130 avionics modernisation upgrade program, the C-17 H22 contract (Boeing BC-17X), the US Navy contract with Boeing for the production and maintenance of 108 civil B737 and their

conversion into long-range submarine hunter Multi-Mission Aircraft, the Missile Defense Agency's Airborne Laser (ABL) Program, and the Army's Comanche Program.

d. by allowing the US LCA industry to exploit the results of government funded research, including, but not limited to, the foregoing or waiving of valuable patent rights or rights in data as such.

4. National Institute of Standards & Technology (US Department of Commerce) Subsidies.

The US Department of Commerce ('DoC') transfers economic resources to the US LCA industry on terms more favourable than available on the market or not at arm's length, through the Advanced Technology Program operated pursuant to the Omnibus Trade and Competitiveness Act of 1988, as amended, and the American Technology Preeminence Act of 1991, by allowing the US LCA industry to participate in this programme, making payments to the US LCA industry under this programme, or allowing the US LCA industry to exploit the results of this programme, including but not limited to the foregoing or waiving of valuable patent rights, and the granting of exclusive or early access to data, trade secrets and other knowledge resulting from government funded research.

5. US Department of Labor

The US Department of Labor transfers economic resources to the US LCA industry on terms more favourable than available on the market or not at arm's length, through the Aerospace Industry Initiative, an element of the President's High Growth Training Initiative, under the authority of the Workforce Investment Act, by granting to Edmonds Community College in the State of Washington funds for the training of aerospace industry workers associated with the Boeing 787.

6. Federal tax incentives

The US Government transfers economic resources to the US LCA industry through the federal tax system, and in particular through the following tax measures:

a. Sections 921-927 of the Internal Revenue Code (prior to repeal) and related measures establishing special tax treatment for 'Foreign Sales Corporations' ('FSCs');

b. FSC Repeal and Extraterritorial Income Exclusion Act of 2000; and

c. American Jobs Creation Act of 2004.

Support to Airbus and Boeing: Seperating the myths from the facts.

What is launch investment?

'Launch aid' is a term used by the US as a misnomer for royalty-based financing granted by certain EC Member States in individual circumstances to a number of companies, that includes Airbus. Since its creation in 1970, some Airbus aircraft development programmes have been financed in part by royalty based financing, otherwise known as 'launch investment'. This kind of finance works in the same way as commercial investments.

The US itself has agreed with the EC in a 1992 international agreement that Airbus may receive such financing within specific and detailed limits. As laid down in the Agreement,

Member State governments advance money to Airbus up to the limit agreed with the US, namely 33% of the total development costs of a new aircraft model. This advance is then repaid by means of a levy on the sale of each aircraft. The levy is set so that, once an agreed sales target is reached, the whole amount should be repaid with a rate of return, i.e. with interest, over a repayment period of 17 years (i.e. 11-12 years from the first delivery).

The sales target is based on a conservative forecast of future sales, which is established when the investment is made.

The interest rate reflects the investing government's objective to earn a good return on its money. It is always in excess of the government's borrowing rate - typically 6-8% nominal - and may be considerably higher, depending, for instance, on the anticipated commercial success of the project and on the Member State. Some Member States insist on a higher return. Once the actual sales exceed the target, as has happened, investing governments continue to collect 'royalties' or 'upside' on the additional sales, which will further increase their rate of return.

Airbus has paid significant amounts of royalties to the Member States which exceed by far the Member States' investments since 1992. Therefore, this instrument is characterised by 'success-sharing' (i.e. extra profit for the investing government) rather than a certain element of risk inherent in any kind of investment (in the present case insofar as payback is linked to the actual sale of aircraft).

None of the individual launch investments granted by the Member States since 1992 has ever exceeded the limits, terms and conditions to which the US government agreed.

If launch aid is such a good investment, why don't other countries do it?

They do. Launch investment schemes are in fact, a widely-used form of financing the development, and outside Europe, also the production, of civil aircraft. They are used, for instance, in Canada and Japan.

Boeing benefits from a Japanese scheme for development and production of Boeing's 787 aircraft, which competes with the Airbus A350. In effect, 35% of the B787 will be produced in Japan and it is understood that Boeing's risk-sharing partners have received financing from the Japanese government of up to 70% of development costs (the ceiling in the EU is 33%). And this is on top of the other forms of support Boeing receives.

The example of Japan demonstrates that even if the Airbus-Boeing dispute is presented as a US jobs issue, Boeing increasingly outsources its R & D projects to non-US firms, and therefore non-US workers, while continuing to receive US government support. The opposite is true for Airbus which imports more and more jobs into the US, but does not benefit from US government funding.

It is also noteworthy that Boeing itself sought royalty-based launch investment from the US government in the 1970's. However, Boeing is significantly better off under the current system since the company benefits from subsidies (e.g. $3.2 billion tax subsidies by the State of Washington for the B787 alone) which do not have to be repaid.

How much launch investment has Airbus received?

Since 1992, the Member States concerned have granted royalty based financing subject to the strict limits agreed with the US in the 1992 EC-US agreement.

Since then, Member States have committed a total of €3.7 billion in launch investment to Airbus. Of the Airbus programmes since 1992 the A330-200 and the A340-500/600 and the A380 received launch investment. The A318 was developed without launch investment.

How much launch investment has Airbus repaid?

Since 1992, Airbus has repaid to the Member States concerned around €6 billion, or €9 billion ($12 billion) in real present value. This means that since 1992, Airbus has repaid over 40 percent more than it has received from EU governments.

Airbus currently repays €300-400 million per year. Principal and interest of launch investment to Airbus have been and continue to be re-paid on the delivery of each aircraft, along with royalty payments thereafter.

How is Boeing supported if it does not receive launch investment from the US government?
Boeing receives different forms of support from the US federal and state governments that benefit the development, production and sales of its civil aircraft.

Taken together (e.g. tax breaks, R&D and infrastructure support), US support has consistently exceeded the limit allowed under the EU-US Agreement of 1992 by 2 to 3 times. These sums have not been reimbursed.

Does Boeing receive R&D support?
Boeing relies on the R& D subsidies it receives from a variety of quarters. In the US, Boeing receives subsidies from NASA's and Department of Defense programmes and contracts (estimated at being at least $22 billion), as well as the Department of Commerce and the Department of Labor, e.g. by providing funds for specific research into composite technology from which the 787 airframe will be constructed and sophisticated software tools that Boeing will use for 787 design and manufacture. Civil R&D support in the EU is granted in the form of generally available programmes (e.g. the EU R&D Framework Programme) in which a large number of companies participate, including Boeing.

Surely, the subsidies Boeing receives benefit only its military or space business?
No. So-called 'military' and 'space' subsidies provide considerable benefits for Boeing's civil aircraft business. Department of Defence and NASA subsidies have helped Boeing develop technologies (e.g. composites) which the company uses in its civil aircraft. Boeing uses DoD centres and testing facilities to work on the design and wings of its civil aircraft. E.g. these subsidies have enabled Boeing to develop the technologies used in its 787 and other civil aircraft, but are not available to Airbus.

This reduces, and effectively subsidises, Boeing's production costs and puts Airbus at a competitive disadvantage. Another issue are non-competitive 'military' contracts at inflated prices which benefit Boeing's civil aircraft business. The situation is therefore problematic: Boeing receives a number of benefits courtesy of US government programmes, its noncompetitive military contracts, awarded at inflated prices by the US government, benefits which are passed on to its civil aircraft production. In other words, R&D for Boeing's civil airplanes is effectively being paid for from US military budgets, rather than Boeing's own pocket.

EU/US Large Civil Aircraft WTO Disputes - Part Two.

The focus in the EU-US aircraft dispute then shifted to the EU's challenge to US subsidies to Boeing, with the Americans putting their case.

The core of the EU's challenge was the lavish R&D support provided by the US Department of Defense and NASA through various means, as well as Boeing-specific support provided at state and local level, such as subsidy packages tailor-made for Boeing in the states of Washington, Kansas and Illinois. The support was aimed at weakening Airbus' position and competitiveness and boosting that of Boeing. Although the US tried to dismiss the challenges using smoke and mirrors, US federal law makers, high-ranking officials, and local politicians have all acknowledged the vital role this support plays for Boeing. Indeed, former Washington State Governor Gary Locke said that the Washington State support is designed to help *'Boeing beat Airbus'* and to *'give Airbus executives many sleepless nights for years to come'*.

Former NASA Langley Director J.F. Creedon was on the record as saying that *'the reason that there is a NASA Langley and the other aeronautics centers is to contribute technology to assure the pre-eminence of US aeronautics'*.

The US filed its reply to the EU's challenge on 6 July 2007. The US acknowledged that FSC and successor schemes were prohibited export subsidies and that Boeing was a main beneficiary. The US, however, claimed that Boeing will not avail itself of any benefits post-2006 despite an internal IRS memorandum which would allow for such benefits to be claimed by companies like Boeing. The US failed provide any documentation that Boeing will actually forego these WTO-incompatible benefits.

For subsidies granted by the State of Washington and the State of Illinois, the US puts up a less than vigorous defence and appears to agree with the EU that subsidies have benefited – and will continue to benefit – Boeing. In both states the subsidies are clearly designed for the exclusive benefit of Boeing. The US claims that these subsidies were generally available, or not designed for the benefit of Boeing lack any credibility. Indeed, these incentive packages had been designed in negotiations with the Boeing company, and even include a contractual promise by the State of Washington that it will provide a US$ 4 billion subsidy regardless of form.

For other subsidies, such as those granted by Kansas authorities, the US makes sweeping statements that Boeing did not benefit – and will not benefit. The US offered essentially no evidentiary support for these claims. The EU noted that these bonds are commonly referred to as 'Boeing Bonds' so how can they not be for the benefit of Boeing?

The US contested the amount of R&D subsidies granted to Boeing as challenged by the EU – an apparent contradiction with the US stance on its challenge of Airbus support where the US grossly inflates the numbers. The EC provided detailed tables and breakdowns of all Large Civil Aircraft-related R&D support and offered to submit all original documentation regarding such support, should the Panel so request. One wonders why the US cannot be equally forthcoming.

The US also sought to argue that certain R&D support should be excluded for purposes of the WTO dispute as it has resulted in military or dual-use technologies which are subject to stringent US export controls and cannot be included in LCAs for exportation. The US conveniently overlooks the fact that while such technologies may not be part of an exported LCA as such, they may be – and frequently are – used in the actual production of LCAs. What is more, the press and even a former Boeing engineer have reported on suspicious Boeing practices of recreating research to 'work around' International Traffic in Arms Regulations (ITAR) controls and use military data for the Boeing 787 despite US restrictions. This is another example of how the US is hiding behind general statements about US laws and regulations while refusing to disclose the actual information and evidence related to R&D support to Boeing.

EU/US Large Civil Aircraft WTO Disputes - Part Three

Finally, in March 2012 the WTO upheld a ruling for Airbus in saying Boeing received illegal US Subsidies. The WTO's Appellate Body backed a March 2011 report finding the US provided aid to Chicago-based Boeing through federal research grants and state support in developing aircraft including the 787 Dreamliner. Airbus parent European Aeronautic, Defence & Space Co. (EAD) has said the aid to Boeing cost it $45 billion in lost sales from 2002 to 2006.

Both the European Union and the US appealed the initial ruling. Appellate judges in Geneva reversed an earlier finding that only two of twenty-three Department of Defense programmes gave illegal aid, saying that subsidies from all twenty-three programs violated global trade rules. They also reversed an earlier ruling that tax breaks from Kansas didn't cause adverse effects.

EU Trade Commissioner Karel De Gucht told reporters in Geneva that the subsidies were *'a blatantly unlawful way of supporting'* Boeing's business.

The Appellate Body backed the US in its argument that aid for Boeing's 777 aircraft didn't harm the Airbus A340. Judges 'dramatically reduced' the harm to Airbus in terms of market share and lost sales and orders, said Bob Novick, external counsel for Boeing in Washington.

The appeals judges reduced the number of lost sales campaigns due to the subsidies to six from twelve in the initial panel report. They also found that Airbus lost 118 orders because of the aid, down from 300 in the first report and below the 436 alleged by the EU. Judges said Airbus was hurt only in one market - Australia - rather than the ten mentioned in the first panel report.

The WTO has also ruled that Airbus received billions of euros in low-interest loans from EU governments, and the US has asked the trade arbiter to approve retaliatory sanctions of as much as $10 billion for the EU's failure to comply with that ruling.

Judges originally found that Boeing received at least $5.3 billion in illegal aid between 1989 and 2006 and was slated to get $3 billion to $4 billion in incompatible future aid based on Washington state tax measures. This appellate ruling means the harm caused by the subsidies may be found to exceed $5.3 billion, though the panel didn't name a figure.

The EU has estimated the total amount of subsidies between 1989 and 2006 at $19.1 billion. The amount of harm is important because it is the basis on which a government can request permission to impose a specific level of sanctions. The illegal aid includes NASA research and development programs for $2.6 billion between 1989 and 2006 and Department of Defense programs with aid as high as $1.2 billion in the same period. There were also three Washington state tax breaks valued at as much as $4 billion from 2006-2024 and foreign sales corporation export subsidies amounting to $2.2 billion until 2006, as well as $476 million in Kansas aid.

Appendix 2

Bibliography/References

747-400 Airport Compatibility Report, section 2.2.1. *Boeing, December 2002.*

747-400 Cross Sections. *Boeing fact sheet.*

747-8 Airport Compatibility Report, section 2.2.1. *Boeing, December 2011.*

A first look inside Emirates' A380s. *The Times (UK).*

A stretch version of the A380? It's in the plans. *Seattle Post-Intelligencer.*

A350 cockpit borrows A380 innovations. *Air Transport Briefing. 6 March 2006.*

A380 – A solution for airports . *Airbus.*

A380 Aircraft Characteristics - Airport and Maintenance Planning. *Airbus fact sheet 1 November 2012.*

A380 convoys. *IGG.FR. 28 October 2007.*

A380 Family. *Airbus fact sheet.*

A380 first touchdown in the United States as part of commercial Route Proving. *Airbus. 12 March 2007.*

A380 flight deck. Airbus fact sheet.

A380 Freighter delayed as Emirates switches orders. *Flight International. 16 May 2006.*

A380 Freighter Specifications. *Airbus fact sheet.*

A380 makes test flight on alternative fuel. *Reuters.*

A380 powers on through flight-test. *Flight International.*

A380 production ramp-up revisited. *Airbus. 13 May 2008.*

A380 pushes 5000 psi into realm of the common man. *Hydraulics & Pneumatics.*

A380 Repairs to cost Airbus 105 million pounds. *Air Transport World. 14 March 2012.*

A380 Specifications. *Airbus fact sheet.*

A380 superjumbo gives thrilling morning air show. *The Standard. Hong Kong.*

A380 superjumbo lands in Sydney. *BBC. 25 October 2007.*

A380 wake tests prompt call to reassess all large aircraft. *Flightglobal. 29 November 2005.*

A380 wake vortex study provides some good news for Airbus. *ATW. 29 September 2006.*

A380-900 and freighter both on 'back-burner': *Flight International. 20 May 2010.*

A380, the 21st century flagship, successfully completes its first flight. *Airbus. 27 April 2005.*

A380: 'more electric' aircraft. *Aviation Today.*

A380: 'More Electric' Aircraft. *Avionics Magazine.*

A380: Milestones. *Singapore Airlines.*

A380: topping out ceremony in the equipment hall. A380: special transport ship in Hamburg for the first time. *Airbus Press Centre. 10 June 2004.*

Advances in more-electric aircraft technologies. *Aircraft Engineering and Aerospace Technology (Emerald Group) 73 (3). 2001.*

Aerospace Notebook: It's no cruise ship of the sky, but A380 is raising the bar for comfort. *Seattle Post-Intelligencer.*

Air Austral Reaffirms its Selection of Engine Alliance GP7200 Engines and Fleet Management Agreement *(Press release). Engine Alliance. 17 November 2009.*

Air Austral selects A380 in single-class configuration for future growth *(Press release). Airbus. 15 January 2009.*

Air Austral signs firm order for two single class A380s *(Press release). Airbus. 17 November 2009.*

Air Austral to take 840-seat A380s in 2014. *Flightglobal.com (Reed Business Information).*

Air France confirms A3XX pre-selection *(Press release). EADS. 24 July 2000.*

Air France gets Europe's first A380 superjumbo. *Agence France-Presse. 30 October 2009.*

Air France picks business seat; eyeing premium economy for A380. *Flight International.*

Air France places major order *(Press release). Airbus. 18 June 2001.*

Air France seeks Airbus compensation for A380 glitches: *report. DefenceWeb.*

Air France set to get Europe's first A380 superjumbo. *MSN News. 30 October 2009.*

Air France to order two additional A380s and 18 A320 Family aircraft *(Press release). Airbus. 18 June 2007.*

Air France to replace 747 fleet with 18 777s and two A380s. *Flightglobal.com (Reed Business Information).*

Air France welcomed its first A380 *(Press release). Air France. 22 November 2010.*

Air France, the first European carrier to offer flights on the A380. *Air France.*

Airbus 380 conducts test flights in Addis Ababa. *Ethiopian Reporter. 21 November 2009.*

Airbus A380 Cabin. *Airbus fact sheet.*

Airbus A380 completes test flight. *BBC News. 4 September 2006.*

Airbus A380 evacuation trial full report: everyone off in time. *Flight International.*

Airbus A380 jets off for tests in Asia from the eye of a storm. *USA Today.*

Airbus A380 Superjumbo. *Aerospace-Technology.com.*

Airbus A380 vortex-revised guidance material *ICAO. 16 January 2007.*

Airbus A380 wake turbulence may double safe distance between planes. *Aviationpros. 23 November 2005.*

Airbus A380 wake vortex study completed. *Airbus S.A.S. 28 September 2006.*

Airbus A380 Wing Flaws May Cost USD$629M *Reuters 24 May 2012.*

Airbus A380: Mehr als 1,5 Millionen Passagiere. *FlugRevue. 11 May 2009.*

Airbus A380: Superjumbo of the 21st Century. Norris, Guy; Mark Wagner (2005). Zenith Press. ISBN 978-0-7603-2218-5.

Airbus A380's bar, flatbeds, showers irk Engineers. *Bloomberg.*

Airbus A380F Wide-Bodied Freighter. *Aerospace-technology.com. 12 December 2006.*

Airbus Adjusts A380 Assembly Process. *Aviation Week. 26 January 2012.*

Airbus aircraft 2011 average list prices. *Airbus S.A.S.*

Airbus Beats Boeing on 2010 Orders, Deliveries as Demand Recovery Kicks In. *Bloomberg.*

Airbus Bust, Boeing Boost. *The Washington Post.*

Airbus Cabin Showroom. *Airbus.*

Airbus conducts A380 alternative-fuel demonstration flight. *Flight International.*

Airbus confirms further A380 delay and launches company restructuring plan. *Airbus. 3 October 2006.*

Airbus could build next Air Force One; 747 due to be replaced. *Seattle Times.*

Airbus delay on giant jet sends shares plummeting. *International Herald Tribune.*

Airbus delivers China Southern Airlines' first A380. *Airbus.com. 14 October 2011.*

Airbus delivers first A380 fuselage section from Spain. *Airbus. 6 November 2003.*

Airbus delivers tenth A380 in 2010 (Press release). 16 July 2011.

Airbus Expects Sharp Order Drop in 2009. *Aviation Week and Space Technology. 15 January 2009.*

Airbus Fell Short with 10 A380s in 2009. *Business Week.*

Airbus Flight Shows Off Troubled A380. *Washington Post.*

Airbus Giant-Jet Gamble OKd in Challenge to Boeing; Aerospace: EU rebuffs Clinton warning that subsidies for project could lead to a trade war. *Los Angeles Times.*

Airbus has no timeline on the A380 freighter. *Flight International.*

Airbus hits the road with A3XX. *Interavia Business & Technology.*

Airbus jumbo on runway. CNN. 19 December 2000.

Airbus names A380 delivery centre in Hamburg after Jürgen Thomas. *Airbus. 4 July 2008.*

Airbus narrowly meets delivery target of 12 A380s in 2008. *Flight International. 30 December 2008.*

Airbus opens its books for the world's biggest jumbo. But is it a plane too far?. *The Independent (UK).*

Airbus Orders and Deliveries (XLS). *Airbus. February 2014.*

Airbus plant Riesen A380 (in German). *Topnews.de. 22 November 2007.*

Airbus poised to start building new higher weight A380 variant. *Flight International. 18 May 2010.*

Airbus ponders A380 thrust reverser options. *Flight International. 3 April 2001.*

Airbus replaces chief of jumbo jet project. *International Herald Tribune.*

Airbus says A380F development 'interrupted'. *Flight International*.

Airbus set for US debut of world's largest passenger jet. *Los Angeles Times*.

Airbus starts painting first A380. *Airbus*. 11 April 2007.

Airbus test flight eith Engine Alliance Engines a Success. *PR Newswire*. 28 August 2006.

Airbus tests A380 jet in extreme cold of Canada. *MSNBC*. 8 February 2006.

Airbus to extend A380 to accommodate 1,000 passengers. *India Times. Thaindian.com*. 29 August 2008.

Airbus to inspect all A380 superjumbos for wing cracks. *BBC News Online*. 8 February 2012.

Airbus to offer higher-weight A380 from 2013. *Flight International*. 20 Feb 2012.

Airbus to reinforce part of A380 wing after March static test rupture. *Flight International*. 23 May 2006.

Airbus Wants A380 Cost Cuts. *Wall Street Journal*.

Airbus will lose €4.8bn because of A380 delays. *The Times (UK)*.

Airbus will reveal plan for super-jumbo: Aircraft would seat at least 600 people and cost dollars 8bn to develop. *The Independent (UK)*.

Airbus' 'big baby' is too big. *Seattle Post-Intelligencier*.

Aircraft movements. *Lufthansa fact sheet*.

Airports Prepare for the A380. *Airport Equipment & Technology*.

Airworthiness Directive regarding Airbus A380 wing cracks. *The Aviation Herald*.

Aluminum Alloy Development for the Airbus A380. Key to metals

Amedeo firms up order for 20 A380s. *Airbus.com*.

Andriulaitis, Robert. B747-8F VS A380F *InterVISTAS, December 2005*.

Asiana Airlines places order for six A380s *(Press release). Airbus*. 6 January 2011.

Asiana orders six A380s. *Flightglobal*.

Asiana Signs Deal to Receive A380 (Press release). *Asiana Airlines*. 20 January 2011.

ATSB Report AO-2008-077 *Australian Transport Safety Bureau*, 9 December 2009.

Aviation giants have Super-jumbo task *Orlando Sentinel*. 27 November 1994.

Barco extends its success in the civil avionics market with new Airbus deal. *Barco*.

BBC News - Airbus A380 wing repairs could take up to eight weeks. *BBC.co.uk*. 2012-06-11.

BBC Two: 'How to build a superjumbo wing'. *BBC*. 23 November 2011.

Boeing Current Market Outlook 2007 . *Boeing Commercial Airplanes*. 20 November 2007.

Boeing looks again at plans for NLA. *Flight International*.

Boeing, partners expected to scrap Super-Jet study. *Los Angeles Times*. 10 July 1995.

Boeing's 747-8 vs A380: A titanic tussle. *Flight International*.

Branson favors planned Airbus 900-seat A380. *Seattle Times*. 21 February 2004.

British Airways and Emirates will be first for new longer-range A380. *Flight International*. 14 May 2009.

British Airways selects Rolls-Royce power for long haul fleet (Press release). *Rolls-Royce*. 27 September 2007.

British Airways to buy 12 Airbus A380 aircraft for long haul fleet *(Press release). Airbus*. 27 September 2007.

Cabin Interior, Mood Lighting. *Diehl Aerospace, Germany*.

Can the A380 Bring the Party Back to the Skies?. *TIME magazine*.

Catering. *Lufthansa fact sheet*

China Southern Airlines receives its first Pearl of the sky A380 jetliner. *Airbus.com*. 14 October 2011.

China Southern Airlines sign for five A380s *(Press release). Airbus*. 21 April 2005.

China Southern Airlines, CASGC sign agreement with Airbus for the purchase of five A380s *(Press release). Airbus*. 28 January 2005.

China Southern Airlines' first A380 makes its maiden flight *(Press release). China Southern Airlines*. 16 February 2011.

Cockpit. *Lufthansa fact sheet*.

Coming Soon: The Innovative Airbus A380. *Aviation Today*. 1 April 2006.

Common Agreement Document of the A380 *Airport Compatibility Group Version 2.1 page 8, European Civil Aviation Conference, December 2002*.

Comparing Airlines' Airbus A380s. *Los Angeles Times*.

Convoi Exceptionnel. Airliner World *(Key Publishing Ltd)*. May 2009.

Creating A Titan. *Flight International*. 14 June 2005.

EADS hopeful A380 could break even in 2015. *Flight International*. 2010.

EADS Sees One-Off Drop In A380 Deliveries

With a spotter on each wingtip and one by the nose A380 A6-EEC, operating as Emirates EK02 from London Heathrow to Dubai is pushed back. (Photo: author)

*All the doors and escape slides are checked on this Lufthansa A380 during regular maintenance.
(Photo: Lufthansa Technik AB)*

Next Year. *Aviation Week, 27 July 2012.*

EADS waves off bid for Air Force One replacement. *Flight International. 28 January 2009.*

EADS: the A380 Debate . *Morgan Stanley.*

EASA AD No.:2012-0013. *EASA. 20 January 2012.*

EASA mandates prompt detailed visual inspections of the wings of 20 A380s. *EASA.*

EASA Type Certificate Data Sheet (TCDS) IM.E.026 Issue 02 *EASA. 23 May 2008.*

EASA Type-Certificate Data Sheet (TCDS) A.110 Issue 05.0 *EASA. 1 December 2009.*

EASA Type-Certificate Data Sheet (TCDS) E.012 Issue 04 *EASA. 24 May 2007*

EASA Type-Certificate Data Sheet TCDS A.110 Issue 03 *EASA. 14 December 2007.*

East Asia's first A380 goes into operation today. *Korea JoongAng Daily.*

Eaton wins hydraulic system contract for A380, $200 million potential for US company. *Business Wire. 10 October 2001.*

Emirates A350-1000 Order 'In Limbo'. *Aviation Week.*

Emirates A380 arrives in New York! *Emirates Press Release 3 August 2008.*

Emirates A380 fever heads to the U.S.. *Emirates Press Release 1 August 2008.*

Emirates A380 flights Dubai - Los Angeles. *Emirates Press Release. 2013*

Emirates A380 Lands at New York's JFK. *Emirates Press Release 1 August 2008.*

Emirates A380. Emirates Press Release.

Emirates A380s to Establish New Airliner Seat Record. *Aviation. 8 June 2008.*

Emirates Airline agrees to buy eight additional Airbus A380s *(Press release). Airbus. 18 June 2007.*

Emirates Airline buys 65 Airbus A350s and 11 additional A380s *(Press release). Airbus. 11 November 2007.*

Emirates Airlines reaffirms commitment to A380 and orders additional four. *Airbus.*

Emirates Airlines reaffirms commitment to A380 and orders additional four (Press release). Airbus. 7 May 2007.

Emirates becomes first to sign for A3XX *(Press release). EADS. 24 July 2000.*

Emirates commits to the A3XX *(Press release). Airbus. 30 April 2000.*

Emirates orders 32 Airbus A380 super jumbos valued at US$ 11.5B. *Emirates Press Release. 8 June 2010.*

Emirates orders 41 additional Airbus aircraft (Press release). Airbus. 16 June 2003.

Emirates orders 50 additional A380s, boosting fleet to 140. *Airbus. 17 November 2013.*

Emirates orders a further 32 Airbus A380s *(Press release). Airbus. 8 June 2010.*

Emirates Selects Engine Alliance GP7200 Engines to Power Latest A380 Aircraft Order (Press release). *Engine Alliance. 19 July 2010.*

Emirates Selects GP7200 Engines for Additional Airbus A380 Aircraft (Press release). *Engine Alliance. 11 November 2007.*

Emirates Triples A380 Order, Selects A340-600 and Adds A330s (Press release). *EADS. 4 November 2001.*

Environment. *Lufthansa.*

Etihad Airways and the Engine Alliance Finalize GP7200 Engine and Fleet Management Agreements (Press release). *Engine Alliance. 7 March 2011.*

Etihad Airways buys 55 Airbus aircraft, including the A380 and A350 *(Press release). Airbus. 14 July 2008.*

Etihad places 55 firm aircraft orders with Airbus. *Etihad Airways. 14 July 2008.*

Etihad Selects Airbus A380 And A330/A340 Family Aircraft *(Press release). Airbus. 20 July 2004.*

Europe – Airbus plans 900-Seat Superjumbo; Emirates would buy. *Bloomberg.*

Exceptional Air France Airbus A380 flights on London-Heathrow to Paris-CDG route. *Corporate.airfrance.com. May 2010.*

Exemption No. 8695. Renton, Washington: *Federal Aviation Authority. 24 March 2006.*

FAA Type Certificate Data Sheet (TCDS) E00072EN Revision 3 *FAA. 29 September 2010.*

FAA Type Certificate Data Sheet (TCDS) E00075EN *FAA. 6 June 2007.*

FAA Type Certificate Data Sheet (TCDS) NO.A58NM Revision 4 . FAA. 26 January 2009.

FAA Type Certificate Data Sheet NO.A58NM Rev 2 FAA. 14 December 2007.

Farnborough 2008: Etihad switching four test A380s for 10 new-build. Flightglobal.com. *Reed Business Information.*

Fascinating figures about the A380. *Airbus.*

FedEx Corporation Quarterly Report. *31 August 2002*.

FedEx Drops Airbus A380 Order, to Buy 15 Boeing 777s. *Bloomberg L.P.*

FedEx Express to acquire Airbus A380-800F *(Press release)*. *EADS. 17 January 2001*.

FedEx Express to Acquire Boeing 777 Freighters *(Press release)*. *FedEx Express. 27 November 2006*.

Fedex pulls out of superjumbo. *Europe Intelligence Wire. 8 November 2006*.

FedEx signs for 10 A380s *(Press release)*. *Airbus. 16 July 2002*.

First A380 for Qantas - The road to delivery. *Flightglobal.com (Reed Business Information)*.

Flight Test: Airbus A380. *Flight International*.

Flying by Nature Airbus Global Market Forecast 2007–2026. *Airbus S.A.S. 31 January 2008*.

Flying the Airbus giant of the skies. *The Times (UK)*.

Furthering fleet growth with world's most eco-efficient aircraft *(Press release)*. *Airbus. 15 November 2011*.

GE joint venture engines tested on Airbus A380. *Business Courier. 25 August 2006*.

Giant plane a testimony to 'old Europe'. *BBC News*.

Global Aircraft – Airbus A380.

GP7200 engine features. Engine Alliance.

GP7200 series specification. *Engine Alliance*.

Green Light For Aircraft Orders *(Press release)*. *British Airways. 27 September 2007*.

High pressure, low weight. *Design News*.

Historical Orders and Deliveries 1974–2009 . *Airbus S.A.S. January 2010*.

How to make an elephant fly. *Scenta. 31 July 2007*.

HRH Prince Alwaleed bin Talal places first order for A380 flying palace (Press release). Airbus. 12 November 2007.

Hydraulic services contract for Airbus A380 wing jigs. *Aircraft Engineering and Aerospace Technology (Emerald Group) 76 (2). 2004*.

ILFC Annual Report. *Morningstar Document Research. 9 March 2011*.

ILFC A380 deliveries pushed back by one year. *Flightglobal.com. Reed Business Information*.

ILFC orders aircraft from Airbus and Boeing *(Press release)*. *ILFC. 8 March 2011*.

ILFC Picks GP7000 for A380s (Press release). GE Aviation. 4 September 2003.

ILFC signs for five A3XXs *(Press release)*. *Airbus. 25 July 2000*.

ILFC to defer its Airbus A380 order until at least 2013, ditching freighter variants for passenger configuration. *Flight International. 4 December 2006*.

ILFC to defer its Airbus A380 order until at least 2013, ditching freighter variants for passenger configuration. *Flightglobal.com (Reed Business Information)*.

Indonesians collect debris from Qantas plane engine. *Australian Broadcasting Corporation. 4 November 2010*.

Inflight engine failure – Qantas, Airbus A380, VH-OQA, overhead Batam Island, Indonesia, 4 November 2010. Australian Transport Safety Bureau, 18 May 2011.

Innovative Honeywell helps to curb A380 weight. Flight International. 15 June 2005. Some systems, like the electromagnetic thrust reversers are a first for a commercial aircraft

Innovative Variable Frequency Power. *Goodrich*.

Interim Aerodrome requirements for the A380. *Civil Aviation Authority of New Zealand. 4 November 2004*.

Interview-Cathay Pacific to wait on next-generation planes. *Reuters*.

It flies! But will it sell? Airbus A380 makes maiden flight, but commercial doubts remain. *Associated Press. 27 April 2005*.

Kingfisher becomes first Indian customer for A380, A350, & A330 *(Press release)*. *Airbus. 15 June 2005*.

Kingfisher defers delivery to wait for A380-900. *ATW Daily News. 6 February 2009*.

Kingfisher Delays Ordered Airbus A380 Deliveries Second Time. *Fox Business Network. Dow Jones Newswires*.

Kingsley-Jones, Max (16 May 2006). Airbus A380 Freighter delayed as Emirates switches orders to passenger variant. Flightglobal.com *(Reed Business Information)*.

Korean Air A380. *Korean Air*.

Korean Air Adds Two A380 to Fleet Order, Upping A380 Order to Ten *(Press release)*. *Korean Air. 3 February 2009*.

Korean Air expands A380 aircraft order (Press release). *Airbus. 19 February 2008*.

Korean Air goes for Airbus A380 *(Press release)*. *Airbus. 18 June 2003*.

Korean Air Launches Inaugural A380 Services. *2 June 2011*.

Korean Air looks to the future with A380 *(Press release)*. *Airbus. 23 October 2003*.

Korean Air orders two more A380s *(Press release)*. *Airbus. 3 February 2009*.

Korean Air Selects Engine Alliance as A380 Supplier *(Press release)*. *Engine Alliance. 14 June 2005*.

Korean Air to buy 3 more A380 jets from Airbus. *Reuters. 13 February 2008*.

Landmark A380 contract signed *(Press release)*. *Airbus. 19 June 2001*.

Lehman puts $18bn price tag on Airbus float. *The Independent (UK)*.

Long Range vs. Ultra High Capacity. *Cannegieter, Roger. aerlines.nl. 21*.

Lufthansa and Airbus partner on inaugural A380 route-proving flight to US *(Press release)*. *Lufthansa. 19 March 2007*.

Lufthansa Annual Report 2011. *Lufthansa*.

Lufthansa flies German team to Johannesburg with A380 *(Press release)*. *Lufthansa. 7 April 2010*.

Lufthansa flies German team to Johannesburg with A380. *Lufthansa. 7 April 2010*.

Lufthansa Signs for 15 A380s Taking Airbus Orderbook to Nearly 100 Superjumbos *(Press release)*. *EADS. 20 December 2001*.

Lufthansa snaps up 2 new Airbus superjumbos (Press release). *Reuters. 29 September 2011*.

Lufthansa Systems database plots route to the paperless cockpit. *Flight International. 5 October 2004*.

Lufthansa übernimmt A380 am 19. Mai – Trainingsflüge in ganz *Deutschland*.

Flugrevue.de.

Luxury living at 35,000 ft. *CNN*.

Major turbulence for EADS on A380 delay. *Forbes*.

Malaysia Airlines goes for Airbus A380 *(Press release)*. *Airbus. 10 January 2003*.

Malaysia Airlines Posts RM226 million Net Profit, Operating Profit Up At RM137 Million For 4Q10 *(Press release)*. *Malaysia Airlines. 25 February 2011*.

Marks, Paul (29 June 2005). Aviation – The shape of wings to come. *New Scientist*.

Marsh, George (11 October 2002). Composites strengthen aerospace hold. *Science Direct*.

Martin, Mike (18 June 2007). Honey, I shrunk the A380!. *Flight International*.

MAS expects first A380 in April 2012 after several delays. *Flightglobal.com (Reed Business Information)*.

McDonnell Douglas Unveils New MD-XX Trijet Design. *McDonnell Douglas. 4 September 1996*.

MDC brochures for undeveloped versions of the MD-11 and MD-12 *md-eleven.net*

Minimum Requirements to Widen Existing 150-Foot Wide Runways for Airbus A380 Operations . *FAA. 13 February 2004*.

More on A380 Special Conditions. *Air Safety Week. 2 June 2005*.

Networking. *Lufthansa*.

New guidelines show shorter A380 separation distances. *Flight International. 22 August 2008*.

New pricelist 2013. *Airbus.com. January 2013*.

Newest superjumbo takes off for Malaysia Airlines. *Sydney Morning Herald*.

Onboard the Airbus A380. *Fodors*.

Operational Evaluation Board Report Airbus A380-800 *Report of the FCL/OPS Subgroup Report, Revision 1 18 July 2011. 18 July 2011*.

Orders & Deliveries summary, spreadsheet. *Airbus, 28 February 2014*.

Orders & Deliveries. *Airbus. 31 May 2013*.

Our history. *Etihad Airways*.

PARIS: Japan's Skymark firms options on two A380s. *Flightglobal. 23 June 2011*.

Pictures: Airbus A380 clears European and US certification hurdles for evacuation trial. *Flight International. 29 March 2006*.

Pilot Report: Flying the Airbus A380. *Aviation Week*.

PMB confirms Airbus A380 purchase for Malaysia Airlines' operation *(Press release)*. *Airbus. 11 December 2003*.

Point-To-Point, Hub-To-Hub: the need for an A380 size aircraft. *Leeham.net*.

Qantas A380 arrives in LA after maiden flight. *The Age (Australia). 21 October 2008*.

Qantas A380 back in the air, 'as good as new'. *Herald-Sun*.

Qantas A380 landing: Airlines were warned in August over engine safety. *Airportwatch.org.uk*.

Qantas A380. *Qantas*.

Qantas and the A380. *Qantas. Adams, Charlotte (1 October 2001)*.

Qantas becomes Launch Customer for the A3XX while also Ordering A330s *(Press* release). *EADS. 29 November 2000.*

Qantas Creates History with Inaugural A380 Service *(Press release). Qantas. 20 October 2008.*

Qantas Orders Additional A380 Aircraft (Press release). *Qantas. 29 October 2006.*

Qantas replaces RR engines. *The Guardian, 18 November 2010.*

Qantas signs firm order for eight additional A380s *(Press release). Airbus. 21 December 2006.*

Qantas signs firm order for eight additional *A380s. Airbus*

Qantas unveils self-serve bar. *Adelaide Now.*

Qatar Airways confirms order for 80 A350 XWBs and adds three A380s *(Press release). Airbus. 18 June 2007.*

Qatar Airways confirms order for 80 A350 XWBs and adds three A380s. *Airbus.*

Qatar Airways Confirms Orders For 80 Airbus A350s At Paris Air Show *(Press release). Qatar Airways. 18 June 2007.*

Qatar Airways confirms orders for A380s *(Press release). Airbus. 9 December 2003.*

Qatar Airways plots Paris A380 and A330P2F deals. *FlightGlobal.*

Qatar Airways selects the A330 and contributes to the launch of the A380 *(Press release). EADS. 27 February 2001.*

Quentin Wilber, Dell (8 November 2006). Airbus bust, Boeing boost. *Washington Post.*

Rapid growth forecast for carbon fibre market. R*einforced Plastics.*

Replay of THAI's First A380 Delivery Ceremony from Toulouse, France *(Press release). Thai Airways International. 27 September 2012.*

Review of the Quota Count (QC) System used for Administering the Night Noise Quota at Heathrow, Gatwick and Stansted Airports

Rolls-Royce to power additional A380s for Qantas Airways *(Press release). Rolls-Royce. 19 September 2008.*

Rolls-Royce Trent 900 to Power first VIP A380 (Press release). *Rolls-Royce. 12 November 2007.*

Rolls-Royce wins Trent 900 contract from Asiana Airlines *(Press release). Rolls-Royce. 16 March 2011.*

Seat Map Singapore Airlines Airbus A380. *Seat Guru.*

SeatGuru Seat Map Qantas Airways Airbus A380-800

Showers, Bars, Lounge – the Emirates Airbus A380 has them all. *Asia Travel Tips. 30 July 2008.*

SIA is ready at last to start flying the A380. *Flight International*

SIA's Chew: A380 pleases, Virgin Atlantic disappoints. *ATW Online. 13 December 2007*

Singapore Airlines – Our History. *Singapore Airlines. 1 November 2012.*

Singapore Airlines A380. *Singapore Airlines.*

Singapore Airlines boosts Airbus fleet with additional A380 orders *(Press release). Airbus. 20 December 2006.*

Singapore Airlines boosts Airbus fleet with additional *A380 orders. Airbus.*

Singapore Airlines celebrates its first millionth A380 passenger. *WebWire. 19 February 2009.*

Singapore Airlines looks to the future with orders for A380 and A350 XWB *(Press release). Airbus. 21 July 2006.*

Singapore Airlines Orders 20 Airbus A350 XWB-900s And 9 Airbus A380s *(Press release). Singapore Airlines. 21 July 2006.*

Singapore Airlines selects Rolls-Royce Trent 900 and TotalCare for additional A380s *(Press release). Rolls-Royce. 15 February 2008.*

Singapore Airlines Signs Agreements With Airbus *(Press release). Singapore Airlines. 20 December 2006.*

Singapore Airlines Suites Singapore Airlines.

Singapore Airlines to be world's first A380 operator *(Press release). Airbus. 16 July 2001.*

Singapore Airlines to order up to 25 A3XXs *(Press release). Airbus. 29 September 2000.*

Singapore, Thai. A380 Fantasy Fares. *thaiairways.com.*

Skymark Airlines of Japan confirms order for four A380s *(Press release). Airbus. 18 February 2011.*

Skymark Airlines orders two more A380s *(Press release). Airbus. 23 June 2011.*

Skymark Airlines signs MoU for four A380s *(Press release). Airbus. 12 November 2010.*

Skymark and Airbus reached a basic

A symphony in white! An A380 in the paint shop in Germany. (Photo: Airbus SAS)

agreement on Introduction of A380 (Press release). *Skymark Airlines. 8 November 2010.*

Skymark signs firm contract with Airbus for purchase of A380s (Press release). *Skymark Airlines. 18 February 2011.*

Strong Euro Weighs on Airbus, Suppliers. *Wall Street Journal.*

Super jet could fit 1000, says maker. *The Age (Melbourne).*

Superduperjumbo Double the size of an Airbus A380? No problem, aerodynamicists say.. *Air & Space Magazine.*

Superjumbo or white elephant?. *Flight International. 1 August 1995.*

Supersizing the superjumbo: Airbus says 1,000 seat A380 due 2020. *Australian Business Traveller. 26 Setpmber 2012.*

Test cards for the Airbus A380. *Aviation Today.*

Thai Airways International selects A380 (Press release). Airbus. 27 August 2004.

Thai confirms A380 delivery delayed until 2012. *Flightglobal.com (Reed Business Information).*

Thai's A380. *Thai Airways.*

Thales technologies onboard the A380. *Thales Group. 30 October 2009.*

The A380 global fleet spreads its wings as deliveries hit the 'century mark'. *Airbus, 14 March 2013.*

The A380 programme . *EADS.*

The A380 Transport Project and Logistics – Assessment of alternatives *Airbus, 18 January 2006.*

The Airbus saga: Crossed wires and a multibillion-euro delay. International Herald Tribune.

The Casino in the Sky. Wired. Associated Press. 19 December 2000.

The Emirates A380: First Class. *Emirates.*

The race to rewire the Airbus A380. *Flight International.*

The triple-deck cargo hauler. *Airbus.*

The world's shortest (and longest) Airbus A380 flights. *Australian Business Traveller. March 2013.*

Thermoplastic composites gain leading edge on the A380. Composites World. 3 January 2006.

Towards Toulouse. *Flight International. 20 May 2003.*

Trent 900 engine. *Rolls-Royce.*

Trent 900 fact sheet. *Rolls-Royce.*

UPS cancels Airbus A380 order. *New York Times. 2 March 2007.*

UPS selects A380 *(Press release). Airbus. 11 January 2005.*

UPS Selects GP7200 Engines for Airbus A380 Fleet *(Press release). Engine Alliance. 18 July 2006.*

UPS signs firm contract for A380 (Press release). Airbus. 13 December 2005.

UPS to Cancel A380 Order *(Press release). UPS. 2 March 2007.*

US considers Airbus A380 as Air Force One and potentially a C-5 replacement. *Flight International. 17 October 2007.*

Use of non-standard 75-foot-wide straight taxiway sections for Airbus 380 taxiing operations . *FAA. April 2006.*

Verghese, Vijay (2011). A survey of the best airline economy seats. *Smarttravelasia.com.*

Vietnam Airlines emerges as possible customer for new A380 variant. *flightglobal. 25 June 2010.*

Virgin Atlantic becomes A3XX Launch Customer (Press release). *EADS. 15 December 2000.*

Virgin Atlantic confirms order for six A380s (Press release). EADS. 26 April 2001.

Virgin orders six A3XX aircraft, allowing Airbus to meet its goal. *Wall Street Journal. 15 December 2000.*

What Grounded the Airbus A380?. *Cadalyst Manufacturing.*

Wing error costs 2B kroner (in Norwegian) *Teknisk Ukeblad 31 May 2012.*

World's biggest super-jumbos must be grounded, say engineers after cracks are found in the wings of three Airbus A380s. London: *The Daily Mail (UK).*

World's Largest Airliner Enters Commercial Service *(Press release). Singapore Airlines. 25 October 2007.*

World's longest superjumbo flight starts 16-hour hauls. *The Sydney Morning Herald. 5 December 2013.*

The first A380 for Asiana Airlines was rolled out of the Airbus paint shop in Hamburg on 24 March 2014, marking the completion of its painting. The aircraft will then have completion of its cabin and enter a final phase of ground and flight tests in Hamburg, during which all cabin systems will be thoroughly tested, including air flow and air conditioning, lighting, galleys, lavatories, seats and in-flight entertainment systems. In parallel, Airbus will also undertake advanced performance tests with the aircraft before it flies back to Toulouse for preparation of its delivery to the airline in the second quarter of the year. (Photo: Airbus SAS)

Index